JOSEPH CONRAD AND MATERIAL CULTURE:
FROM THE RISE OF THE COMMODITY TRANSCENDENT
TO THE SCRAMBLE FOR AFRICA

CONRAD: EASTERN AND WESTERN PERSPECTIVES
Editor: Wiesław Krajka

VOLUME XXXI

Merry M. Pawlowski

JOSEPH CONRAD AND MATERIAL CULTURE:
FROM THE RISE OF THE COMMODITY TRANSCENDENT TO THE SCRAMBLE FOR AFRICA

MARIA CURIE-SKŁODOWSKA UNIVERSITY PRESS, LUBLIN
COLUMBIA UNIVERSITY PRESS, NEW YORK

2022

Cover Design
Marta and Zdzisław Kwiatkowscy
Agnieszka Muchowska

Typesetting
Agnieszka Muchowska

ISBN 978-83-227-9638-2

All rights reserved

Copyright 2022

© Maria Curie-Skłodowska University Press, Lublin, Poland
and the Author

Publication financed by Maria Curie-Skłodowska University, Lublin

MARIA CURIE-SKŁODOWSKA UNIVERSITY PRESS
ul. Idziego Radziszewskiego 11
20-031 Lublin, Poland
tel. (81) 537 53 04
www.wydawnictwo.umcs.eu
e-mail: sekretariat@wydawnictwo.umcs.lublin.pl

Sales Department: tel./fax 81 537 53 02
e-mail: wydawnictwo@umcs.eu

Printed by
„Petit" S. K., ul. Tokarska 13, 20-210 Lublin, Poland

For my four grandchildren,
this is my legacy to you

TABLE OF CONTENTS

Introduction: The Commodity Transcendent	1
Chapter One: "Autocracy and War," the Age of Capital, and the Rise of the Commodity Transcendent...	17
Chapter Two: Spectral Sightings, Mapping, and Exploration in "Geography and Some Explorers"........	65
Chapter Three: A Witness in the Congo: Conrad's "The Congo Diary" and "Up-river Book"	131
Chapter Four: "An Outpost of Progress": "The lightest part of the loot I carried off from Central Africa"...	187
Chapter Five: "Heart of Darkness": Conrad's Centerpiece in the Congo.........................	235
Conclusion: Conrad, Commodities, and the Work of Art..	289
Notes..	295
List of Illustrations and Permissions	307
Works Cited.....................................	313
Index of Nonfictional Names	329

A NOTE ON THE TEXTS

Unless otherwise noted in my text, quotations from Conrad's published works are taken from the Cambridge University Press editions for several reasons: I've made extensive use of the supplemental materials in each of the editions, and the texts of Conrad's works are designed to be accurate and authoritative by editors who have conducted extensive research using existing manuscripts, typescripts, and published documents to produce a definitive text. Each edition includes an introductory essay, the body of the Conrad text or texts included in the volume; an extensive list of variations among manuscripts, typescripts, serial and book publications; textual notes; and explanatory notes, among other materials. All of these editions are listed in the Works Cited.

For each of the editions where I have quoted from the supplemental materials, I have so indicated in parenthetical citation including the editors' names and page numbers; these references are also listed in the works cited under the name of the editor/s as author of the supplemental item.

In addition to the Cambridge editions, I have used two other editions of Conrad's works: *The Mirror of the Sea*, Harper & Brothers, 1906, and "Autocracy and War" in the *Uniform Edition* published by Dent, 1924, and have listed full publication information for both in the Works Cited.

I have relied heavily, too, on several of the earliest publications of Conrad's works selected here for discussion, as well as manuscripts and typescripts; these are listed by title below, with complete publication information included in the Works Cited:

"Autocracy and War" in *The Fortnightly Review*
"Autocracy and War" in *North American Review*
"The Congo Diary," Untitled Manuscript, 1890

"Geography (The Romance of Travel)," Original Manuscript

"'Geography': *Ur*-Version of 'Geography and Some Explorers'" in Stevens and Stape

"The Romance of Travel," *Countries of the World* (the earliest publication, in February 1924, of "Geography and Some Explorers: under a different title)

"Heart of Darkness," GEN MSS 1207

"The Heart of Darkness," Incomplete typescript

"The Heart of Darkness," [Part One] *Blackwood's Edinburgh Magazine*

"An Outpost of Progress," GEN MSS 1207

"An Outpost of Progress," The Macmillan Co.

"An Outpost of Progress," (Part I), *Cosmopolis* 18

"An Outpost of Progress," (Part II), *Cosmopolis* 19

"Up-river Book," Manuscript 1890

"Up-river Book, 1890," in Najder, *Joseph Conrad: Congo Diary*

Richard Curle published Conrad's manuscript "Congo Diary" in several publications; these are listed in the Works Cited under Curle's name as the editor, since the titles for the untitled manuscript were assigned by him. These include:

Conrad's Diary published in *The Yale Review*

Joseph Conrad's Diary of His Journey up the Valley of the Congo in 1890, privately printed by Strangeways

Joseph Conrad's Diary of His Journey up the Valley of the Congo in 1890, published in *The Blue Peter*

Other editions of these manuscript journals, including Najder's and Stevens and Stapes's appear in the Works Cited under the name of the respective editor.

Robert Hobson produced an edition of "An Outpost of Progress" as his PhD dissertation entitled *A Critical Edition of Joseph Conrad's "An Outpost of Progress"*; full publication details of the dissertation are included in the Works Cited.

ABBREVIATIONS

I. Conrad's Texts:

AW	"Autocracy and War"
CD MS	"The Congo Diary" Manuscript
CD	*The Congo Diary* as published by Richard Curle with a reference to the publisher of the edition in parenthetical citation
GSE	"Geography and Some Explorers" in *Last Essays*
HD	"Heart of Darkness" in *Youth, Heart of Darkness, The End of the Tether*
HD MS	"The Heart of Darkness" Manuscript
HD TS	"The Heart of Darkness" Typescript
HD Blackwood's	"Heart of Darkness" in *Blackwood's Magazine*
MS	*The Mirror of the Sea*
OP	"An Outpost of Progress" in *Tales of Unrest*
OP	"An Outpost of Progress" with a reference to the publisher, *Cosmopolis* or Macmillan, in parenthetical citation
OP MS	"An Outpost of Progress" Manuscript
PR	*A Personal Record*
UB MS	"Up-river Book" Manuscript

II. Conrad's Letters

CL	*The Collected Letters of Joseph Conrad*. Gen. ed. Laurence Davies. 9 vols. Cambridge UP, 1983-2008

ACKNOWLEDGMENTS

I am fortunate to have as revered colleagues and friends scholars from whose work I have learned so much. I want to thank Andrea White, Laurence Davies, Keith Carabine, Robert Hampson, and Chris GoGwilt, Johan Warodell, and Mirela Altic, who have offered advice and guidance through this process; and most of all, I offer my thanks to Wiesław Krajka, who has been such an important supporter of my work. I owe a debt to several wonderful librarians at the Berg Archive in the New York Public Library, the Special Collections at Texas Tech University, and the Huntington Library, where I am privileged to be a reader. Lastly, I am indebted to the California State University Emeritus and Retired Faculty and Staff Association for a travel grant that funded my research for this project.

Introduction:
The Commodity Transcendent

Elephant Tusk with Scenes of African Life.[1] Courtesy of the Walters Art Museum, Baltimore

During the nineteenth century, trading between Europeans and Africans grew exponentially, resulting in the development of numerous multinational trading stations or "factories" all along the Loango coast down to the mouth of the Congo River and beyond. By the late 1850s, the Vili, Kongo peoples located on the Loango coast, were renowned as sculptors of ivory and produced works of extraordinary beauty and detail while also providing commentary on the cross-cultural environment in which they were immersed. The sculptures were produced as exports largely in response to European demand, and a large number are still extant in Europe and the United States, scattered in various museum exhibits or private collections. The carvers oriented the tusks vertically to portray scenes of a continuous procession of figures arranged in a spiral display moving up (or down) from the bottom of the tusk to the top. At the tip of the tusk, there was often a figure which could be interpreted as capping the themes of the procession below; equally remarkable is the fact that almost all of these tusks display not only African figures but also Europeans and Arabs as well – clearly indicating the impact of European and Arab incursion on African life. The carved ivory tusk depicted in the illustration above, in the collection of the Walters Art Museum in Baltimore, Maryland, is an especially fine example of the work of the Vili folk.

In reading the spiraling map on the tusk from the bottom rising to the top, I should note that the scenes are not necessarily meant to constitute a consecutive narrative; rather, as Strother suggests, scenes may be juxtaposed "across different registers"– a vignette in a circle above another, for example, may interact with that below rather than a scene on either side (52). The carvers may also have had a repertoire of scenes of trading posts to use as the sources for their art, mixing the life of the interior with the acknowledgment of trade on the coast.

One scene featured at the bottom of the Walters tusk portrays a European, clearly dressed in a plaid suit and a hat, presumably a carpenter measuring on a table with his assistant – perhaps working on the plans to build another storehouse. Below the table sits a chimpanzee with his paw in his mouth, a satiric twist apparently meant to register his quandary and/ or to mock the actions above him. An adjacent African figure to the left is secured to an oil palm, tapping it to collect the sap for palm wine into a calabash attached to the palm, and around the other side of the tusk, not visible in the illustration above, three African figures drag a prone naked man by a rope around his neck. Just above these scenes on the bottom circle, an enslaved African chain gang proceeds upward, the bights of their chains and their neck collars carved in great detail while the last man visible in the image seems to look at the viewer. A European, not visible on this side of the tusk, holds the neck of the last man in the slave gang with his right hand and what looks like a switch in his left. In the circle above the enslaved men, a boy offers a European a light for his cigar, signifying the European's lack of concern for the violent scenes that surround him. In the second circle up from the chain gang, an African has a stranglehold on another one, threatening him with a knife, and just above that, near the center, African bearers carry ivory tusks on their heads. Nearing the top, another African stabs a man in the back, the wound marked by a splotch of red. The scenes of violence, though, are interrupted by those that represent everyday life – tapping for palm wine, carrying huge fish to market, grinding and chopping food, and butchering a hog.

While the scenes swirl up to the top of the tusk, not all the figures are in motion, nor are they all traveling the same way. One European figure is seated in a rattan chair, while others stand still performing their tasks. Most of the figures in the processional march upward, but the bearers of the fish are traveling down the column, while other figures stand or kneel facing each other in some interaction, whether of trade or violence. There seems to be, too, an admixture of clothing representing a blurring of identities; for example, some Europeans are depicted wearing suits and hats, while others may have on a suit coat and hat but a waist wrapper instead of pants. Africans generally wear loin cloths or waist wrappers with bare torsos, their hair appearing almost helmet-like. Three rows from the top of the tusk, women, both bare breasted and covered, wear patterned textile waist wrappers, bangles that could be ivory or brass, waist beads, and anklets. In addition to Africans and Europeans, the carver has included Arabs sporting fezzes, shirts or coats, and waist wrappers. Commodities, trading, acts of violence, and scenes of everyday life mingle in the spiraling vignettes while ivory dominates the center. "The strategy of the Vili carver," Strother suggests, is to indicate that "ivory symbolizes the European trade for which the tusk itself serves as the nexus" (53). Ivory and slavery, violence and the disruption of everyday life, are inextricably linked in the Vili carver's symbolic structures.

The capping symbol, though, is the monkey on the top. Strother discusses the fact that the portrayal of apes on African carvings cuts two ways. For Africans, monkeys were a disgusting nuisance, while Westerners seemed to find them entertaining. Yet there is an undercurrent perceptible in reading this tusk – the monkey as a symbol of African inferiority in Western texts – so "the image of the primate could never be innocent for an African carver" (54). Balancing the image of the monkey at the bottom of the tusk, the monkey who sits prominently at the top is carved in greater detail, eating a banana and scratching his rump. This strikes me as the ultimate act of the carver mocking the scenes of European domination, violence, and interference in African life below. Of course, as an obvious phallic symbol, the tusk goes even further to mock Western power as a Western buyer is meant to be the recipient of the tusk.

Indeed, this tusk does not ignore violence enacted by Africans upon Africans, but it centralizes the Western lust for ivory which forever changed life as Africans knew it. The tusk is a potent map of central African life carved for European consumption, but the carver producing it may never have meant for the buyer to have the keys to the codes he embedded in the sculpture.

The Walters ivory tusk is significant to me for the themes it introduces that are central to this book. To begin: it is a palimpsest to be decoded, a work of art carved upon an ivory tusk to be consumed as a commodity by a European buyer; as such, it becomes a prime example of a fetish. Furthermore, it serves as an introduction to the African continent as the setting for mapping and exploration in the nineteenth century, to the overwhelming power of European colonialism met by African resistance powerless to undo its damage, to the presence of transculturation through trade not widely examined in Conrad's African fictions, and to the rise of the commodity, especially

Introduction: The Commodity Transcendent 5

ivory, as the transcendent symbol of colonial and imperial power. But most of all, in my view, the tusk embodies the desire for the primacy of art inflected by its complicity with the transcendent commodity.

Beyond the complicated identification of the commodity and the work of art, transculturation, as the complex conflation of cultures, is another important component of this study. I define it as a combination of three elements: acculturation, deculturation, and neo-culturation: a fluid process involving the acquisition of elements of a culture and the loss of elements of another, resulting in a newly formed cultural combination.[2] These may be constantly moving parts, combining and recombining to constitute new cultures in the progression of time. Acknowledging the presence of transculturation in Conrad's African works is especially important because, as Mirzoeff argues, "the Congo was in fact a key locus of transculture since the fifteenth century" (132). "Kongo," Mirzoeff writes (referring to the Kingdom of Kongo eradicated by European, specifically Belgian colonization),

> was integral to the unfolding history of modernity. For it was and is a dramatic example of the power of transculturation to create and destroy at once. Its peculiar reputation as the very origin of the primitive made it a key site for the constitution of Western notions of modernity that are always in tension with the primitive and primitivism. (133)

The Congo was, for nineteenth century thinkers in the West, the most "primitive place in Africa" (133), the Dark Continent left behind by the rest of the world. Mirzoeff goes even further to designate the Congo as "the most primordial point of space-time" (134), so that nineteenth century explorers, forgetting an African material past, could imagine themselves *inventing* an untouched wilderness. Marlow's feeling that "[g]oing up that river was like travelling back to the earliest beginnings of the world, when vegetation rioted on the earth and the big trees were kings" (HD 77) is rooted in this pervasive Orientalist construct of Africa as virgin territory, waiting to be explored and bent to a European will to power.

The Congo is at the center of my study - each text I've chosen is tied to Africa whether set there in a symbolic representation of African space or alluded to, seemingly in passing; and the order in which I take up the discussion of the works connects them through the overriding themes I pursue, developing from the initiation of a cult of the commodity in the mid nineteenth century to the devastation of an indigenous African culture wrought by European greed for African ivory by the century's end. I begin with a discussion of Conrad's 1905 essay for the Pandora's box of global issues it opens at its core, not the least of which is the hint at the scramble for Africa and the rise of an untethered power of the global commodity enabled and promoted by the international exhibition.

In Chapter One, "'Autocracy and War,' the Age of Capital, and the Rise of the Commodity Transcendent," I examine details that emerge in the genealogy of Conrad's composing process – a practice that I follow in my analysis of each of Conrad's works discussed in this study. The origins of "Autocracy and War" (1905) are fascinating for the revelations about how Conrad comes to think about a global problem – for example, the reason for Conrad's choice of the epigraph "Sine ira et studio" both left in and out of early publications, and the irony of its application to his writing as a historian of his times, when, in fact, he, like Tacitus before him, wrote propelled by passion and partiality.

Early in the chapter, I tease out the significance of a rather minor detail in Conrad's brief reference to the Great Exhibition of 1851 – the scene for numerous scholars of the beginning of the age of the commodity transcendent (Richards 1). For Conrad, though, the Great Exhibition – the Crystal Palace – crammed full with that variegated rubbish which it seems to be the bizarre fate of humanity to purchase for the benefit of a few employers of labour" (88) – heralded, instead of dreams of peace, a future in which rampant capitalism could give rise to imperialism, colonialism, and war. My discussion of Conrad's essay traces his arguments about the Russo-Japanese war for their spatial metaphors and their prescience in laying out the

Introduction: The Commodity Transcendent

case for the demise of the Russian "spectre" (75) and the rise of Prussian imperialism. Conrad's warnings about the future are potent and passionate.

Inextricably linked to the rise of imperialism, and in its wake, colonialism, are the international world's fairs which followed the first, the Great Exhibition, and touted the commodity, creating a "phantasmagoric commodity fetishism" (Leslie 116), a concept that resonates with European misperceptions of African fetishism and its power. To balance the Great Exhibition in mid-nineteenth century, an exhibition that focused squarely on Africa appeared in London in March 1890, *The Stanley and African Exhibition* trumpeted the achievement of European explorers in Africa, predominantly Henry Morton Stanley, of course, to solidify public support for carving up the African continent for its rich natural resources – especially ivory.

My discussion of the contested space of a nineteenth century Africa as an exhibitionary model and a real space pried open to the European gaze yields to a deeper examination of another contested space in Conrad's essay – the battle in Sha-ho for control of the island of Saghalien (Sakhalin) and its commodities and ice-free ports. But the space of that battle for Conrad is seen only through the eyes of the newspaper which dulls the reader's senses to the tragedy. Naturally, in his 1905 essay, Conrad gloats over Russia's failures in its war with Japan but warns against a world that will become a "House of Strife" (AW 89) and the rising imperialist power, the "German eagle with a Prussian head look[ing] all round the horizon […] for something *good to get*" (93, emphasis added).

From an examination of Conrad's recognition of a global threat in 1905 and his writing as a contemporary historian, I turn to his focus on geography and the map in "Geography and Some Explorers." By 1924, some of Conrad's warnings in "Autocracy and War" had come true; the world had experienced global warfare, but geography and mapmaking now center his thoughts in this late essay. And the geopolitical and geocultural state of the world, especially on the continent of Africa, forms the spine of my study.

Chapter Two, "Spectral Sightings, Mapping, and Exploration in 'Geography and Some Explorers,'" shifts my narrative to African soil, where the German eagle had already dug in his beak for something good to get, but more directly to the Congo as King Leopold II's personal fiefdom. Written nineteen years after "Autocracy and War," "Geography and Some Explorers" offers, amid so much else, a brief glimpse at the specter of Henry Morton Stanley. I take up the rise in nationalism in the nineteenth century and the determination on the part of numerous European nations to dissect Africa in their mad rush to establish colonies. The overt message of "Geography and Some Explorers" is indeed to celebrate travel and exploration, and to applaud those explorers that Conrad felt were driven by the purest instincts to seek new lands. In his brief, tantalizing mention of the "vilest scramble for loot" and the "unholy recollection of a prosaic newspaper stunt" (GSE 14), Conrad raises the ghost of Stanley, arguably the single most important African explorer. Conrad will have nothing more to say about him, though, perhaps the irony of the portion of his title "*Some* Explorers" (emphasis added) makes clear that he has no intention of including Stanley in his pantheon of greats.

As a precursor to the published essay, we have a complete manuscript, entitled simply "Geography," which is revelatory for its denial of a "great figure" haunting the space below the thundering sound of Stanley Falls ("Geography," Original Manuscript 49). The irony is, of course, that Stanley is there in his own name imposed upon the space. Another feature of the manuscript I find significant is the doodled map at the top of page 37. While Stevens and Stape, in their introduction to *Last Essays* (Introduction xliii) identify this doodle as a map of the Western Hemisphere, I disagree and argue that it is a map of Saddle Island, where Conrad anchored for more than ten hours during his passage through the Torres Strait – the connection between image and text illustrates my analysis of Conrad as cartographer and explorer.

One of the major themes of this chapter is the theory of cartography centered on Conrad's own maps as well as on a proliferating succession of maps of the African continent. After a discussion of the map of Saddle Island in the manuscript, I look closely at two more detailed maps, Conrad's "Map of the Russias" and his "Map of Congo Basin," to begin theorizing about how to read map codes and how Conrad's own maps might illuminate his writing.

Central to the study of the African map is Conrad's pronounced passion for maps, the fascination of the blank spaces of Africa, which, conversely, had been filled in with the colors of the rainbow, the emblems of European colonizers, by the time Conrad traveled to the Congo. The single most important explorer to fill that African map was Henry Stanley – most notable for his discovery of the entire trajectory of the Congo River, the second longest river on the African continent, and its snaking course above and below the Equator. Before Stanley, the interior basin of the Congo was largely unknown and unexplored by Europeans – Africans, of course, knew the big river quite well.

With Stanley's discoveries came the influx of European commodities to fill the space of central Africa and drive out locally produced goods. Additionally, with Stanley's opening of the interior to Europeans, ivory hunters discovered new herds of elephants to be killed for their tusks and Africans were forced to serve as bearers, either enslaved or indentured, to transport that ivory to the coast – all to slake European greed.

After a discussion of Stanley's four major African expeditions and the scramble for African colonies that they engendered and promoted, I turn briefly to Conrad's well-known disgust with journalism to tie Stanley to that "prosaic newspaper stunt" – being a journalist must have made Stanley, in Conrad's eyes, even more a figure to be reviled. I close the chapter with a return to Conrad's essay to look at his own feat of exploration, his passage through the Torres Strait as captain of the *Otago*, his opportunity to "pass through a central place in the history of sea exploration which has been for long a place of mystery to the civilized world, and even in my time was very imperfectly charted and very lonely" ("Geography," Original Manuscript 50-51).

My next chapter ("A Witness in the Congo: Conrad's 'The Congo Diary' and 'Up-river Book'") moves backward in time to read more deeply into Conrad's experience as an explorer marching overland and sailing upriver in central Africa. These experiences not only form the foundation of Conrad's knowledge of African geography in "Geography and Some Explorers," but they also act as the catalyst for the creative eruption that formed his African fiction. It takes a close look at Conrad's two manuscript journals composed during his Congo journey. Since Conrad arrived in the Congo in the wake of Henry Stanley's last, failed expedition to free Emin Pasha, what he saw and the paths he traveled had been irrevocably transformed and shaped by Stanley's sustained presence in the Congo for almost two decades – the 1870s and the 1880s. In early 1890, Conrad signed on as an employee of the *Société Anonyme Belge*, the trading company founded by Albert Thys in 1888 to capitalize on Stanley's work in founding the Belgian Congo Free State. Conrad's journals record his brief experience in the Congo traveling both overland on the lower Congo River and by steamer on the upper Congo; it's remarkable that these journals still exist as Conrad's wife retrieved them from the "waste-paper basket" twice! Richard Curle acknowledges that information from Jessie Conrad in his introduction to his editions of Conrad's manuscript "The Congo Diary" (Introduction, *CD*, Strangeways 10).

I begin the chapter by reinforcing the importance of Stanley's impact upon the Congo, focusing more in detail on Stanley's work in founding the Congo Free State, especially his river and overland journeys both upriver and down. For Stanley, the Congo River was preeminently "the grand highway of commerce"; he was convinced that any European power that could possess this river would "absorb to itself the trade of the whole of the enormous basin behind" (*The Congo* 1: vi). For Conrad, however, such unabashed commercialism could only be repugnant.

In the first of his journals, "The Congo Diary,"[3] Conrad records his experiences traveling from Matadi to Stanley Pool on foot – the cataracts from Matadi to the Pool made the

Introduction: The Commodity Transcendent

lower portion of the Congo River unnavigable. What is most extraordinary about this journal, whose fragmented narrative reveals few details about the journey, are the sketches that Conrad drew at the end of the daily travel. They are maps, not reproduced in Curle's editions of the diary nor in Najder's, but pivotal for combining the visual sketch with the textual log to decipher what Conrad meant to convey – perhaps only to himself – but clearly preliminary to the narratives that would emerge later. In reading Conrad's map sketches and daily log, I work in, where possible, additional historical information from Stanley and others to enhance our understanding of what Conrad saw.

My reading of the "Up-river Book" follows a similar pattern: again, Conrad has left sketches that are navigationally significant for steering a steamer through the rapidly changing current and dangerous snags, rocks, and sandbars of the upper Congo River. Here, though, Conrad engages in virtually no chatter about what he sees beyond the scope of his work assisting Captain Koch as navigator. Thus, to enhance the discussion of what Conrad might have seen but did not describe, I include more details about the same route by George Grenfell, T. J. Comber, W. H. Bentley, and Emory Taunt.

Up to this point in my study, I've looked at Conrad's nonfictional texts, exploring their revelations about contemporary history, geography, mapmaking, and major geopolitical change; but Conrad was not only writing in his own voice about his experiences, he was also an artist, and it is to that major dimension of his craft that I now direct my attention. Building on the foundation of Conrad's Congo journals, Chapter Four, "'An Outpost of Progress': 'The lightest part of the loot I carried off from Central Africa,'" sharpens the focus on the emotional "loot" Conrad carried back from Africa which explodes in the mordant irony of his initial tale of the Congo. I explore the genesis of the tale as Conrad first began to think of it, tracing information in his letters about his wavering opinions of the story as well as his growing sense that he had achieved a "scrupulous unity of tone" (qtd. in Hamner 173).

Perhaps, as Gérard Jean-Aubry surmises, the impetus to begin the story came with the arrival of Conrad's trunk carrying the effects from his Congo journey, including his two Congo journals along with other manuscripts (220).

Like the manuscripts for the Congo journals, we have a complete manuscript of "An Outpost of Progress," written in ink, although no typescript survives. My attention is directed to significant changes between the manuscript and the story's first appearance in *Cosmopolis* as well as the extremely rare Macmillan pamphlet, produced to obtain an American copyright. Critical changes I examine include not only substitutions in the publications for what was written in the manuscript as well as sections Conrad deleted from the printed versions. These changes do help to account for an evolving irony that grows stronger as Conrad revises.

From there I move to a discussion of space/place in the African setting, considering Conrad's identification of Makola, one of the central characters, as a native of Sierra Leone. Both Sierra Leone and the Loanda coast, the home of Makola's wife, are clearly implicated in the history of the slave trade.

A key space in the story is the setting on the Kassai River, not the Congo. While there is no direct mention of the location in the text, we do know from Conrad's letter to Fisher Unwin that the tale is about "the life in a lonely station on the Kassai" (*CL* 1: 294). This adds an ironic twist to the setting since we know that Conrad was denied the opportunity to command a steamer on an expedition up the Kassai River. I add to the scant details about the Kassai that we find in Conrad's text by including historical information from missionaries and explorers who did travel up the Kassai and founded outposts and stations there. Maps play a large part here again in the visualization of the space, and I include details of maps by George Grenfell and Stanley to enhance and anchor the reader in the space.

The space of the outpost itself is critically important, especially for the appearance of the "fetish," the storehouse for European trade goods and for the opportunity its name affords for my discussion of both African and European conceptions of

Introduction: The Commodity Transcendent

fetishism and the relationship of those opposing conceptions as an expression of transculturation. Other spaces in the outpost, especially the grave of the first white manager of the station, are significant for their representation as "heterotopias" – counter-sites or spaces of the other – which are different, disturbing, and transforming. The manager's grave, for example, represents the absolute space of otherness and suggests the sealing of the fate of white Europeans who are destined to be buried in Africa.

Of course, ivory and slavery take center stage in this tale with the arrival of natives from the coast carrying magnificent tusks to trade with Makola for slaves. The other major characters, the bungling duo of Kayerts and Carlier, presumably Belgian, become complicit in the slave trade, but are also produced as characters to be satirized from the beginning of the tale. Their incompetence, spiraling into insanity, possibly brought on by fever, results in the demise of both, leaving Makola in charge at the end as the corpse of Kayerts sticks out its blackened tongue at the European attempt to invade and conquer this space.

The fifth chapter, "'Heart of Darkness': Conrad's Centerpiece in the Congo," is the culmination of the intertwining themes pursued throughout the preceding chapters and the high point of Conrad's artistic rendering of the African Other. In examining the evolution of the tale, I work with both the surviving manuscript pages and the surviving typescript to evoke Conrad's "authorial withdrawal" (Knowles, Introduction xlii) in the enhancement of the universality of the finished tale.

Here too, as in previous chapters, mapping is key to the view of the text both as dreamscape and historical landscape. My approach is to unveil, as much as can be done, a "political unconscious" of the text, following the lead of Fredric Jameson's landmark study. Marlow is surely, in a sense, a dreamer moving through an unreal space, while trying to penetrate to the Real where Kurtz, and his ivory, lie. Jameson's potent suggestions invoke both Freud and Lacan in their theorizing a "navel" toward which the dream, and in this case, the narrative, must go, but which cannot be ultimately unravelled to penetrate to absolute meaning. This concept comports with Conrad's narrator's description of the meanings of Marlow's tales "like misty halos that, sometimes, are made visible by the spectral illumination of moonshine" (HD 45).

While Marlow travels in a dreamscape, though, he is also on solid ground where commodities inhabit the space. Ivory is predominant but is accompanied by the "holy trinity" of commodities: cloth, beads, and brass wire. These commodities, though far less prominent in the text than ivory, still reveal a material history which Conrad, and Marlow, witnessed, and which must be further unpacked to develop the devastating ramifications for African freedom, culture, and economy.

Cloth is the first of the holy trinity I discuss, including details that implicate not only the Belgians in an immoral colonialism but also the British. Cloth largely from Manchester as well as other countries, flooded the African continent with "about 57 million yards of textiles" in the 1860s (Eltis and Jennings 953). Just as important as the volume of European cloth is the mixing of textiles as the result of transculturation – for example, African patterns printed on Manchester cloth. Additionally, an African taste for European cloth that was viewed as exotic drove out the native market in raphia palm cloth.

Marlow's mapping continues as he follows Conrad's overland trail from the Outer Station (Matadi) to the central station (Leopoldville/Kinshasa on Stanley Pool). Several observations from Conrad's diary of this journey resurface in Marlow's description. Once he arrives at the Central Station, Marlow sees a grass shed (the fetish?), containing both cloth and beads, burst into flames.

Beads appear next in my discussion of the trinity; here transculturation once more takes center stage as the trading of beads in Africa dates all the way back to the fifteenth century when the Portuguese first began to explore the African coast. Beads were essential for any African explorer to have in his kit, and the wrong kind of bead – one that didn't appeal to a particular tribe – could result in the explorer's starvation or even worse. Beads were central to African culture, a fact that Marlow's minimal contact with Africans in the tale prevents

Introduction: The Commodity Transcendent 15

him from knowing; yet beads, Lois Dubin argues, played a major role in African culture through rituals which were meant to ensure the endurance of the community (151).

Marlow's journey continues from the Central Station to the Inner Station as he navigates the big river, based largely on what Conrad must have remembered of his own log as he assisted Captain Koch in navigating the Congo. Onboard the steamer, Marlow will refer to the third of the holy trinity, brass wire, given as payment to the cannibal crew. Here again, with Birmingham brass flooding African markets, the native trade in indigenous copper was put out of business as the use of brass for trade grew. Brass was used not only for trade, but also for adornment, as were cloth and beads. Brass bangles were the fashion with African women in the nineteenth century. Livingstone left a comic account of one African woman whose brass rings "around her legs impeded her walking, and chafed her ankles; but as it was the fashion, she did not mind the inconvenience" (*Narrative of an Expedition to the Zambesi* 283-84).

The epitome of commodities in the Congo is ivory, to reach that ivory hoard is the destination toward which Marlow has been traveling all along, and toward Kurtz, who has become little more than an ivory skeleton. Ivory pervades the atmosphere of the tale, becoming the supreme fetish around which the "faithless pilgrims" seem to surge (HD 65). Ivory metonymically links European capitalism in the Congo to desire and death, and yet caught in a web of associations, Marlow seems unable to express the "unreal" nature of his experiences.

Transporting that ivory is the tinpot steamboat, and Marlow's singular reference to the Huntley and Palmers biscuit tin rises to the forefront of my discussion. The biscuit tin, itself a representative commodity fetish, becomes, once kicked in the gutter, a metaphor for the strength of the tinpot steamer, which in turn is a metaphor for work and art; for Conrad work *is* art (*The Mirror of the Sea* 24).

Steaming toward the narrative's, and the dream's, navel, Marlow encounters the apparition of the magnificent African woman. She represents not only an Africa unbowed in my opinion, but she also embodies the clash of cultures in the cross-cultural ornaments she wears. She is both a real woman fantastically adorned and the wilderness – its mirror image – woman unknowable as the reflection of the Real. As Rebecca Stott suggests, woman is the "horror at the centre of the text." "To lift the veil, to penetrate too deeply into the mysteries of woman or into the mysteries of Africa, is to risk releasing something dangerous and potentially deadly" (75). And the African woman is a threat. She reappears in Marlow's imagination at the end of the tale, echoing, in the outreach of her arms the gesture of Kurtz's pale Intended.

With the keynote of "Heart of Darkness" summoned at the tale's end – "darkness" – I conclude with reinvoking the tragedy visited upon the African continent by the onslaught of European colonialism, evident throughout Conrad's texts, and symbolized by the enforcement of the European map on African soil, the enforcement of European culture on African communities through an inevitable transculturation, and the reinforcement of African slavery through the unslakable European desire for ivory, the commodity transcendent. Finally, I argue that Conrad's signature African tale complicates the notion of the commodity transcendent by asserting the ascendance of art over the commodity, of timelessness over the mundane. Out of the bedrock of mapped space where cultures merge and clash and commodities flood the global market, "Heart of Darkness," as eternal myth, prevails.

Chapter One:
"Autocracy and War," the Age of Capital, and the Rise of the Commodity Transcendent

In Medias Res: History in the Present Tense

In 1905 Joseph Conrad embarked on a significantly different venture; he chose to write as a public intellectual, with the gravitas to command attention as he advanced opinions on world historical events. This was a new departure in Conrad's career, and, as Keith Carabine observes, the essay resonates with "his terrible anger and almost unimaginable despair as he contemplates the inevitability of a huge European war" ("Conrad the European" 84). Imbued with the fervor for Polish activism exhibited by his father and his wide reading of Polish historiography, political theory, and philosophy, Conrad's thinking about war began to crystallize as he read newspaper accounts of the Russo-Japanese war (Stape, Introduction xlvi). While Poland seems only to appear as the almost invisible elephant in the room in "Autocracy and War," its centuries-long partitioning provides a backdrop as the essay predicts the geographical space of a Europe divided against itself and trending ever closer to war. At the heart of Conrad's essay lies a prescient analysis of the foregrounding of capitalism in the Great Exhibition of 1851; he believed that the ascendant commodity in Western capitalism at the midpoint of the nineteenth century was the foundation of global conflict. Conrad wrote that, despite numerous contemporary accounts of the splendor of the Great Exhibition of 1851, frequently referred to as the Crystal Palace: "A swift disenchantment overtook the incredible infatuation which could put its trust in the peaceful nature of industrial and commercial competition" (AW 88).[4] In this view, peace is not possible in future "democratic," capitalist societies. Thinking about the rise of capitalism in an exhibitionary age at the midcentury, Conrad decried the illusions and misperceptions of the past:

> The dreams sanguine humanitarians raised almost to ecstasy about the year fifty of the last century by the moving sight of the Crystal Palace–crammed full with that variegated rubbish which it seems to be the bizarre fate of humanity to purchase for the benefit of a few employers of labour–have vanished as quickly as they had arisen. (88)[5]

These comments about the first international exhibition crammed full of commodities suggests an alignment with the view of Richard Ruppel, that imperialism is "a natural outcome of late-stage capitalism" (79). Both "isms" are critical components of Conrad's complex argument in "Autocracy and War." In a trenchant, ironic observation, Conrad writes that by delimiting territories, as in the scramble for Africa, the late nineteenth century European land grab that Conrad witnessed firsthand, consuming nations could learn from the "model of the territorial spheres of influence marked in Africa to keep the competitors for the privilege of improving the nigger (as a buying machine) from flying prematurely at each other's throats." The main goal of the European scramble, Conrad recognized, was unquestionably "the supremacy of material interests" (AW 88).

Thinking spatially, Conrad writes of the universe expanding "some few inches" through the "giant strides" of science while the globe shrinks "beneath our growing numbers by another ell or so" (88), and imagines a yet inconceivable "universal city," not built upon a foundation of material interest, whose erection can only be accomplished once the world "has been cleared of the jungle" (89). Through these observations, Conrad emphasizes the commercialization, as Andrew Francis observes, of time and space, an expansion of time and contraction of space accomplished by rapid, steam-propelled motion across sea and land speeding time and bending it to the service of global trading (Francis 88). "Industrialism and

Commercialism" are linked directly to "picking up coins" in the wake of science that has widened our horizons for trade, and both stand ready with sword in hand to act in the interest of material gain (AW 88).

These observations are critical to understanding the core of Conrad's view of the potential failure of world order and assist in supporting his blatantly stated objective to attack Russian autocracy and warn against the rise of Prussianism in the void that Russia's demise leaves. To unpack Conrad's assertions, my intention is to examine aspects of the essay through the lens of the rise of capitalism and the role played in that rise by the phenomenon of the nineteenth century exhibition. My approach to the essay differs from that of other scholars; I take up what at first blush appears to be a minor theme, signaled by the reference to the Crystal Palace, but upon further examination, this rarely acknowledged allusion points to Conrad's belief that the root cause of war is the new world order in the age of capital.

Described by Zdzisław Najder as Conrad's most "extensive and ambitious political statement" (qtd. in Hampson, "Polish Problem" 22), the creative origin of "Autocracy and War" unfolds in a series of letters dating from mid-January 1905, when Conrad wrote Henry-Durand Davray for help finding a book on Russia – one from the "French point of view" (*CL* 3: 204) – to bolster his knowledge before writing what, at this early stage, he conceived as a series of three articles on the future of Russia. Instead of thinking of a novel, which was an earlier intention for productive use of his time in Capri, Conrad had begun to think politically about the fate of Russia in the light of internal burgeoning strikes matched by conflict with Japan abroad. From January through July 1905, Conrad continued to make brief mention of his essay to various correspondents, dropping hints at its changing shape in response to rapidly moving events in Russia and the world.

These hints of ongoing composition toward publication culminate in a June 30th letter to Galsworthy in which Conrad announces the appearance of the essay in *The Fortnightly*

Review, bearing the motto "Sine ira et studio" (272).[6] But even though Conrad clearly intended it to, the motto did *not* appear in *The Fortnightly Review,* apparently removed by *The Fortnightly Review*'s anonymous editor without Conrad's knowledge. It does, however, appear in the Syracuse typescript, in *North American Review* published on the same date as *The Fortnightly Review* version, and later reprinted in the Cambridge edition of *Notes on Life and Letters.* Its meaning "without prejudice [also translated as anger] or partiality," the epigraph comes from Tacitus' *Annals* and would seem to act as an emblem for historical objectivity. Tacitus writes:

> The history of Tiberius and of Caius, of Claudius and of Nero, during the lives of these Emperors was distorted by terror, and after their deaths coloured by the hatred that survived them. It is my purpose therefore to relate a few incidents of the latter part of the reign of Augustus, and thereafter to deal with the reign of Tiberius and subsequent events, without either prejudice or partiality – motives from which my mind is necessarily free. (2-3)

Whether Conrad had recently read Tacitus or had his Tacitus through Gibbon, whom he acknowledged reading on board the *Torrens,* we can't know, but regardless, there has been little critical commentary on Conrad's use of the quote from Tacitus other than recognition that the motto denotes Tacitus' impartiality in describing Roman emperors who lived generations before he wrote. However, in his *Annals,* Tacitus, despite his stated intention, *fails* to be impartial, as classical scholars widely acknowledge. Written almost a century after the death of Tiberius, Tacitus' *Annals* are notable for style, selection, and moral purpose; for Tacitus, Tiberius was a villain, and where Tacitus' heroes, like Germanicus, were painted with a white brush, Tiberius was painted all black (Wells 33-34).[7] J. S. Reid argues that "'saeva indignatio' gnaw[s] at the hearts of all the trio" (of great Roman writers: Lucan, Tacitus, and Juvenal) (191). Tacitus writes against autocracy and empire, privileging liberty instead, looking back to the days of the Republic, while articulating despair about his own time. Some of that strikes a similar chord in Conrad; furthermore, Tacitus' determination to attempt impartiality and Conrad's adoption of his Latin phrase for a historian's impartiality raise the broader issue of the very possibility of historical objectivity. A Polish philosopher of Conrad's father's generation, Henryk Kamieński, for example, rejected Hegel's theory of the "Absolute knowledge of history," arguing instead that facts are not "'something ready-made [...] they have to be selected and endowed with meaning'" by "'the knower'" (qtd. in Niland 23). Richard Niland argues that Conrad subscribed to this method of subjectively rendering the past whose meaning can only be inscribed in the present (23). Why, then, would Conrad use this motto from Tacitus?

Its use by Conrad – and by Tacitus – suggests an irony in both their historiographical approaches to subjects about which they are not at all impartial, but passionately partial (savagely indignant!). Najder confirms, for example, that the "tense flourish" of Conrad's prose in "Autocracy and War" creates an essay which is "emotionally charged, sometimes to excess," preventing Conrad's ability to dismiss his subject "with a despondently sceptical shrug" ("Conrad's European Vision" 48). Carabine adds that Conrad's "polemic is written against the grain of both his Flaubertian aesthetic of detachment and of his sceptical temperament" (*The Life and Art* 84). Thus, possibly relying on his memory of Gibbon's *The History of the Decline and Fall of the Roman Empire*, which he acknowledged discussing at some length with W. H. Jacques on board the *Torrens* in 1892 (*PR* 28), Conrad embarked on his own analysis of the decline of Russia and the rise (and hopefully future decline) of Prussia as an emblem of the West. Gibbon offered exposure to Roman history which relied a good deal on Tacitus both in manner and matter, and through Gibbon's reconstructive narrative, Conrad saw Rome and Roman Empire as the ancient model for Britain, clearly evidenced in the references to Roman occupation of Britain in "Heart of Darkness," for example, among others.

In fact, as both Andrea White (40) and John Griffith (104ff) have pointed out, an anonymous piece entitled "From the New

Gibbon" appeared on pages 241-49 in the same February 1899 issue of *Blackwood's Magazine* as the first installment of "The Heart of Darkness"; its sentiments would have and did attract Conrad's attention, as he wrote to William Blackwood, "I was delighted with the number. Gibbon especially fetched me quite" (*CL* 2: 162). The Gibbon essay is a deeply pessimistic view of Britain's *fin de siècle* and a dire prediction for the decline and fall of her empire in the twentieth century. Imbued with the spirit of degeneration which seemed to permeate the age, the essay quickly moves from an opening which extols an empire "at the highest pitch of its power" ("From the New Gibbon" 241) to decry the cause of its latent "decay and corruption": British commerce (242). The effect on Britain caused by the advancement of manufacture and trade was reflected in the pollution of its air by poisonous coal, the penning up of its poor into tenements, the dilution of manliness in its army, the concentration of industry into "huge establishments controlled by a few heads" (246), and even "the debasement and final extinction of English letters" (248). "[T]he British Empire," the "New Gibbon" concludes, "entered upon the twentieth century under the gloomiest auspices" (249). Such sentiments about the fate of empires echo Tacitus as well as Edward Gibbon and would have aligned with Conrad's views of European world order in 1905. Conrad's portrait of Britain's past as "one of the dark places of the earth" (HD 45) occupied by a Roman Empire in decline, suggests that the fate of British empire nineteen centuries after Roman occupation could very well end in its fall if it participated in the greed and lust for trade of other European empires; thus "Autocracy and War" is a cautionary tale for multiple empires.

Distinct from Tacitus, though, and even more so from Gibbon, Conrad, as a historian of his own time, writes *in medias res* in a unique way, witnessing the unfolding of events *without* knowing their outcome. Conrad had begun to adopt a role as public intellectual and "interpreter of his epoch" as both Hampson and Carabine observe (Hampson, "Polish Problem" 27; Carabine, *The Life and Art* 84). Months after "Autocracy

Chapter One: "Autocracy and War," the Age of Capital...

and War" appeared in print, Conrad wrote Ada Galsworthy in November 1905, reflecting on history evolving in the aftermath of his essay. Seeing his work as "a piece of prophecy both as to Russia and Germany," he acknowledged significant change in Russia, change that before a year ago he had not envisioned (*CL* 3: 294). What was still to come in Russia and Germany, of course, he could not know in November of 1905.

The main thrust of Conrad's essay develops as a prequel to the unleashing of revolution and war nine years in the future and incorporates prophetic observations about change in the world order. Russia, Conrad's *bête noir* hovers over the essay in spectral form, both literally and figuratively, in its inevitable loss to Japan and Conrad's narrative shaping of the result of that loss: "the spectre of Russia's might still faces Europe from across the teeming graves of Russian people"; but through the surging power of the Japanese military, "the ghost of Russia's might is laid" (AW 75, 76). In the background of Conrad's vitriol is the powerful example of his father's "Poland and Muscovy," Apollo Korzeniowski's satiric diary of his transfer from the Warsaw Citadel to the *zsyłka,* his place of exile, where he condemns Muscovy unequivocally as the "plague of humanity," the would-be destroyer of all civilization, most importantly, that of Poland (77). "Countless swarms of Muscovites, corrupted and infested with vermin," Korzeniowski writes, "are out to destroy everything that man, conscious of his human dignity, has built, in the course of a centuries-long effort of the mind, and for the price of blood" (79). Korzeniowski's essay is filled with a spirit of defiance that, nonetheless, sadly recognizes Muscovite power and the potential to attack Europe: "The most hideous slavery […] hangs over Europe" (79). With the passage of almost half a century, his son can gloat that Russian might has met its match in Japan.

Despite his celebration that "the ghost of Russia's might is laid," Conrad's essay is haunted, as Hampson cogently points out, by "the erasure of Poland's national boundaries" ("Polish Problem" 31). With Poland gutted and virtually nonexistent, Conrad seems to train his focus not on that enormous loss, but on the balance of power shifting from autocracy in Russia to the rising threat of Prussia. He argues that the Russo-Japanese war arises from the "expansionist policies" of both empires – as Hampson observes, the war's origins lay in the struggle for wheat and rice as well as the command of Eastern waters and "ice-free ports" (23). And with the slippage of autocratic Russia from the status of world power to a "Néant" (AW 79), the West is primed for Prussian (German imperial) expansion as an economic force contributing to the rise of capitalism, itself synonymous in Christopher GoGwilt's view, with the West (31). "*Il n'y a plus d'Europe –*" writes Conrad, "there is only an armed and trading continent" (AW 92), echoing the views of a close friend of his father, Stefan Buszczyński, whose *La Décadence de l'Europe* further asks "'which form will the future take?'" (qtd. in Niland 37). Conrad seeks to answer that question, singling out the threat as, "'Le Prussianisme – voilá l'ennemi!'" (AW 93).

At the heart of these major observations in Conrad's essay is his reference to the Crystal Palace, which seems to have little to do with Russia, Germany, or Poland. It docs, however, serve as a potent symbol for both future and failure. If the dreams of humanitarians were so bolstered by the sight of the Crystal Palace, they were made so by the promise of world peace. But for Conrad, the Crystal Palace, stuffed with "that variegated rubbish" (88), that the many forms of the Victorian commodity took, and offering powerful testimony to the advancement of technology, signals instead the rise of a culture of "Industrialism and Commercialism" which will inevitably bring about war. Even delimitation of geographical spheres of trade, like those effected in Africa by colonizing European nations and outlined by Conrad so cogently in "Heart of Darkness" seems preferable over the mass destruction of European nations at war. In a way, then, the Crystal Palace is the beginning of the end – the direct ancestor of World War I.

As GoGwilt observes, "Autocracy and War" is a hinge text; one century turns into another, and Conrad's essay moves from the map of Empire to the map of Europe with the imaginary space of Poland as the emotional center (27). While the essay frames time spanning the decades between 1851 and 1905, invoking the course of half a century in the trajectory of the rise of capitalism, it also moves spatially across Eastern and Western Europe, even skipping south for a brief mention of Europe's African colonies. In fact, we can extrapolate further from Andrew Francis' observations about commerce, space, and time in Conrad's *Victory* (168-69) that in "Autocracy and War" commerce cuts two ways: its rise to primacy and control as manager of Western and colonial geographical space and chronological time predicts its future as the source of the eventual decline of the West into global warfare. For Russia, "*le néant*" time has, in Conrad's view, stopped, and space exists only as an unfathomable chasm; but the West, the "armed and trading continent," stands poised to spread through the conquest of geographical space and the inevitable evolution of trade and commerce across continents, projecting into an unknowable but threatening future.

The Crystal Palace as the Centerpiece for Commercialized Space

Conrad's Europe in 1905, that "armed and trading continent, the home of slowly maturing economical contests for life and death, and of loudly proclaimed world-wide ambitions" (AW 92), had begun its transition to "Industrialism and Commercialism" in the long aftermath of the Great Exhibition. But how much do we, readers of "Autocracy and War" in the twenty-first century, know about the impact of the Great Exhibition in initiating capitalism through the nineteenth, the twentieth, and into the twenty-first centuries? For Conrad's recognition is salient to the long age in which we have lived. Even though Conrad responded negatively to the rise of the commodity imaged in the Great Exhibition; in 1851, the luminous Crystal Palace dominated discourse worldwide and provided a watershed moment in modernity, ushering in sweeping cultural change in Great Britain and the world, and announcing the arrival of a new world order dominated by commodity spectacle. Mass culture merged with commodity spectacle to mark the triumph of emergent capitalism as the defining characteristic of modern life. No longer a trivial thing as it was in the first half of the nineteenth century, the commodity, spectacularly displayed at the Crystal Palace, began its transformation to become "the focal point of all representation, the dead center of the modern world" (Richards 1).

Conrad's prescience about a spectacle he could not have seen, is remarkable. Time and space in the early twentieth century had been shaped by the explosion of technological advances in steam powered machinery like the steamship and railroad; the shrinking of the globe through networks of trade, transatlantic cables, and the telegraph; and the unhinging of the commodity as a thing of use to become globally traded and virtually autonomous, inviting want rather than need. Enhanced by its appearance on the world stage at this transformational moment, "phantasmagoric commodity fetishism reaches its acme in the spectacular display of the world exhibitions" (Leslie 116). The Crystal Palace served as a monument to production and consumption in an age where spectacle would become paramount as commodities were organized to incorporate and export an ideology, specifically, the ideology of England (Richards 3, 5). Thomas Richards suggests that the exhibition at the Crystal Palace sealed the visual inviolability of the object displayed within a building flooded with light where the objects could not be touched and where no prices were assigned (19-20). Marx's analysis of commodity fetishism underscores this almost mystic quality of the commodity emerging in the mid-nineteenth century – as a transcendent object no longer important as an object of exchange but now "a powerful and essentially unstable form of representation" (69). "World exhibitions," Benjamin wrote, "are places of pilgrimage to the commodity fetish" (*The Arcades Project* 7).

Though the dreams of peace imaged in the Crystal Palace, as Conrad observed, would vanish before the dawn of the

Chapter One: "Autocracy and War," the Age of Capital...　　27

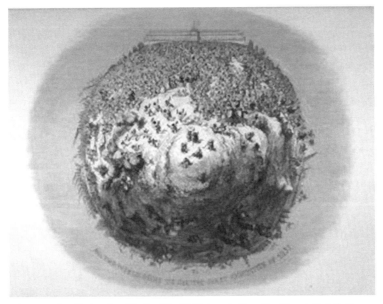

George Cruikshank. *All the World Going to See the Great Exhibition of 1851*[8]

twentieth century, the new world in mid-nineteenth century set in motion by that palace of light had just begun. Conrad's view of the Crystal Palace's "variegated rubbish" aligns with what Esther Leslie would later claim (following Walter Benjamin): that the new commodity society was a "fetishized thing-world, [where] phantasmagoric and frozen commodity-forms belligerently beset people, only to be tossed, through technical change and economic stimulus, on the rubbish heap of the outmoded" (9). While Conrad saw the commodities displayed in the Crystal Palace as junk; for Benjamin, rags and scraps provided proof of an alternative history of society, told by its discards. Beyond this, however, Douglas Smith argues that Benjamin offers a "'redemptive' view of trash, as a source of creativity and alternative history" (qtd. in Pye 9). The refusal of rubbish to stay in the trash can – following Benjamin and his critics – suggest new dimensions for examining Conrad's notion of the "variegated rubbish" filling the Crystal Palace, including a prize-winning commodity container that Conrad knew well and referenced by name as "kicked along a gutter" (HD 71) – the Huntley and Palmers biscuit tin – on the world stage for the first time at the Great Exhibition.

Contemporary visitors to the Great Exhibition, though, many without Conrad's disdain for commercialized rubbish, thronged to the Exhibition, and their senses were besieged by hundreds of commodities, the Huntley and Palmers biscuit only a small part of that massive display. Most visitors, like art historian Julius Lessing, found the event exhilarating. For Lessing, the Great Exhibition heralded the dawn of a new age:

> The great new thought found a great new form [...]. In every land rang out the news of something fabulous and unprecedented: a palace of glass and iron was going to be built [...]. It is in the highest degree remarkable and significant that this Great Exhibition of London – born of modern conceptions of steam power, electricity, and photography, and modern conceptions of free trade – should at the same time have afforded the decisive impetus [...] for the revolution in artistic forms. (qtd. in Benjamin, *Arcades* 183-84)

Lessing's emphasis is on the commodity form as *artistic* rather than commercialized and materialistic; and while Lessing's adulation was not shared by all – John Ruskin, among others, protested the lack of artistic significance in the huge greenhouse which housed the Great Exhibition (419) – nonetheless, from May Day to October 15, the Crystal Palace afforded more than six million visitors (approximately one-fifth of the population of Great Britain) the opportunity to witness one of the greatest spectacles of the age. Housed in a vast, novel architectural space in Hyde Park encompassing nineteen acres covered by a structure of cast iron and plate glass, the display of exhibits marked the first world's fair, the origin of industrial design, and the "'advent of modernity'" (qtd. in Auerbach, *The Great Exhibition* 1).

The broad theme of the exhibition was announced as education – an education in taste for the consuming public and in aesthetics for the producers of British goods, whose designs had been measured against European goods and found wanting. Even though mid-century Britain was the workshop of the world – producing two-thirds of the world's coal and half of its iron and cotton cloth – British manufacturing design lacked appeal (Auerbach, *The Great Exhibition* 122). That the concept of arts manufactures was one of the "fundamental ideological building blocks" of the exhibition was made clear in the division of its displays into raw materials, machinery, manufactures, and fine arts (98).

Innate in the very structure of the exhibition project was an intended tension in establishing the boundaries between the artistic object and the commercial one, so the thrust of the Exhibition was to enable not only a transformation in industry but a transformation in the wider culture and its aesthetics as well. For the organizers, it was signally important to find ways to combine "commerce and culture, arts and manufactures, taste and profits" because at the heart of the critique of British production was the recognition of lack in aesthetic design (113). The tensions outlined in Auerbach's quotation would help transform British society at the mid-century, and the commodity, as the product of tension and transformation, took on a life of its own. For Richards, "the Crystal Palace turned you into a dilettante, loitering your way through a phantasmagoria of commodities" (35); indeed, the mid-century Victorian who visited the Crystal Palace had become, like Benjamin's "*flâneur*," seduced by spectacle, by "the intoxication of the commodity around which surges the stream of customers" (Benjamin, *Charles Baudelaire* 55).

"The spectacle is *capital* accumulated," wrote Guy Debord, "to the point where it becomes image" (24), an observation that applies to the spectacle of consumerism offered by the Crystal Palace. Architecturally the huge greenhouse flooded its interior spaces with light to illuminate objects, many of which were additionally housed within glass cases. The "glass surfaces [were] themselves practically dissolved in light," signifying a "new valuation of space at work in the Crystal Palace" (Benjamin,

Arcades 541). Glass, transparent and clear, made the "things" visible as the transparent medium itself receded into invisibility. Unreadable, glass pressed upon a Victorian "cultural imaginary," standing in for the "invisible nature of mediation in complex, 'modern,' nineteenth-century experience" (Armstrong 58).[9] The Victorian visitor witnessed an interior space mediated by glass, making the objects within "strange," disrupting the meaning of exchange value, and calling the relationship of things, which were not overtly priced, into question. Spectacle becomes the cultural form for "the representation of manufactured things" (Richards 54), operating in similar fashion to Benjamin's notion of phantasmagoria in which "commodities displayed within the Universal Exhibitions manifest themselves in phantasmagorical terms" (Cohen 22). "The world dominated by its phantasmagorias," writes Benjamin, following Baudelaire, "is [...] 'modernity'" (*Arcades* 26).

The commodity, argues Richards, had become the "centerpiece of everyday life," and the "era of the spectacle," as a cultural form for representing manufactured things, had begun (1, 3). Following the argument of Debord, the consumer within the society of the spectacle sees a series of related images in which "the world of the commodity rul[es] over all lived experience" (26). In a society initiated in large part by the spectacle at the great Crystal Palace, the commodity had become a fetish, an object of power and desire, around which, to paraphrase Benjamin, the stream of *worshippers* surged.

Tony Bennett argues that nineteenth century expositions highlight their ideological organizing principles, so that displays of machinery and industrial processes become material signifiers of progress, of "progress as a collective national achievement with capital as the great co-ordinator" (80). Following this principle, the Great Exhibition organized its displays on two levels, with booths arranged on north and south sides of a long central avenue running west to east; exhibits were divided by nationalities, with the majority of displays, naturally, devoted to Great Britain and its colonies. British and colonial goods were arranged in the west half to the center, while foreign exhibitors were located in the east half, divided by the sparkling centerpiece of the north/south transepts, the great 4-ton, solid glass crystal fountain, designed and built by Follett Osler of Birmingham.

Lighter articles were placed in the galleries, heavier articles, like machines, were found on the northwest side close to the steam pipes which powered them. Manufactures and fine arts were spaced intermittently along the central avenue, but machines in motion and machines at rest, like locomotives, carriages, agricultural machinery, and railway equipment, provided the biggest draw for visitors, followed by raw materials and textiles. Eric Hobsbawm notes that the increasing need to expand global markets was met by the explosion in steam machinery technology, and the development of railways was a crowning achievement of Britain's early industrial society (33). "History," in Hobsbawm's words, "from now on became world history" (47). The age of the machine and the exhilaration of technological progress dominated the exhibition.

Providing the initiatory impulse for world exhibitions to follow, the Great Exhibition ordered the displays along the principles of mass production, prefabrication, mass communication, and urbanization. All these factors stemmed from the Industrial Revolution, and Great Britain experienced all of them first (Greenhalgh 142). "The physical abundance" of man-made commodities in circulation, writes Paul Greenhalgh, "allowed empire to expand at an unprecedented pace until most of the known world was brought under the yoke of the industrialised nations" (142). Great Britain hardly lacked the commitment to Empire visible throughout exhibitions to 1940, providing the foundation for propaganda justifying the subjugation of native colonies and inspiring Britons with imperial pride (59).

Accordingly, British exhibits privileged raw materials, machinery, and manufactures, while neglecting representations of fine arts. In raw materials, British and colonial exhibits displayed substances which could be converted into manufactured articles and those which provided power for manufacturing, like coal, iron ore, and wool from Australia.

Heavy machinery, described in the *Official Descriptive and Illustrative Catalogue* as "the most direct representation of one of the principal sources of the industrial success and prosperity of Great Britain" (qtd. in Auerbach, *The Great Exhibition* 104), included examples of cotton processing machinery – fifteen machines which operated from opening the cotton boll to weaving spun cotton – and locomotives, seen as the primary example of steam engines which would eventually do all the work of the world (107). In manufactures, Britain presented itself as the "'workshop of the world,'" "'an enormous pantechnicon'" of objects on display, including multipurpose furniture, model working class houses, and decorative household goods (gaudy objects largely derided by art critics who visited the Crystal Palace) (109).

With imperial displays located centrally and dominating the west wing of the Crystal Palace, non-mainland British displays were divided into foreign countries and colonies. Among the colonies, commodities included mostly raw materials and some manufactured items, like sugar from the West Indies, birchbark canoes from Canada, specimens of native cotton and palm oil from West Africa, and exotic artifacts like the Indian Koh-i-Noor diamond. Foreign countries, including Russia, Prussia, Holland, Belgium, Austria, France, Spain, Portugal, Switzerland, Italy, Sweden, Denmark, Tunisia, and Turkey, all sent representative products including furs, minerals, tapestries, carpets, porcelain, merino wool, and Toledo ware. These foreign displays of raw materials and manufactured commodities offered little in the way of technological advances, but the United States provided sensational inventions and popular items like the McCormick reaper, the Hobbs lock, a collection of daguerreotypes by Matthew Brady, rubber goods displayed by Charles Goodyear, the Leroy and Blodgett sewing machine (but not the Singer which wasn't patented until August 1851), and the Colt revolver (Cunliffe 118).

However, the United States exhibit also created controversy for its life-sized marble statue "The Greek Slave" by Hiram Powers (Cunliffe 120; Hyman 218).

Chapter One: "Autocracy and War," the Age of Capital...

The statue symbolized an important shift from objects as commodities to bodies as commodities, its imagery literally linking it to the commodified body enslaved. In 1850, while so many other countries had long before declared the abolition of slavery, the United States countered world opinion and

John Absolon. *The Greek Slave*

passed the Fugitive Slave Law, authored by Henry Clay, which required the return of escaped slaves to their owners regardless of whether they were found in a free or a slave state. Thus, Powers' statue – wherever it toured both before and after the Great Exhibition – served as a flashpoint for discussions of slavery, even inviting a performance at the Crystal Palace by fugitive slaves William and Ellen Craft and William Wells Brown, who demonstrated next to the "Greek Slave" on June 21, 1851, to counterpoint the irony and hypocrisy indicated by the juxtaposition of black bodies and the white marble female form of Powers' statue (Knadler 348). However, Ellen Craft's appearance provided an additional layer to the performance of race, for she was so light skinned that she was able to pass as white, enabling the couple's escape from the United States to Great Britain. Her pale skin also invoked a powerful icon in nineteenth century literature – the "tragic octoroon," one of the most famous of abolitionist tropes – the figure of a light skinned woman, raised as white but sold into slavery after the death of her white, slave-owning father to repay his debts. Harriet Beecher Stowe's *Uncle Tom's Cabin* is a well-known example among many which include this character type from pre-Civil War sentimental romance.

Hiram Powers' intention, however, did not seem to reflect views on the status of slavery in America but rather, according to his own gloss on the statue, the figure signified a young Greek Christian woman being sold into slavery in Constantinople (Hyman 216). In the 1840s, Powers was very aware of the revolutions sweeping Europe at the time, specifically the short-lived revolutionary "springtime of the peoples" in 1848 (Hobsbawm 13), and more concerned for freedom in his adopted country Italy rather than for slavery in his native land. Powers would produce six versions of the statue, each one, though almost identical to the others, considered an original. The earliest versions were displayed in both Great Britain and the United States in the 1840s to widespread acclaim. In the last version, crafted in 1866, Powers changed the chains to manacles, more closely reflecting the statue's connections to the passing of the Civil War and the abolition of slavery in the United States.

The first version of the statue was the one sent to the Great Exhibition in 1851 and set on a revolving pedestal, so that viewers could examine all angles of the life-size figure. The whiteness of the marble form suggested the image of whiteness set against the darkness of the Ottoman Empire and was meant to link contemporary neoclassical form to the ancient Greeks, representing the pinnacle of civilization. But the statue, in addition to its unintentional connection to slavery sanctioned in the United States, also represented female vulnerability to sexual slavery, thus adding a gendered dimension to the display. Contemporary audiences in both Britain and the United States saw the statue as the model of ideal womanhood, "cloaked in a veil of moral sentiment" (Hyman 219), but the statue's feminine nudity allowed a male audience to see her as an erotic sex object – both passive and in bondage to masculine power.

While inviting discussion of racism and slavery in America, the Great Exhibition, cloaked its own unexamined prejudices. As an English audience expressed abhorrence at an American culture that insisted on the preservation of slavery, the Great Exhibition itself preserved rather rigid class distinctions present in Britain while privileging European, more specifically British, productivity over that of darker skinned nations. Following the lead of Paul Greenhalgh, Jeffrey Auerbach argues that the exhibition was meant to do more than enlighten and educate, it was also meant to serve as a "purveyor of coded messages about the alleged racial superiority of European civilization" (*The Great Exhibition* 228; Greenhalgh 27-29, 52-44, 226). Furthermore, while the organizers created the appearance of bringing together the whole of English society, admission prices were staggered to segregate the classes, based on fears that the working classes might cause trouble while rubbing elbows with the upper classes. Fears engendered by the revolutions of 1848, which convulsed European capitals, and the rise of the working class lingered among the exhibition organizers who set aside "shilling days" for the working-class attendees while the upper class could dominate attendance on "pound days" when the workers were virtually excluded by the high cost. The British satirical journal *Punch* had a field day with this segregation by price in its June 1851 issue's illustration "The Pound and the Shilling. 'Whoever Thought of Meeting You Here?'" (Auerbach, "The Great Exhibition and Historical Memory" 103). In it, a working man in his stocking cap with his family comes face to face with the Duke of Wellington surrounded by fashionable ladies, depicting an encounter that was hardly likely to happen.

Other illustrations, like those from Thomas Onwhyn's *Mr. and Mrs. Brown's Visit to London to see the Great Exhibition of All Nations*, highlight "dark gentlemen in their bed-clothes with spears" and a group of purported cannibals with dark skins and monkey faces threatening to eat the Browns' child (Auerbach, "The Great Exhibition and Historical Memory" 106). These views of the exotic, darker skinned, and even repulsive other, were balanced by the exhibits offered by the British possessions in Africa, which indicated instead that Africans were extremely active, knowledgeable, and savvy producers and consumers on their own continent. Improving Africans as "buying machines," as Conrad thought, was exactly the goal of European imperialists, who rigorously ignored African culture and values as well as a long history of African trade practices in order to cultivate a desire for European goods.

The introduction to African exhibits in the *Official Descriptive and Illustrative Catalogue* implied that Africa was useful to Britain only for its raw materials (Auerbach, *The Great Exhibition* 101). As listed in the *Official Descriptive and Illustrative Catalogue*, exhibitors brought raw materials from the African colonies such as woods, lead, iron, minerals, animal skins, elephant tusks, and ostrich feathers as well as products of native industry like woven baskets, weapons, cloth made of native cotton, and glass amulets made from melted European beads (2: 949, 952). While Africans were the producers of manufactured objects largely made by hand and gatherers of the raw materials exhibited, they were not the exhibitors; for the items were brought exclusively by British exhibitors interested in the colonies. The fact that Britons exhibited the artifacts certainly underscores a patriarchal attitude that Africans were incapable of managing and providing the displays from their own country. *Official Descriptive and Illustrative Catalogue* identifies "textile productions of native industry" (952) as the most extensive and interesting part of the collection from West Africa; for example, specimens of female dress made from silk gathered from the silk cotton tree on the banks of the Niger River were on display. But items from two ports on the west African coast are of particular interest to readers of Conrad:

from Popo on the Oil Coast came Popo cloth, "the whole of the material, except the red, grown, spun, and dyed in the country" (954), and from Grand Bassam, a dagger. In "Heart of Darkness," Gran' Bassam and Little Popo are: "names that seemed to belong to some sordid farce acted in front of a sinister backcloth" (HD 54). Both, however, were, from the 1880s, trading places on the Ivory Coast and the Slave Coast, especially Grand Bassam, the most important trading post and original capital of the French colonial Coté d'Ivoire.

Additionally interesting to readers of Conrad is an item from the river Congo: a "[f]etische […] in the garb of a slave traveling through the country" (*Catalogue* 2: 954). Thus, especially in the case of the "fetische," the items from African colonies would have been favored for their exotic appeal, but, in the eyes of the European observer, could hardly have held sway against the "superior" technological productions of European colonial powers. Africa, however, offered enormous potential both as a new market for European-produced goods and for its wealth in natural resources.

"Trade," argues Greenhalgh, "was at the theoretical core of exhibitions, perhaps because it was at the heart of European and American society. Trade had created Western power; the exhibitions were no more than an expression of that power" (22). Certainly, at the core of the Great Exhibition, British and colonial displays were meant to emphasize European hegemony and to indicate European ability to manipulate and control trading systems. Greenhalgh uses a significant passage from William Cowper's "Charity" (1782) to underscore the centrality of trade to the Great Exhibition: "And if a boundless plenty be the robe // Trade is the golden girdle of the globe" (qtd. in Greenhalgh 22; Cowper 529). Further lines from "Charity" underscore the link between trade and slavery:

> But ah! What wish can prosper, or what prayer,
> For merchants rich in cargoes of despair,
> Who drive a loathsome traffic, gauge, and span,
> And buy the muscles and bones of Man? (Cowper 529)

Cowper, whose poem appeared seventy years before the Great Exhibition, understood the unavoidable connections making slavery necessary to global trade, connections which resurface in the Crystal Palace not only in the American exhibition of Hiram Powers' statue but also in the pervasive belief in the superiority of European culture and technological advances, the centrality of trade, and the transcendent commodity (both human and inanimate).

The Rise of the Commodity and the Contraction of the Globe in International Exhibitions

Tucked away in the North Transept Gallery between cutlery and china, listed as an item in "Miscellaneous Manufactures and Small Wares," Item 107, Class 29, of the *Official Descriptive and Illustrative Catalogue*, was a display by Huntley and Palmers of "Various fancy biscuits, made by steam machinery; the biscuits being mixed, rolled, cut out, and conveyed to the ovens without kneading the dough, as in the ordinary way" (2: 796). No mention of the tins, but the biscuits were displayed in the distinctive Huntley and Palmers tin. The Huntley and Palmers display was located directly above the exhibits of machinery in motion like lathes and mills, railroad engines, steam machinery, and printing presses. Even though this appearance of Huntley and Palmers in the first international exhibition did not result in a prize, the company would learn from this appearance,[10] going on to win its first medal in the 1867 Paris Exposition Universelle, a medal a year at exhibitions for the next eleven years, and the Grand Prix gold medal at the 1878 Paris Exposition Universelle, which established its brand name as one of the great exhibition winners. Through the years, Huntley and Palmers learned not only how to expand its global reach for trading its biscuits, primarily to Britons abroad in British zones of control, but also how to promote its sales through sharp advertising. In its appearance at the universal

Chapter One: "Autocracy and War," the Age of Capital...   39

exhibition, *Weltausstelung*, in Vienna, 1873, the company's exhibition space had grown large enough to display its wares in an elaborate showcase.

Universal Exhibition of Vienna. Courtesy of Reading Museum (Reading Borough Council)

In 1846, with the arrival of George Palmer as partner, Huntley and Palmers proved itself to be a technical innovator in the mass production of biscuits as well as the development of aesthetically pleasing tins, which became an integral part of the product. For example, in the 1850s, three companies, including Huntley and Palmers, produced six million pounds of biscuits; but by the 1870s, that figure jumped to 37 million pounds. As Felipe Fernandez-Armesto argues, both "the Reading biscuit and the Huntley and Palmers *biscuit tin*, with its distinctive blue livery, became symbols of the global reach of British industry and imperialism" (197, emphasis added).

And the global reach of British industry and imperialism, symbolized by Huntley and Palmers, found ample support back home in a succession of exhibitions and shows, international, colonial, and otherwise, that followed in the wake of the Crystal Palace. Just two years after the close of the Crystal

Palace, for example, colonial displays like the performance of Zulu "kaffirs" in London in 1853, prompted Charles Dickens to claim that "if we have anything to learn from the Noble Savage, it is what to avoid," adding that the Zulus should be "civilised off the face of the earth" (337). Dickens wrote rather extensively and satirically on the performance and lecture, using onomatopoeia to reproduce animalistic sounds:

> I am the original physician to Nooker the Umtargartie. Yow yow yow! No connexion with any other establishment. Till till till! All other Umtargarties are feigned Umtargarties, Boroo Boroo! But I perceive here a genuine and real Umtargartie, Hoosh Hoosh Hoosh! in whose blood I, the original Imyanger and Nookerer, Blizzerum Boo! will wash these bear's claws of mine. O yow yow yow! (338)

Yet, despite Dickens' disdain and his tirade in print, the Zulu show was the biggest hit of the season in London in the summer of 1853, offering three performances a day by eleven men, one woman, and a baby born on the journey to London, and dramatized as scenes from tribal life rather than a sideshow (Lindfors 65). The show followed on the heels of the eighth Zulu/Xhosa wars from 1850-1853, the longest and most bitterly fought, which inspired intense British interest in the Zulus and encouraged promoters like Charles Caldecott to capitalize on the moment by bringing one of the most famous exhibitions of the exotic "other" to London in 1853. One journalist who attended the performance described it in terms somewhat similar to Dickens:

> After a supper of meal, of which the Kaffirs partake with large wooden spoons, an extraordinary song and dance are performed, in which each performer moves about on his haunches, grunting and snorting the while like a pair of asthmatic bellows ... no description can give an idea of the cries and shouts – now comic, now terrible – by which the Kaffirs express emotions. (qtd. in Qureshi 192)

The show appeared at a seminal moment during the earliest stages of European exploration in Africa, seeding interest in the vast unknown of the continent; David Livingstone, for example, had already begun missionary activity and exploration in southern and central Africa in the 1840s, to be followed by Burton, Speke, Grant, and Stanley from the 1850s onward.

A few years before the Zulu performances, the discovery of a "man-ape" in Africa captured the attention of the Western world. Scientific proof of the existence of the gorilla began to appear in the 1840s; then, in 1861, shortly after the publication of Darwin's *On the Origin of the Species* (1859), Paul du Chaillu arrived in London to display skins and skeletons of gorillas he claimed he had killed in Africa. For centuries, the gorilla had existed on the periphery of human knowledge, largely hidden in African forests; now evidence of their existence had come to London as an exhibition for entertainment as much as for zoological research. In time, du Chaillu's integrity, authority, and authenticity would be challenged by the scientific community and the Royal Geographical Society, prompting a scientist like T. H. Huxley to claim:

> If I have abstained from quoting M. Du Chaillu's work, then, it is not because I discern any inherent improbability in his assertions respecting the man-like Apes; nor from any wish to throw suspicion on his veracity; but because, in my opinion, so long as his narrative remains in its present state of unexplained and apparently inexplicable confusion, it has no claim to original authority respecting any subject whatsoever. It may be truth but it is not evidence. (71-72)

In fact, to further discredit du Chaillu, several scientists speculated on his racial origins, intimating that his mother was mixed-race, making him a "mongrel," therefore, susceptible, based upon his "negro" origins, to provide a romanticized rather than scientific account of his discovery and incapable of proper preservation of the animal skins he collected (Miller 164). As popular as the exhibition might have been early on, the display of gorillas became a mere sideshow:

> The gorilla became a creature not just of serious scientific discussion but of side shows and tabloid newspapers. A "gorilla ballet" went thumping across the London stage, and in parlors around Europe and the United States, amateur pianists performed a "Gorilla Quadrille." (qtd. in Miller 159)

"Gorillas," John Miller concludes, "in their eerie familiarity and abyssal difference appear as an uncanny shadow of humanity that necessarily, it seems, inhabit a territory on the edge of fiction" (166). Exhibitions, displays, and productions such as the Zulu troupe performances and the gorilla exhibits served to heighten a public fascination with the spectacle of an "other" frighteningly close to oneself, to commodify and objectify that "other," and to orient a public gaze toward Africa.

From the Great Exhibition to World War II there were 35 international exhibitions hosted by the United States, France, Belgium, Italy, and the United Kingdom, among others, clearly resulting in delivering to the world a Western vision of trade, technological advancement, and imperialism. Moreover, such exhibitions offered the opportunity to view "'anthropological' exhibits," turning the display of other cultures into spectacle (Gold and Gold 80).

Writing of ancient societies, Bettina Bergmann points out "[s]ocieties and people define themselves through spectacle" (9), and it was spectacle with a capital S that international exhibitions offered for decades. Adding race and otherness to the mix, the colonial nature of ensuing world's fairs, especially in the nineteenth century, could celebrate cultural hegemony in the west, turning the world into an exhibition of Western power and technological advancement.

Two *Expositions Universelles* in France, the first in 1867 and the second in 1889, are powerful examples of raising ethnic display to new levels. While still serving as showcases for commodities and prioritizing global trade, both fairs sought to render all spaces of the globe visible to the gaze of metropolitan fairgoers. Beginning in 1867, exhibitions regularly featured anthropological exhibits and even native villages. While visitors from many parts of the British empire attended the Great Exhibition, colonial subjects and foreigners first became a part of the exhibits at the 1867 Paris fair in "tableaux-vivants" from North Africa (Greenhalgh 85). There were bazaars with Egyptian crafts and vendors, a camel stable with camels and their attendants, and Egyptian, Tunisian, and Algerian cafes.

Chapter One: "Autocracy and War," the Age of Capital... 43

By 1889, at the largest *Exposition Universelle* to date, the scale of display had expanded to an unprecedented level of peopled exhibits where, partly fueled by the rise of anthropology as a discipline, "people were degraded to the level of zoological exhibits" (87). This fair, in its erection of native villages, forged a prototype for imperial sections of fairs to follow. Native tribes appeared to demonstrate every aspect of humanity through all of its evolutionary stages. Among the main attractions in 1889, the Congolese village served as an example of what one enthusiastic, but condescending visitor described as

> Each village is built in its own grounds, enclosed by a fence, and inhabited by its own natives .... All these natives have been specially imported for the exhibition. They have brought with them the materials for their huts, their tools, and everything necessary for them to reproduce in the capital of the civilized world the everyday life of Africa. (qtd. in Greenhalgh 88)

From 1889, the native village was a regular feature in international exhibitions, culminating in the White City exhibitions of 1908-1914, but these could not surpass an exhibition devoted exclusively to the exploration of Africa.

The Stanley and African Exhibition at the *Fin de Siècle*

While not on the scale of an international exhibition, but unquestionably the most popular colonial exhibition in 1890, *The Stanley and African Exhibition* opened in London on the very eve of Conrad's departure for Africa. The exhibition, lodged at the Victoria Gallery on Regent Street and open to the public in March 1890, provided ample advance advertisement for Henry Morton Stanley's heroic return to London in May and presented Stanley, whose busts and portraits were prominently featured and whose collection formed many of the exhibit's displays, as the conquering hero of African exploration. Though later accounts of the real nature of the 1887 expedition to rescue Emin Pasha would seriously mar

Stanley's reputation; in the spring of 1890, he was lionized in the national and illustrated presses as the representative of "'the new journalism'" and the "'intrepid explorer'" (qtd. in Coombes 66), the Victorian equivalent of a rock star. The language of romance, argues Coombes, citing the lavish adulation heaped upon Stanley in the *Anti-Slavery Reporter*, informed the "dramaturgy" of the exhibition, painting Stanley as "'the great African leader'":

> From the untracked depths of one of Nature's densest and most deadly forests, saturated with the tropical rains of countless ages, and alive with malignant pigmies, skilled in the use of poisoned arrows, Stanley like a hero of Romance, has once more emerged into the light of civilization. (qtd. in Coombes 68)

The Stanley and African Exhibition was enthusiastically publicized by *The Times*, which proclaimed: "'never has there been an Exhibition on anything like the scale of the present'" (qtd. in Coombes 66). Indeed, we know from Helen Chambers that Conrad was a devoted reader of *The Daily Telegraph* from 1885 on (*Conrad's Reading* 159), and Stanley was a correspondent for *The Daily Telegraph* beginning with his African adventures to find David Livingstone in the early 1870s. According to Annie Coombes, the Stanley exhibition, though only one among many exhibitions related to Africa at the time, outstripped them all in the exhaustive coverage it received, especially in *The Times* – coverage that it seems impossible for Conrad to have missed, even though he was not a habitual reader of *The Times* until after the turn of the century (66). However, as a "devoted reader" of the *The Daily Telegraph*, Conrad may have noted that his favorite newspaper reported Stanley's return to England in late April 1890, highlighting the crowds that awaited Stanley at the docks of Dover, lined his route to London, and greeted him at Victoria Station (Berenson 144). Capitalizing on this public fervor just before Conrad left for the Congo, *The Graphic* published an extensive "Stanley Number" on April 30 detailing Stanley's triumphant return from the Congo, filled with illustrations, African history, description of the exhibits, and reports of the Emin Pasha relief expedition. While there is no proof that Conrad ever saw that issue of *The Graphic*, its extensive circulation indicates how much information about Stanley and the Congo was widely disseminated throughout European culture. A journalist in *The Contemporary Review* commented at the time that "one of the most remarkable features of the century has been the phenomenal interest in all things African" (Introductory Note, *The Stanley and African Exhibition Catalogue* 5). *The Stanley and African Exhibition*, far more than the earlier Great Exhibition and those that followed in its wake through 1889, focused specifically on the spectacle of the exotic "other" and "set the standard for public performances of race and empire" (Gerzina 76). The exhibition featured a binary opposition where British enterprise was set against African primitivism; British visitors viewed a coherent representation of the "British displayed to themselves," in their own superiority to races so vastly inferior, tamed and conquered by a hero like Stanley who had exploited Africa and made it "marketable" (Driver 155). Indeed, the *Catalogue* for *The Stanley and African Exhibition* proclaimed that, in addition to reclaiming "myriads of people steeped in the grossest idolatry" (5), the fascination of Africa offered the possibility of exploiting this virgin territory, for there were

> Frightful wrongs to be wiped out, deeds of high emprise to be achieved, virgin countries to be *commercially exploited*, valuable scientific discoveries to be made, myriads of people steeped in the grossest idolatry, and regions more or less capable of colonization, where no civilized flag floats – these are some of the varied elements which have thrown a glamour and fascination over Africa and taken men's minds captive. (Introductory Note 5, emphasis added)

Culture, commerce, and civilization, but most importantly, as Conrad would write later, the "nigger" to be turned into a "buying machine."

Patrons for the exhibition included Queen Victoria and Leopold II of Belgium, with Stanley, of course, as vice-patron.

The Committee consisted of notables among explorers (including several from Stanley's expeditions), missionaries, and representatives from Great Britain and Belgium: among them, Sir Richard Burton (famed explorer of the African great lakes in the 1850s), Paul du Chaillu (of gorilla fame), Colonel Grant, (African explorer with John Speke), Dr. Parke (a member of Stanley's Emin Pasha Relief Expedition), Horace Waller (British missionary to Africa and anti-slavery activist), Major Thys (a leader in forming the Société Anonyme Belge), and Lieutenant Stairs (also with Stanley on the Emin Pasha Relief Expedition). These, as well as the more than seventy other members, display a broad diversity among the men (there were no women on the Committee) who controlled in text and image the representation of Africa to the British public for the next several decades (Coombes 68).

Like the Crystal Palace, *The Stanley and African Exhibition* satisfied a public lust for spectacle, with the spectator constructed as an explorer in the image of Stanley, "[e]*n route* for the Heart of Savage Africa" (*The Stanley and African Exhibition Catalogue* 9), moving through a jungle, encountering native villages and stuffed wild animals, simulated native

Stanley and African Exhibition. Cover Illustration. Courtesy of the Smithsonian Librairies and Archives, Washington, D.C.

attacks, and live African boys depicting a "typical" African scene. The entrance was through a "'palisade of ... tree stems ... ornamented with skulls' which led to a simulated explorer's camp, surrounded by a composite landscape supposedly representative of the key feature of Central African territory as 'discovered' by the European" (qtd. in Coombes 69). In addition to the native scene created to invite the spectator in as an explorer and among the hundreds of items displayed, the exhibition featured numerous busts and portraits of Stanley, maps, photographs, cases of specimens of African insects, native clothing and ornaments, stuffed lions, the head of an African elephant, the largest African elephant tusk yet found (184 pounds), relics from Mungo Park's possessions, and relics from Dr. Livingstone's possessions. Many of the artifacts came from the collections of European explorers and missionaries via Paris, Germany, and Brussels, including items from Speke, Grant, Livingstone, Stanley, of course, and a large number from Leopold II's Congo State Collection.

The exhibition was arranged into five sections: the Native Section, which contained many of the artifacts collected by explorers and missionaries; the Geographical Section, which displayed maps and information about the geography of Africa from the time of Ptolemy; the Section of Portraits, displaying those of prominent European travelers to Africa, including three women: Alexandrina Tinne, a "lady traveller on the upper Nile" (*The Stanley and African Exhibition Catalogue* 57); Florence Baker, Hungarian-born wife of explorer Samuel Baker and herself a former white slave; and Annie Hore, who, accompanying her missionary husband, was the first European woman to visit Lake Tanganyika); the Slave Trade Section, containing artifacts used in slave trafficking; and the Department of Pictures and Photographs, where images of the people, dwellings, and scenery of Africa were displayed. Mounted on the walls and arranged on tables beneath the wall displays in the Native Section, African weapons–including shields, spears, and bows and arrows–were artfully and symmetrically arranged but also powerfully representative of their inadequacy against far more advanced European firepower. Even the introduction to the catalogue of the Exhibition, describing the various items displayed, identifies them as "the arms, implements, domestic utensils, musical instruments, dresses, and adornments of the peoples of *savage* Africa" (Introductory Note, *The Stanley and African Exhibition Catalogue* 6, emphasis added). As Coombes argues, the exhibition reinforced "the dominant narrative of European exploration, and the hagiography of those figures involved in mapping the continent according to European principles of visibility and geography" (74-75).

In addition to the popularity of the displays of native weaponry, the exhibition emphasized the need for eliminating the slave trade in Africa, especially in light of the ongoing "scramble" by European nations to consume the African continent. Visitors thronged to anti-slavery exhibits, enhanced by the artistic rendition of a peaceful forest village scene followed by the scene of a farming village raided by slave-traders:

> The men have been confined in slave yokes, the women tied neck to neck with chains. Over all this scene illustrating "man's inhumanity to man," the giant mountain of Ruwenzori rears in the distance its snowy summit, looking the emblem of infinite purity against the blue sky in striking contrast to the deeds of blood enacted at its base. (*The Stanley and African Exhibition Catalogue* 49)

Balanced against the repudiation of slavery was the image of superiority of white Europe – a sculpted group in the main hall, an original quarter-size scale model of a larger group by William Theed for the Albert Memorial, delivered the European vision of Africa:

> The centre figure represents Egypt seated on a camel, on the right an Arab merchant, on the left a figure of a Troglodite, formerly dwellers on the Nile, at the back a figure of civilization instructing a negro, who is trampling on his broken chains, indicative of freedom. (39)

Tied to the Great Exhibition of 1851 as Albert's signature achievement, four of the Albert Memorial sculptures represent the major themes in the Exhibition of manufacturing,

Chapter One: "Autocracy and War," the Age of Capital...   49

commerce, agriculture, and engineering, and larger sculpted groupings representing the four continents span the corners of the memorial. The full-size sculpted African grouping differs slightly from *The Stanley and African Exhibition Catalogue*'s romantic description of the smaller, original model loaned to the Stanley exhibition by Theed. But the model metaphorically and metonymically links the Great Exhibition of 1851 to the Stanley exhibition, reinforcing, near the end of the century, all the major themes introduced at its midpoint.

The central figure of the sculpted group *Africa* at the Albert Memorial is an Egyptian princess with a pharaonic headdress astride a kneeling camel, to her right is an upright figure described in contemporary accounts[11] as a Nubian, to her left is a figure in Arab dress, and at her back is a female figure dressed in Grecian, classical style, her hand raised instructing a figure whose negroid features mark him as the "savage" receiving instruction in civilization. As the monument neared completion in 1873, awaiting only the bronze statue of Albert to complete it, the weekly magazine *Bow Bells* printed a detailed account, including a description of Theed's Africa group. The princess appears as a representative of Egypt as "the great early African power and the precursor of civilization" (180). The Nubian represents the eastern limits of the continent, "his hand resting on a half-buried statue, in allusion to the glories of the past" (180). The figure that appears in Arab dress denotes "the merchant of the northern states" (180). While

> [t]he negro leaning on his bow is the representative of the uncivilized races of this continent. He is listening to teachings of a female figure typifying European civilization, in allusion to the efforts made by Europe to improve the condition of these races; the broken chains at his feet refer to the part taken by Great Britain in the emancipation of the slaves. (180)

Behind the smaller model of this grouping in the Stanley exhibition was an "adult male gorilla from the Gaboon" (*The Stanley and African Exhibition Catalogue* 40). Presumably

William Theed the Younger. *Africa*

one of du Chaillu's, although not so acknowledged, the gorilla's positioning in relationship to African racial types in the sculpture, ranging from higher (and lighter skinned) civilizations to the lowest, suggests that the black African's position on the scale of evolutionary progress is just above the apes.

There was a plan for detailed documentation of the exhibits at the Stanley exhibition, and William Steains, with the Royal Geographic Society, was tapped to execute the drawings. While no final document of this exists, Steains' prototypes for the catalogue are located in the British Museum, and indicate, according to Coombes, an emphasis on drawings of carvings of figures and furniture (75). One of Steains' figures is listed in *The Stanley and African Exhibition Catalogue* as "an idol or fetish Boma Congo." Accompanying his drawing, Steains wrote the following description:

> The little wooden figures, of which there are five attached to the idol, are furnished with red glass bead anklets – necklaces – and have all very protruding abdomens – into which cowrie shells have been inserted in order to imitate navels. The grooved portion down the center of the forehead is highly polished for [the next word is unclear [...]. Small circular pieces of looking glass are inserted for the eyes. On breast yellow handkerchief with blue pattern. On right side red torn flannel. Rags very dirty of blue, white yellow and red. Blue and red predominating.

Chapter One: "Autocracy and War," the Age of Capital...   51

> A-A [the base] is a lot of *old* rope (thin) of a pale Burnt Umber colour – nails and knives rusty black and brown. Head shaded dark brown light brown and dull red (ochre?) as shown. Abdomen feet and stand pale brown wood. (qtd. in Crush, Appendix F 7)

While the colors are not apparent in the illustration offered here, the viewer can discern at least one of the smaller "idols" attached to the figure, the nails and knives inserted into the figure, and the rags and rope that drape its body. Given its position on a table in the Congo section, it is overwhelmed, despite its 4-foot size, by trophy presentations of spears, shields, and arrows on the walls above, and most likely obtained from Stanley's collection resembling "idols" and their potency described by him in *The Congo and the Founding of Its Free State*:

> In this village there is a double-headed wooden bust, with its crown adorned (?) [sic] with old iron scraps and bits of mirror glass, and

Fig. 24 *Nkisi*, item 35 "An idol or fetish from Boma", from the table in front of Panel 11 "The Congo State Collection" in the Stanley and African Exhibition

An Idol or Fetish from Boma.[12] With kind permission by Peter Crush

two wooden idols, about 4 feet high, ferocious in appearance, placed under a small shed, as a chapel, I suppose. These are the great gods of Banza Uvana. (1: 199)

The European misunderstanding of these objects is exemplified in the Western belief that Africans worshipped them, when, really, the "fetish" (an imperfect term to describe an *nkisi*) was a receptacle of power, a vessel whose contents were believed to bring about a desired result, whether it was the cure of disease, destruction of an enemy, or punishment of an evildoer. *Minkisi* (plural of *nkisi*)[13] in the Congo were

> lodged at the core of the economic and power relationships of society, thus they were used to control commerce in that business oaths were made before them, and the objects had the power to punish those who broke the rules of trade. They were used in the investiture of chiefs, and persons, jostling for power, would work to suppress the *minkisi* of their opponents. (Crush 7)[14]

The idol from Boma is barely visible in photographs taken of the interior of the exhibition, but its cultural importance is unmistakable, for, like all *minkisi*, it signals power. In an African society which valued mystical beliefs, the *nkisi* served as a dominant force for its society, just as the European commodity dominated an emergent consumer society. *Minkisi* were not only emblems of power but also internally dynamic, containers of powerful forces that could be harnessed to control the uncontrollable and pushed, through the insertion of knives and nails, into action. Like the commodity, *minkisi* were central to native government and trade, but they also constituted a threat to Western trade, so missionaries and explorers attempted to suppress them. As European empires pushed further into the interior, *minkisi* increasingly became symbols of resistance to Western colonization, while at the same time, evolving to become more representative of transculturation by using beads, cloth, and mirrors imported from the West. The *nkisi* in the Stanley exhibition, for example, incorporated numerous European items with the native wood and fiber. Glass beads, mirrors, flannel, and handkerchief cloths would have come from Europe. Like Conrad's textual representation of the Huntley and Palmers biscuit tin in "Heart of Darkness," the African *nkisi* symbolizes not only an important point of intersection between conflicting cultures but also the presence of power in both; thus, with a biscuit tin loosely representative of a Western concept of fetish, both the *nkisi* and the fetishized commodity can be symbolically bound.

While *The Stanley and African Exhibition* did not highlight the spatial partitioning of the African continent by European nations in the wake of the great scramble for Africa which Conrad briefly alludes to in "Autocracy and War," it does highlight Africa as the exotic Other waiting to be vanquished, balanced against the clear superiority of European imperialism – and materialism. Long before 1905, Africa had become the contested place where new markets, so desperately needed for trading European goods, gradually emerged.

Commercialized, Contested Spaces in "Autocracy and War"

Conrad's essay opens to a different contested space: the battlefield, Sha-ho, in the Russo-Japanese war, a space of contention over commodities – Russian wheat, Japanese rice, and for trading those commodities – ice-free ports, command of the waters of the East. And even further, for the contested space of Sakhalin Island (Conrad refers to it as "Saghalien"), in the northern Pacific Ocean, north of the Japanese archipelago and off the eastern coast of Russia.[15] At the end of the Russo-Japanese War, Russia would yield the southern portion of the island to Japan, but at Conrad's writing the entire island remained Russian despite a centuries-long tug of war between the two powers. And Conrad's mocking reference to the island as "that jewel of [Russia's] crown" (AW 76) points obliquely to the widely known fact, bolstered by Anton Chekhov's remarkable piece of journalism, *The Island: A Journey to Sakhalin* (1895), that Sakhalin was the "'most notorious penal settlement in the world'" (qtd. in Gentes 28).

"Saghalien," Sha-ho, these names conjure up fluid control of space, for Conrad senses that even if *"the"* great battle has been won, the war is not over (AW 71). And there are past battlefields which yield to this present, still fluid one: battlefields during the Napoleonic wars; battlefields of the Crimean war; Sadowa and Sedan, battlefields in the Austro-Prussian and Franco-Prussian wars of the 1860s and 1870s. These battle spaces in the past all lead to shifting geopolitical spaces in Europe through the rise of nationalities, the demise of the Ottoman empire, the gradual demise of Russia, and the emergence of Prussia as an increasingly aggressive world power.

The end of the Napoleonic Wars and the defeat of Napoleon's France resulted in a rather fragile balance of power as European states sought to develop a long-term plan for peace; however, once more, parts of Poland – the duchy of Warsaw, specifically – were ceded to Russia and Prussia. Both Russia and Prussia gained power through increased territory. But peace is transitory, and, as Conrad observes, after the close of the Napoleonic wars there would follow "a series of sanguinary surprises held in reserve by the nineteenth century for our hopeful grandfathers" (AW 72). For Conrad, these "sanguinary surprises" defeat the dream of world peace through decades-long struggles which lead inevitably to Russia's tumultuous decline and the rise of Prussian might. And Conrad balances the wars of the nineteenth century emerging from the corruption of the French Revolution to this one at the dawn of the twentieth century, from which, he predicts "a new political organism [will] take the place of a gigantic and dreaded phantom" (73).

Conrad gloats at the "powerlessness" of Russia's territorial aggression over the course of the last century. In the Crimean War, for example, Russia's efforts to absorb more territory in the Balkans resulted, instead, in the loss of its ability to maintain a military fleet and control of the Black Sea, and, as Conrad observes, in "the end of what remained of absolutism and legitimism in Europe" (78). As the allies against Russia in the Crimean War began to employ modern technologies in advanced weaponry, communication, and transportation, Prussia, most notably, built upon these early developments in the battles to follow.

The Austro-Prussian War followed just a decade after the Crimean War (1853-1856), where the Battle of Königgrätz (July 3, 1866) – Conrad refers to it as "Sadowa," – was one of the most decisive battles of the modern era and the largest battle in nineteenth-century Europe, employing advanced weapons technology as well as telegraphy and railways, all combining to display the rising power of the Prussian military. Within just four years, Prussia was on the march again, provoking France into the Franco-Prussian War (1870-1871), with the insidious help of Prussian Chancellor Otto von Bismarck. During the Battle of Sedan, to which Conrad refers, Prussia utilized telegraph and railroad systems to the fullest potential available at the time, while over one million Prussian soldiers took the field; and the French, fighting with obsolete weapons, were hopelessly outmaneuvered, bringing on the end of the old order in Europe, as Conrad rightly observes (78), and the end of the French Empire. Indeed, for Conrad, since Sadowa and Sedan, *"il n'y a plus d'Europe!"* (92); the concept of European solidarity had been extinguished in favor of "the doctrine of nationalities much more favorable to spoliations that came to the front" (86). All this while Russia, militarily far weaker than Prussia, stayed on the sidelines and watched the growing military strength and unification of Germany. But the growing weakness of the Ottoman Empire throughout the nineteenth century offered Russia another avenue for military aggression to recover territorial losses suffered during the Crimean War, and despite Russia's success in winning the Russo-Turkish War (1877-1878), Conrad sees this as another example of Russia's striking with "a withered right hand" (78).

With so many conflicted spaces leaving the balance of power in Europe during the nineteenth century in continual crisis, the ground was prepared for the inevitable demise of Russia as a military power at the mercy of Japan. Conrad's hatred for Russia finds expression through spatial imagery: the space of the grave, the abyss, the chasm, are invoked to express empty space, nothingness. Conrad fixes upon Otto von Bismarck's declaration of Russian impotence which he had engraved in a ring: *"La Russie, c'est le néant"* (94). For Bismarck, Russia was "nothing" to fear, an accomplice whose inevitable weakening could only add to Prussia's strengthening as it became the German Empire he envisioned. For Conrad, though, Bismarck's pithy phrase conjures the spatial imagery of a "yawning chasm open between East and West; a bottomless abyss" (83). Fueling much of Conrad's disgust with Prussia and Bismarck is the role that Prussia played in the partition of Poland.

Fueling much of Conrad's disgust with Prussia and Bismarck is the role that Prussia played in the partition of Poland. Poland is at the heart of Conrad's essay; his reference to another contested, partially Polish space, Pomerania, points obliquely to that fact in his connection between Bismarck and the Pomeranian grenadier. Conrad uses a famous quotation from Bismarck to fault the "last comer amongst the great Powers of the Continent," Prussia, for its "envious acquisitive temperament" (92). Fueled by sarcasm, Conrad writes of "Pomerania, the breeding place of such precious Grenadiers that Prince Bismarck (whom it is a pleasure to quote) would not have given the bones of one of them for the settlement of the old Eastern Question" (92). For Bismarck, only German self-interest, not the Balkans, mattered; but for Conrad, the vexed issue of the erasure of Polish space is captured by the reference to Prussian Pomerania and the loss of Polish Pomerania (Pomorze), and Poland's access to the Baltic Sea in the course of the Polish partitions (*Polish Pomerania* 7-8). Conrad refers even more directly to the crime of partition, writing, "[t]he common guilt of the two Empires (Russia, Prussia) is defined precisely by their frontier line running through the Polish provinces" (AW 80). Further, it is tempting to suspect, as we read Conrad's passionate appeal for justice and imagine his dictating in a powerful emotional outburst – he was dictating this essay to Jessie Conrad (Stape, "The Texts" 264) – that he might just have been thinking in Polish. In the surviving typescript, Conrad has dictated the Polish word *organizator* ("Notes" 417), which is editorially changed to "*organiser*" in *The*

Fortnightly Review (13) and Americanized to "*organizer*" in the *North American Review* (47) but restored to the Polish form in the Cambridge edition of *Notes on Life and Letters*. The textual note to the Cambridge edition of *Notes on Life and Letters* further suggests that Conrad's use of the word *provocator* in the typescript and *The Fortnightly Review* indicates a blend of the Polish *prowokator* and the French *provocateur*, and was editorially changed (and, I would argue, Americanized) to "provoker" in the *North American Review* ("Notes" 414).

With Poland as the contested geographical center of his emotional space, Conrad creates a link to textual space which acts as a pale reflection of the reality of the battlefield: newsprint. Conrad's antipathy to the press has been well documented, but his complex engagement with the press within the context of these pages is worth deeper examination. The first connection between material and textual space occurs when Conrad decries the ineffectiveness of newsprint to convey the reality of the battlefield: "We have seen these things, though we have only seen them in the cold, silent, colourless print of books and newspapers" (AW 71). Thus, a distant war, for Conrad, can only be known as a "grey reflection," "a reflection seen from the perspective of thousands of miles, in the dim atmosphere of official reticence, through the veil of inadequate words" (71). We, the readers of newsprint, Conrad avers, are mercifully immune to the horrors of "tens of thousands of decaying bodies tainting the air of the Manchurian plains" (72) because the "veil of inadequate words" fails to convey what the eye can't see. Thus, Conrad seems to undercut the power of sensationalist journalism so rampantly prevalent in Britain beginning in the late nineteenth century. Admittedly, Conrad's attitudes to the nature of the "new journalism," journalists, and newspapers were most often antagonistic, but also frequently ambivalent and at times even ambiguous.

For, while initially emphasizing the failure of newsprint to convey reality, Conrad performs a subtle shift as he moves through the progression of the essay to reveal the power of

The Shattered Remains of Russian Heroes Who Were Killed Near 203 Metre Hill, Port Arthur

Watching the Battle of the Yalu

newsprint to manipulate the reader. First, of course, Conrad the artist must stake out the position of art in the modern world: only "direct vision of the fact, or the stimulus of a great art" can awaken faculties numbed to sleep by a constant stream of reports "appalling in their monotony" (71). In fact, Conrad's sense of the inadequacy of words to convey the horror of death and mutilation on the Manchurian plain gathers further weight in the light of the amply documented

Chapter One: "Autocracy and War," the Age of Capital...   59

difficulty of journalists to get anywhere near the battlefields on the Japanese side during this war. While Conrad attempts to summon to the reader's imagination the horrific images of broken bodies in the "stream of reports," in fact, press coverage of this war was strictly censored and reporters' movements were restricted, more so on the Japanese side than on the Russian.

There is a sharp distinction between the two photographs above: the photo of Russian remains suggests the relative access that journalists and photographers had to the Russian side of the battlefields; however Jack London's photograph of Japanese soldiers and Korean laborers indicates the distance of the battle taking place on the other side of the river. London's well documented efforts to get close to the battlefield, for example, were made impossible by the Japanese who "were not eager to relinquish control over the narrative framing and reporting of the war" (Swafford 85). London was even thrown in jail several times as he struggled to get closer to the scene of the action. As Kevin Swafford argues, London's war story was "the story of the writer struggling to get a story – which in turn becomes *the* story" (86). Thus, London was largely unable to participate in the ideology of the popular press controlling war correspondence: it was meant to be "propagandizing entertainment, intended to sell newspapers and books" (88). Nor was London alone in his experience; in "The Japanese-Russian War: Battles I Did Not See," Richard Harding Davis, a highly regarded American war correspondent, wrote:

> We knew it was a battle because the Japanese officers told us it was. In other wars I had seen other battles, many sorts of battles, but I had never seen a battle like that one [...]. So far as we were concerned it consisted of rings of shrapnel smoke floating over a mountain pass many miles distant. (213)

Conrad, though, may well have been unaware that reporting on this war was so strictly censored by the Japanese, and so saw what reporting there was as little more than sensationalist pap dulling the senses with its repetitiveness. Indeed, Conrad was also reminded of that "mist of print" that veils the image of the "blood freezing crimson upon the snow of the squares and streets of St. Petersburg" sparked by the devastating news of Russian losses in Manchuria (AW 73-74).

Newsprint is dangerous, Conrad avers, for its power to rob the reader of true feeling while instilling the lust for sensation: "there must be something subtly noxious to the human brain in the composition of newspaper ink; or else it is that the large page, the columns of words, the leaded headings, exalt the mind into a state of feverish credulity" (76). And Conrad follows with a powerful image, the "still uproar" of the printed page, an oxymoronic reflection of how newsprint can "still" reflective thought while fomenting "uproar" in the senses. In Conrad's view, a newspaperman like W. T. Stead, as the founder of "new journalism" in Britain may well have represented the epitome of the "yellow" journalist. Stephen Donovan argues that Stead makes several oblique appearances in Conrad's fiction, one, notably, in "The Black Mate," to "'that newspaper fellow – what's his name'" who saw ghosts (qtd. in "That Newspaper Fellow" 4). Stead, a well-known spiritualist, edited the spiritualist quarterly *Borderland: A Quarterly Review and Index* in addition to the "new journalist" *Pall Mall Gazette* and the monthly distillation of the British Empire's best journalism, *The Review of Reviews*. Famous for revolutionizing journalism as sensationalist, Stead, ironically, took Conrad to task for his "fantastic rhetoric" in "Autocracy and War" in the July 1905 issue of *The Review of Reviews* ("Russia: 'Ghost, Ghoul, Djinn, etc." 51-52). A supporter of the Tsar and Russia, Stead would naturally have taken offense at Conrad's position against Russia as ghost, ghoul, djinn, old man of the sea, but Stead should have bristled even more at Conrad's depiction of journalism. Somehow, though, Stead missed the opportunity to skewer Conrad on that score, preferring instead to mock what he perceived as Conrad's pretentious pronouncements on Russian and global politics. Stead is silent on the fact that in both *The Fortnightly Review* and *North American Review* versions of "Autocracy and War," Conrad makes incendiary comments about journalists which he later edited out of the essay in *Notes on Life and Letters*. Those comments are well worth repeating here. Inserted between the sentence that later would end with the words "painful intimacy" and one that would begin with "It is not absurd," Conrad described journalists as "the apostles of war's sanctity [who] will crawl away swiftly into the holes where they belong, somewhere in the yellow basements of newspaper offices" (*The Fortnightly Review* 19; *North American Review* 53). How did Stead miss the clear reference to "yellow" journalists as rats?[16] If Conrad knew of or read Stead's scathing review in July, it certainly doesn't show in his November letter to Ada Galsworthy, where he characterizes his "political article" as "a piece of prophecy both as to Russia and Germany I think it comes off rather" (*CL* 3: 294).

But questionable journalism, of course, dates back before Stead's sensationalism. Conrad alludes several times in "Autocracy and War" to the dangerous policies initiated by Otto von Bismarck; he was equally aware of the suspicious practice of muzzling the free press by Bismarck's German government. Referring to the "amiable Busch," Bismarck's "pet 'reptile' of the Press," Conrad demonstrates keen awareness of the dangerous "war-temper" revealed in Busch's "prattle" (AW 87). Matthew Rubery argues that the notion of a slithering "reptile press" originates with Bismarck's policy of bribing editors to support Prussian aims in 1866 (*The Novelty of the Newspapers* 84). Rubery also makes an interesting claim that would be relevant to Conrad's distaste for the press; he argues that Victorian novelists including Eliot, Gissing, Meredith, Thackery, and Wells introduced fictional journalists into their work at a time when it appeared that "the newspaper was beginning to challenge the novel's preeminence in terms of the realistic representation of daily life" (84).

In this context, Stead comes back into play, addressing the issue of Bismarck and his reptile press in ways that, unlike much of his politics, would have pleased Conrad. In an issue of his *Review of Reviews*, Stead reviewed Moritz Busch's recently published slavish celebration of his idol, entitled "Bismarck, Some Secret Pages of His History" (1898). Stead wrote:

> Prince Bismarck, who neglects nothing, and presses everything into his service, has converted the German press into a vulgar and blatant speaking-trumpet of the German Administration. What with the Reptile Fund for corruption, and the immense power which the Administration has over the press for the means of intimidation, the Chancellor has converted German journalism into the most effective and the most disreputable of the instruments by which he governs Germany. ("Bismarck and His Boswell" 404)

In December 1904, just six months before the concurrent journal publications of Conrad's "Autocracy and War," Austin Harrison published an exposé entitled "The German Press." In it, he echoes much of what Stead and others had written several years before, insisting that the German press "is the pulse of the German government—the mirror of modern Bismarckian statecraft" (632), and added that Bismarck's aim in molding the press to his vision was to mold the German public, which he could keep profoundly ignorant of events in other countries. As an example, argues Harrison, German newspapers clearly demonstrated, despite widespread anti-Russian sentiment in the German populace, a sympathy for the Russian cause by writing up Russian victories and predicting Japanese defeat (638).

Though deleting the reference to journalists as rats referred to earlier, Conrad edited back into the essay in *Notes on Life and Letters* his insistence on journalists as "apostles" of war, "preaching the gospel of the mystic sanctity of its sacrifices and the regenerating power of spilt blood to the poor in mind – whose name is legion" (AW 90). With war and capitalism inextricably linked in Conrad's view, newspapers and journalists participate not only in war mongering but also in the production of capitalism. While daily or weekly news had long been a feature of everyday life, with the advancements of technology and machinery in the nineteenth century, as witnessed at the Crystal Palace, newspapers could reach a global market in ways never before possible, just as ships were carrying trade goods all over the world. Instead of the peace dreamed of in the era of the Crystal Palace, newspapers, capitalism, and war had become inextricably linked.

Conrad predicts the devastation to come; instead of Europe, there is left only "an armed and trading continent" (92). Indeed, two continents, Africa and Europe, had become "armed and trading" grist for a vast capitalist mill. As Conrad argues, "the architectural aspect of the universal city remains as yet inconceivable [...] the very ground for its erection has not been cleared of the jungle" (89). Instead, there is a globe become a "House of Strife" (89) and the "German eagle with a Prussian head look[ing] all round the horizon [...] for something good to get" (93). With the space of the whole world beneath his eye, the German eagle "gazes North and South," Conrad writes, "and East and West"; he "has learned to box the compass" (93).

Chapter Two:
Spectral Sightings, Mapping, and Exploration in "Geography and Some Explorers"

Geography, Imperialism, and Selling the Congo

While two specters – one of dying Russian imperialism and the other of Bismarck's German eagle "boxing the compass" – haunt "Autocracy and War," the specter of European imperialism and colonialism more broadly brushed haunts Conrad's much later "Geography and Some Explorers." This chapter takes up that issue raised in Conrad's essay from a new perspective, echoing many of the themes of the previous chapter, while moving backward in time to examine the devastating effects of European domination of the African continent and its relationship to the production of the future. That global war would explode within nine years of his 1905 essay, Conrad seemed to sense, and even Bismarck, the architect of German imperialism, predicted its impending threat in 1898: "One day the great European war will come out of some damned foolish thing in the Balkans" – a shockingly prescient awareness of the global stage and the source of the coming conflict (qtd. in Bingham 118).[17] The "German eagle" of course would be on the wrong side of history once the "foolish thing in the Balkans," the assassination of Archduke Ferdinand, lit the match of global conflagration.

One important imperialist precursor to World War I begins in the rise of nationalism in the West fueling the colonialist land grab in the scramble for Africa. As indicated in the previous chapter, the European and American public had already been primed for expanding interest in the exotic "Other" through the prevalence of universal exhibitions which featured colonial displays as well as the explosion of interest in exploration of unknown areas of the globe. As a result, by the second half of the nineteenth century European nations were flexing their imperialist muscles to dissect the continent of Africa into slices of that "magnificent African cake," Leopold II's expression of colonialist desire and greed (qtd. in Pakenham 22). African colonies, in the 1880s-1890s were, for much of Europe, something good to get, and mapping that space as "blank," marking boundaries, and dividing the locales of colonial domination set the table for slicing that cake. Of course, no one invited the Africans to the party.

In "Geography and Some Explorers," written several decades after the devastating effects of European colonial occupation of the African continent and in the aftermath of the Great War, Conrad, while celebrating the "romance" of travel, focuses his attention more intently on historicizing geography and privileging the map, but he also leaves, as is often his method, inviting gaps, half-veiled innuendoes, and silences in the text. At the core of the essay lies his reminiscence of the Congo, linked to four significant memories: the lure of the African map, the "vilest scramble for loot that ever disfigured the history of human conscience and geographical exploration," "the unholy recollection of a prosaic newspaper stunt," and the "yet unbroken power of the Congo Arabs" (GSE 14). The veiled allusion to Henry Morton Stanley buries his name and minimizes his fame, but the specter of Stanley looms over the history of exploration of central Africa, perhaps leaving Conrad aggrieved at remembering his own presence there. But Stanley represents more than exploration through warfare, his expeditions wink at slavery while proposing to abolish it; and Stanley insistently promoted the commercialization of Africa while ignoring that it was on black backs that tons of ivory were carted out of the interior to slake Western greed.[18] Conrad's memories of the map, the scramble, the newspaper stunt, and the Arab slavers – provide a structure for examining his essay through the expansion of his hints and his theory of geography, while filling in gaps and silences with historical context. Threaded throughout this chapter is the constant theme of the commodification of the African continent superimposed upon the material conditions prevalent there during the second half of the nineteenth century.

In the early stages of composition, Conrad was clearly thinking about the ramifications of the veiled charges he makes against Congo atrocities as an example of the reduction of Africa and its natural resources to something good to get for the West. In the manuscript "Geography," the earliest version of the essay, Conrad adds the following before "the unholy memory of a newspaper stunt": "no great figure haunted that spot, so unknown to the civilized world" ("Geography," Original Manuscript 49; Stevens and Stape, "Geography" 389).[19] The phrase "no great figure haunted that spot" changes in the published version to "But there was no shadowy friend to stand by my side in the night of the enormous wilderness, no great haunting memory" (GSE 14). Conrad's denial of a "great figure" haunting the spot in his manuscript may be yet another veiled reference to Stanley who was no great figure there, but, in Conrad's view, infamous. Yet Conrad seems to mute recollection of Stanley even further, longing for a shadowy friend instead of erasing a great figure. Another significant change, "unseemly scramble" in the manuscript to "*vilest* scramble" (emphasis added) in two of the typescripts and the final printed versions, strengthen Conrad's attack on colonialism ("Geography," MS 49; Stevens and Stape, "Emendation and Variation" 14.30a, 283). In fact, Conrad even refuses to take up the attack further in the manuscript, writing: "But I won't dig up that old hatchet now" ("Geography," Original Manuscript 50; Stevens and Stape, "Geography" 389). That reluctance evaporates, though, as the composition of the essay evolves; Conrad erases that sentence and leaves the indictment in place.

The evolution of the essay's published forms designed for distinctive readerships results in two appearances of the essay – apart from the limited pamphlet edition released by Strangeways in January 1924 – on either side of the Atlantic. In subsequent months, the essay appeared as the introduction to a volume of

Countries of the World in February 1924, and next in the March 1924 issue of *National Geographic*. The title changes from "The Romance of Travel" in *Countries of the World* to its final title, "Geography and Some Explorers" as the lead article in *National Geographic*. The change in title certainly suggests a shift in Conrad's recognition of audience, context, and even the major thrust of his theme, though the text remains essentially the same. Each version displays subheadings added in the first case by the Amalgamated Press and in the second by *National Geographic* editors to make the format of the essay more adaptable "to the magazine's [North American] audience" (Stevens and Stape, "The Essays" 209). For example, subheadings in "The Romance of Travel" tend more toward advancing the notion the title suggests, leading the reader to reflect more on the lure of travel than on geography as science. Several headings include "Lure of the Unknown Places," "Luckless Searchers for El Dorado" and "Balboa's Moment of Elation." On the other hand, those in the *National Geographic* version emphasize the attention to science: "Geography is the Science of Action," "Early Geographers Sought in Vain for Great Southern Continent," and "Captain Cook Laid the Ghost of Terra Australis Incognita." Further, although the repeating illustrations lining the headers and footers of the pages in *Countries of the World* at least display some reference to the subject of the text – ships under sail, waves on the ocean, a camel with a view of pyramids – those interspersed with the text in *National Geographic* display little direct relevance to Conrad's essay, with the exception of an image of the memorial tablet indicating where Stanley found Livingstone, another of Stanley Falls with a caption quoting Conrad's text, even though Conrad pointedly ignores Henry Morton Stanley in his text. Also, in the *National Geographic* version there are a number of images of icebergs at the Antarctic related to Robert Scott's Terra Nova Expedition which would have had only an oblique connection to Conrad's mention of John Franklin and Leopold McClintock at the opposite end of the world, in the Arctic. These factors all contributed to massaging the packaging of Conrad's text to serve the editorial mission of the journal and even included, as

Chapter Two: Spectral Sightings, Mapping, and Exploration... 69

Stevens and Stape note in their essay on the text, the exclusion of "arm chair" in reference to casual geographic observers, those who comprised the majority of the journal's readership and who would have therefore been offended by the term ("The Essays" 209).

Conrad's "Passion for Maps" Performed

While the two early publications place Conrad's essay within different contexts and for different readerships, both preserve a text whose close attention to maps shapes the final version printed posthumously in *Last Essays*. Indeed, Conrad drew his own doodled map in the marginalia of the manuscript "Geography," perhaps to trigger his memory about a scene he recalls later in the essay. Stevens and Stape point to that bit of marginalia, but identify it incorrectly, in my view, as a map of the Western Hemisphere (Introduction xliii). Indeed, the manuscript "Geography" contains several doodles in the marginalia and even what appears to be a tiny map on page 37, whose meaning may become clear when we read in the manuscript (but not in the published version): "Thirty hours afterwards of which about ten were spent at anchor under Saddle Island, I was at the other end of the Strait" ("Geography," Original Manuscript 37; Stevens and Stape, "Geography" 390).[20]

Conrad's Drawing of Saddle Island

As Laurence Davies points out in an email, the drawing must be Conrad's rendering of Saddle Island – he did have at least ten hours to observe it. There's an arrow pointing to the direction N and then the drawing indicates what appears to be one larger island, a smaller one or sandbank or even coral reef to its right, and then maybe a chain of sandbars – or – coral reefs lining a bay on the southwest side of the island. Conrad's image includes topographical markings for hills with possibly bamboo groves, which did exist there as late as 2014 (McNiven 44); there are *x*s marked to the east of the island, and the number 2½ appears below its southern shore, possibly Conrad's measurement of the depth in fathoms near the shore (approximately 30 feet), which would conform with the shallow depths of the entire Torres Strait – from approximately 30-40+ feet. This island is further described in terms that match Conrad's image – "a small island with two hills of a rounded contour [...] between the two hills is a low, flat isthmus, which possesses all the characters of a typical coral island: in other words, it is merely a beach" (Haddon, et al. 461). The island is geographically located at 10°10" latitude and 142°40" longitude. Ian McNiven's beautiful aerial photo of Saddle (indigenous name "Ulu") Island bears remarkable similarities to Conrad's drawing (45):

Ulu (Saddle Island), an Ephemerally-used Continental Island, Naghi Cluster. With kind permission of Ian McNiven

Perhaps the xs in Conrad's image mark sand bars or coral reefs to avoid, or Conrad's path to sail past the island, or even

Chapter Two: Spectral Sightings, Mapping, and Exploration...   71

spots where he anchored. Is Conrad thinking ahead to writing about his own exploratory journey through the Torres Strait?21 We know he'll record that grand and dangerous adventure near the end of his text, and in rendering this image of a tiny continental island where he lay anchored, he fills blank space with his own knowledge.

Conrad drew more sketches: his map of the Russias, his sketches of his overland trail and navigational maps in his Congo notebooks, and an unpublished map of a section of the Congo River. Robert Hampson writes that Conrad "was more involved with maps and mapping than any other major nineteenth- or twentieth-century British novelist and, this leaves its mark on his fiction" ("'A Passion for Maps'" 44). And, I would add on his nonfiction as well.

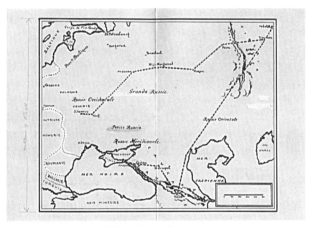

Map of the Russias

In concert with Hampson's view, I would argue that one such map that may be directly connected to Conrad's fiction, the undated and unsigned map entitled "The Map of the Russias" depicted above. Johan Warodell's description in *Notes and Queries* identifies it as Conrad's production through the handwriting, though its provenance is unknown ("Query" 682). So the question arises: why did Conrad produce this extraordinary map? The map suggests to me that Conrad has imposed meaning through drawing the map, very possibly, as part of his compositional process in writing "Prince Roman" (1911). If drawn at some point during the six years between "Autocracy and War" and "Prince Roman," the map offers intriguing insights into Conrad's creative processes and reinforces his revulsion of all things Russian. The map also suggests that Conrad worked on changes and revision, as shown in the erasures created by white correction fluid and the use of that correction fluid to create the white spaces in the marked path. The place names on the hand drawn map are written in French in ink, an important appropriation of Russian space through the use of French to name cities, seas, lakes, and territorial sections. The map extends over a portion of Russia from the boundaries with its neighbors to the west to the Ural Mountains and Lake Aral at the northeast and southeast edges with "*Siberie*" marked in the upper righthand corner. Scale, Warodell argues, is "almost completely out of scale with actual Russia" (682). Yet scale, Denis Cosgrove insists, is fundamental, bringing questions of representation and reality into sharp relief (9). The representation of actual space and distance, it would seem, are unimportant in this map, which is meant, rather, to make a private statement. Conrad's map does bear a scale legend at the bottom righthand corner but the map doesn't show latitudinal and longitudinal grids, so scale and orientation can be extraordinarily deceiving. Even more perplexing is the meaning of the numbers in the scale – what, for example, does 500 stand for? Miles? Kilometers? There appears to be a previous owner's or librarian's measurement of the document suggesting the measurement of the actual map space as 15.5 centimeters on the side[22]; however, the size of the entire page measures at 24.4 centimeters across the top and 19.4 down the side, or 9.11 x 7.12 inches. So, the map is quite small, smaller than a standard 8 x 11 inch sheet of paper, and without knowing the ratio of the scale legend, whether inches to miles or centimeters to kilometers, it's not possible to measure the geographical space accurately. Geographical distance, after all, may not have been the main point.

Chapter Two: Spectral Sightings, Mapping, and Exploration...   73

Furthermore, Conrad divides the map into geographical sections: *"Grande Russie," "Russie Occidentale," "Petite Russie," "Russie Meridionale,"* and *"Russie Orientale,"* all printed in ink in italics, with *"Pologne"* and *"Volynie"* clearly situated in the west and printed in smaller block capitals. Such designations for Russia are historic French names dating from as far back as the seventeenth century and even before – *"Petite Russie,"* for example, is now part of the Ukraine, *"Grande Russie,"* designated central territories of Russia. *"Russie Occidentale,"* forms the western portion of Conrad's map dominated by Poland (*"Pologne"*) and Volynia (*"Volynie"*), which appear in larger block print than *"Moscou,"* and are known alternatively as *"Russie Européene." "Russie Orientale"* slips over the Urals into Siberia. My conjecture is that Prince Roman Sanguszko and perhaps Conrad's father may have used French to designate Russian space, and thus the map as it stands would certainly suggest Conrad's rejection of Russian autocracy through its connections to two Polish patriots.

My conclusion about the path markings is that they indicate the path of Prince Roman Sanguszko's journey into exile in 1831 for his participation in the November Uprising, an armed rebellion in the heart of partitioned Poland against the Russian empire. Sanguszko was forced to walk the entire way to Tobolsk, Siberia, in chains, passing through Moscow, Yaroslavl, Nizhny Novgorod, Kazan, Perm, and Tyumen. From Tobolsk, Sanguszko was drafted into the Russian army and relocated to the Caucasus – note the long trajectory of the path from Tobolsk to Tiflis in the Caucasus on Conrad's map, the path then turns west tracking Prince Roman on military duty to Stavropol (a garrison town), Kuban (a frontier town fortified by the Cossacks), and Anapa (fought over between the Turks and the Russians and changing hands between 1820 and the Crimean War). Finally, after displaying bravery in the army, Sanguszko was released and allowed to return to his manor in Slavuta in the Ukraine (Krzyżanowski 34). I would also note that Conrad's family came from Podolia, not featured on this map, but he lived part of his childhood in Zhytomyr, "*Jitomir*" on the map, and the origin point of the path.

Conrad's father, Apollo Korzeniovski, was, like Prince Roman, exiled, a victim of Muscovite oppression, imprisoned in Warsaw in 1861 (Warsaw appears on Conrad's map), and exiled to Vologda, northeast of Moscow, so the personal connections to Prince Roman's story are clear and a Polish narrator is featured in Conrad's tale "Prince Roman." But Conrad's father didn't provide the only link; his maternal uncle, Tadeusz Bobrowski wrote about Prince Roman in his *Memoirs* (Krzyżanowski 46-47). The question remains, though, why such a detailed map if most of the details of Roman's path would not be included in the tale "Prince Roman"? The map becomes, in my view, an extension of the tale, a visualization of space that could lend reality to the prelude of a narrative whose real focus is on an aging Prince Roman after his exile and military service. The map is a witness to Conrad at work visualizing and revising a narrative that exists *hors du texte*. Such a visualization also provides important links to Conrad's thinking about Russian imperialism in "Autocracy and War" and, through his acknowledged passion for maps in "Geography and Some Explorers," his view of imperialist aggression in Africa near the end of his life.

Another of Conrad's extraordinary map productions more directly related to themes in "Geography and Some Explorers" is the map of his overland Congo journey; as readers of Conrad, we might expect him to map some part of the trajectory of his travel – but the reason for this level of detail and its purpose, like that of the "Map of the Russias," is unknown. According to Warodell, this is Conrad's first professionally drawn full-scale map of a portion of the Congo, larger than the map of the Russias, measuring approximately 13 x 17 inches. ("Conrad's Unpublished Map" 64). The map, which follows the Congo from its mouth at Banana to Stanley Pool, is held in the Beinecke library, and as is the case with its counterpart map of the Russias, the provenance is unknown. More questions may be raised here too than answered; for example, why does Conrad plot this map that follows closely his own overland journey detailed in his "The Congo Diary"? Is there a connection between the map and the brief plotting of Marlow's overland journey in "Heart of Darkness"? Or could it have a connection to Conrad's seminal reminiscence of the Congo in "Geography and Some Explorers"? And, most importantly, when did he draw it? The Beinecke tentatively attributes the date of the map to 1910, but with a question mark. All the place names are written in Conrad's distinctive hand and he has inked the river and the names of its tributaries in green with place names lettered in black. This map, unlike that of the Russias, includes longitudinal and latitudinal coordinates based on Greenwich as the Prime Meridian – from 4 degrees to 7 degrees latitude south of the equator and from 12 degrees to 16 degrees longitude – as well as a legend in the lower left corner that indicates an "Old [Path]" and a "Present Path." There is no legend for scale here, so geographical distance isn't meant to be measured, but Conrad has clearly entitled the map "Map of Congo Basin / Showing Path Travelled / by /Joseph Conrad Korzeniowski." By using his full name, it may be that Conrad is pointing to that period of his life between the sea and the shore, between voyaging and writing, and between experiencing the Congo and writing about it nine years later. We don't know why Conrad marked one route the "Old Path" which appears to be a detour to Lutete (on his map "Gomba-lutete"), perhaps this was an earlier detour from the present path. In marking the "Present Path," Conrad appropriates the space of his overland journey alongside the river from Matadi to Stanley Pool. While not including all of the stops Conrad names in his "Congo Diary," the map does name quite a few, including Matadi, Pataballa, Congo da Lemba, Banza Mateka, and Manyanga, among others, and also includes the names of several rivers he passed along the way. In his introduction to his publication of *Conrad's Diary*, Richard Curle writes that "mapping of the Congo is not in a very advanced state, and with the paucity of the entries and the contradictory nature of the information, precise accuracy is not attainable" (*CD*, *The Yale Review* 256).

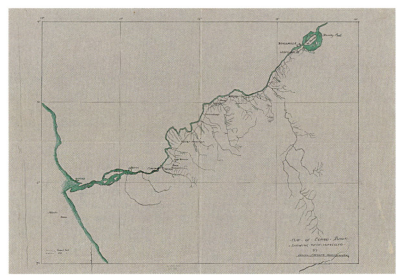

*Map of Congo Basin: Showing Path Traveled by
Joseph Conrad Korzeniowski*

Curle fails to acknowledge, however, Stanley's mapping of the entire course of the Congo beginning in the mid-1870s, and with much more detail for *In Darkest Africa* in 1890, but it's impossible to confirm if Conrad consulted Stanley's maps or those of other explorers in drawing his own. Warodell indicates that there are tributaries on Conrad's map that were not mapped until F. Delhaye's "Croquis Hypsometrique du Congo Occidentale" drafted sometime after 1898. Delhaye's map, which does not indicate its date, was clearly produced after the completion of the Matadi-Kinshasa-Leopoldville railway in 1898 while other railways were still under construction – these are shown on his map.

In looking at Stanley's "A Map of the Route of the Emin Pasha Relief Expedition through Africa" which appears later in this chapter, I agree that Conrad sketches more details of the tributaries than are found on Stanley's map; however, this seems understandable given Stanley's much broader scope. But what is equally fascinating is that Conrad didn't travel

Chapter Two: Spectral Sightings, Mapping, and Exploration... 77

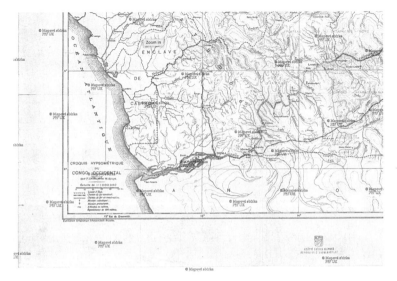

Section from F. Delhaye. *Croquis Hypsometrique du Congo Occidental*

those tributaries, so he's clearly relying on other maps or on knowledge gleaned from local natives. Just as important is the fact that Conrad uses place names that are found in Stanley's 1890 map: Brazzaville, Leopoldville, Stanley Pool; and he includes other place names also found on Stanley's map, most notably Banza Manteka, Pozo (inked in green) for Mpozo on Stanley's map, are a few examples. Conrad includes no tributaries or place names on the north side of the river other than Brazzaville, which seems logical given that he's tracking his own overland journey along the south shore. As Stanley did before him for the entire stretch of the river, Conrad marks his footprint on the short stretch from Matadi to "Kinchassa" (sic), adding new information about tributaries as he sketched. It is intriguing to speculate that, instead of using the color blue, the more logical mapmaker's choice for coding waterways, Conrad chooses green instead – a veiled link perhaps to the image of the snake so powerful in Conrad's depiction of the Congo River in "Heart of Darkness."

Warodell cogently observes that Conrad's maps "occupy a liminal space between private imagination and public discourse" ("The Writer at Work" 36). Exactly my impression. Even though he's writing about other sketches Conrad made in various manuscripts, Warodell's observation about liminal space holds especially true for Conrad's Congo map; although never published, and perhaps never meant to be published, the map occupies that space between the manuscript text of "The Congo Diary," where Conrad journeyed on foot in real time and real space, and his visual, imaginative reconstruction of that footprint later in "An Outpost of Progress," "Heart of Darkness" and "Geography and Some Explorers." Conrad's sketches of numerous daily treks in "The Congo Diary" and his navigational sketches in the "Up-River Book" add a further visual dynamic to his overland journey and navigation of a dangerous river, and in that light, form companion pieces to the map of Conrad's footpath, a connection I will explore in the next chapter.

The Lure of Blank Spaces: Filling in the Map of Africa

Clearly there is significant private appropriation of space in Conrad's own efforts at mapping discussed thus far, but it seems clear that Conrad didn't intend his manuscript sketches and unpublished maps for public viewing. Instead, as I suspect is the case of both maps discussed above, Conrad must have been working on visualization of his writing projects, his mapping of a text under construction, and near the end of his life, thinking about maps dominates his consciousness in the text of "Geography and Some Explorers."

The most prevalent map image in the essay is Conrad's childhood memory when "putting my finger on a blank spot in the very middle of the, then white, heart of Africa I declared that some day I would go there" (GSE 14). Much earlier, in "Heart of Darkness," Conrad depicted this same scene in an oft quoted, seminal moment in the evolution of his geographical consciousness, complicated by the filling of the

Chapter Two: Spectral Sightings, Mapping, and Exploration... 79

spaces of the continent: "It had ceased to be a blank space of delightful mystery – a white patch for a boy to dream gloriously over" (HD 48). Later, in *A Personal Record*, published in 1912, Conrad wrote again of the fascination the blank map of Africa held for him as boy:

> while looking at a map of Africa of the time and putting my finger on the blank space then representing the unsolved mystery of that continent, I said to myself with absolute assurance and an amazing audacity which are no longer my character now: "When I grow up I shall go *there*." (*PR* 26)

While this scene acts as a foundational memory in "Geography and Some Explorers" and elsewhere, Conrad speculates on mapping in the service of geography throughout. He begins by drawing us, his readers, into agreement with him that "a map is more fascinating to look at than a figure in a treatise on conic sections" (GSE 3), privileging thereby the tangible and visual nature of the representation of geographical space over mathematical abstractions, even though geography uses mathematical tools to acquire and analyze its data. It was the "pictorial" quality of medieval cartography, Conrad suggests, that fired the imaginations of medieval map readers no matter how fantastical or ridiculous the images might have been (3). Moving forward in time, Conrad celebrates Abel Tasman's voyage charting the Australian continent that laid the groundwork for more scientific projections of land masses and for Captain Cook's voyages and resultant charts to follow. "Geography," Conrad argues, evolved into "a science of facts" (9).

Conrad acknowledges the power of McClintock's narrative *The Voyage of the Fox in the Arctic Seas* to engage his attention and send him into "romantic explorations of [his] inner self; to the discovery of the taste for poring over maps"; for such exploration "revealed to [him] the existence of a latent devotion to geography" (GSE 10). These comments suggest that Conrad continuously mingles both the romance of the imagination and the science of facts. For Conrad personally, map-gazing brings the "problems of the great spaces of the earth into stimulating and directive contact with sane curiosity and gives an honest precision to one's imaginative faculty" (11). Now Conrad is writing about *gazing upon*, not *making* maps; but by letting his imagination fly, presumably slipping from the grasp of scientific precision, Conrad indicates that his is the gaze of the artist, not the scientist. Curiously, given this ambiguous approach to the scientificity of geography and its maps, Conrad nevertheless insists upon mapmaking "growing into an honest occupation registering the hard won knowledge" but also "recording the geographical ignorance of its time" (11). So, Conrad accepts the record of factual data which must, in his view, constitute the field of the map, but he also acknowledges the map as a *process*, evolving as more knowledge and discovery impact what has already been drawn or left undrawn as unknown – the map functions as a palimpsest of place. "The heart of its Africa," on maps drafted before 1852, "was white and big" (12); Conrad's reference here marks his excitement at blank spaces, those spaces gradually disappearing as European explorers nibble away at the edges of the unknown; but he also takes credit for his own boyish achievement of "entering laboriously in pencil the outline of Tanganyika on my beloved old atlas which having been published in about 1852 knew nothing of course of the Great Lakes" (12). "Thus," Conrad writes, "I could imagine myself stepping in the very footprints of geographical discovery" (12). But Conrad's acceptance of geography as a pure and transparent science fails to acknowledge that geography, as the editors of *Geography and Imperialism* point out, "illustrates better than any other 'imperial science' the soaring proprietorial ambition of the European imperial mind" (Bell, et al. 4).

Those blank spaces that Conrad imagined himself filling existed on *European* maps. Conrad does not acknowledge or perhaps even consider as he writes that those spaces were already inhabited by an indigenous populace for whom space was not blank, as Edward Said would argue, therefore, African space was blank only as far as the European, colonizing gaze was concerned ("Narrative, Geography, Interpretation" 86). For Said the "relationship between European scientific advance and the process of European imperial expansion had become so intimate and mutually dependent that the two seemed virtually synonymous" (qtd. in Bell, et al. 3). As a suggestive corrective to the Eurocentric view of African space, indigenous *lukasa*[23] were maps designed on a board covered with beads and cowrie shells to be read or sung in praise of the king of a pre-colonial Luba kingdom in the Congo basin. The tactile map "charts the journeys of the king, the location of sacred lakes and trees, and residences that later became spirit capitals" (Bassett 32).

Certainly, during the colonial period, European ethnographers maintained the view that Africans did not have the cognitive ability to make maps (24); this view would validate the need for "superior" Europeans to invade and map African space. An examination of indigenous maps shows, however, that Africans understood and could reproduce the configuration of material space while at the same time positioning that space between the real and the spirit worlds in which they lived.

Of course, like most Westerners at the time, Conrad may not have been aware of these indigenous practices of mapmaking, but his comments on mapping raise important questions when aligned with more recent theories of cartography, beginning with the recognition of a map as a system of signs (indeed, the indigenous map, for example, functions as a system of signs for those being initiated into Luba history and myth). The map serves as the principal geographic tool, and as the blank spaces of any map are filled, that map increasingly becomes a text to be read. In fact, even before the blanks are filled with newly recorded geographical information, they can be populated by the imagination, as Conrad contends. Thus the map is an evolving entity, continually adapting as the mapmaker learns and records new discoveries and measurements. But it is also a symbol – a "symbolic mimesis" of geographical reality in a moment of time that bears markings and codes which facilitate in its interpretation (Vivan 49). Warodell adds to this observation that looking at the textuality of the map underscores J. B. Harley's claim that a map is "inherently rhetorical," "'a graphic language to be decoded'" (qtd. in "Writer at Work" 31). A well-known figure in contemporary critical cartography, Harley makes significant claims about how we should read maps in the wake of poststructuralist and postmodern theory, while offering valuable reminders about the lack of map transparency. Maps, Harley argues, encode power, and while their objective may *seem* to be to mirror nature transparently, they are never value-free (4, 5). The map can create a hierarchy of space by manipulating seemingly innocuous features – for example, the attribution of color, the thickness of lines, the size of letters in the textual legends, the size of symbols – even, I would add, in the distortion of scale. For Harley, a map's rhetorical codes can be used to propagate a mythology: "Much of the power of the map, as a representation of social geography, is that it operates behind a mask of a seemingly neutral science" (7). "Maps," Harley contends, are more appropriately viewed as "*cultural* text[s]," rather than mirrors of nature (7, emphasis added). Now, even more importantly, maps generated in the West are by their very nature Eurocentric, their measurement of longitude based on 0 degrees located at the prime meridian in Greenwich, England – every place on earth is mapped according to its distance east or west of this point. From 1871-1880, European and American geographical societies and other civic institutions "helped shape geography as a sternly empirical science of empire and of commerce" (Withers 142). A primary reason for choosing Greenwich as the Prime Meridian? The fact that standardizing time "was by the mid-nineteenth century vital to commerce" and four-fifths of the world's commerce depended on sea charts which used Greenwich as the Prime Meridian (15, 95, 142). Thus, Greenwich became the center of world time and longitudinal space because commerce and trading needed it to be there.

    There are more features of mapmaking and map decoding that unmask the apparent transparency of the science. For example, there is always the problem, especially in the late

Chapter Two: Spectral Sightings, Mapping, and Exploration... 83

nineteenth and early twentieth centuries – before the advent of computer modeling – of plotting three-dimensional space on a two-dimensional plane, whether paper or cloth or another flat surface. One example of the solution of that problem is clearly Eurocentric – the Mercator projection, designed in the sixteenth century, perhaps the best known of all map projections and most useful for navigation. But its distortions are notorious; it inflates the areas toward the poles and renders Africa smaller than it is in contrast with North and South America.

Even the Gall-Peters projection, designed to correct errors in the Mercator projection, created new areas of distortion and raised a great deal of controversy in the cartographic community. Subsequently, in 1989, the American Congress on Surveying and Mapping drew the line on geographic representation by means of rectangular maps, adopting a resolution that denounces the Mercator as promoting:

> serious, erroneous conceptions by severely distorting large sections of the world, by showing the round earth as having straight edges and sharp corners, by representing most distances and direct routes incorrectly, and by portraying the circular coordinate system as a squared grid. (qtd. in Robinson 101)

Despite evolution in cylindrical and other methods of projection, it may well be that there is no world map developed to date free of distortion – even Google Maps uses the Mercator projection to preserve the angle of roads but only recently (2018) introduced an update that displays the earth as a 3D globe when the user zooms out. In 2003 the International Cartographic Association composed a succinct and generalized definition of the map which touches on themes raised by Conrad the map-gazer and mapmaker as well as European explorers like Stanley and others mapping the "blank spaces" of Africa:

> A map is a symbolized representation of geographical reality, representing selected features or characteristics, resulting from the creative effort of its author's execution of choices, and is designed for use when spatial relationships are of primary importance. (qtd. in Kainz 56)

What Stanley Has Done for the Map of Africa

> Trying to remember how they ever came to this place, both speak of passage as by a kind of flight, all since Tenerife, and the Mountain slowly recessional, having pass'd like a sailor's hasty dream between Watches, as if, out of a sea holding scant color, blue more in name than in fact, the unreadable Map-scape of Africa had unaccountably emerg'd as viewed from a certain height above the pale Waves, tilted for a look at this new Hemisphere, this haunted and half of ev'rything known, where spirit powers run free among the green abysses and sudden mountain crests. (Pynchon 58, qtd. in Cosgrove 1)[24]

Thomas Pynchon's image of Africa rising from the sea as Charles Mason and Jeremiah Dixon sailed to the Cape to study the transit of Venus in 1761 epitomizes the lure of the exotic in this "unreadable," virtually unknown geographical space. Before Henry Morton Stanley, little was known of the interior of Africa; maps drawn before Stanley's own mapping of the trajectory of the Congo River show only the smallest portion of the great river, a fact amply supported by those maps drawn prior to 1873.

In January 1890, James Keltie published an article in *Science* entitled "What Stanley Has Done for the Map of Africa." In it, Keltie, a geographer with the Royal Geographical Society, detailed the vast changes made on the map of Africa as a result of Stanley's successive trips through the interior. Additionally, the maps he included offered powerful visual evidence of Stanley's impact as they underscore Conrad's own early examinations of the blank spaces of the African map as well as his lament that African space had become one of the dark places of the earth. Keltie offers the maps figured below as examples of what the interior of Africa looked like before and after Stanley's Anglo-American expedition, 1874-1877. Stanley traveled from the east in Zanzibar to the west, from Bagamoyo to Boma, circumnavigating Lake Tanganyika and tracing accurate details of its outline, reaching the Lualaba river that Livingstone had seen before him, and at last becoming the first *white* man to record a journey "down this majestic river,

Chapter Two: Spectral Sightings, Mapping, and Exploration...   85

which for ages had been sweeping its unknown way through the centre of Africa" (Keltie 50). Of course, Stanley's maps evolved through successive journeys on the river and along its shores, and by 1890, Keltie observes: "The blank has become a network of dark lines, the interspaces covered with the names of tribes and rivers and lakes" (51).

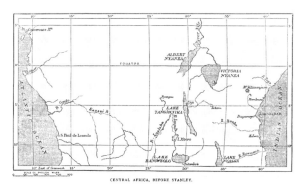

J. Scott Keltie. *Central Africa before Stanley*

Contrasting the two maps reproduced in Keltie's article (52, 53), the second one clearly indicates the major discoveries made by Stanley, especially limning the trajectory of the main course of the river, indicating its numerous tributaries, and extending greater detail about the lakes. "The few great geographical problems in Africa," Keltie concludes, "that Livingstone had to leave untouched, Stanley has solved" (55). Because of Stanley's field work and manuscript maps, Mirela Altic adds, "the first accurate maps of the Congo River were compiled and printed for the very first time" ("Henry Morton Stanley").

Keltie's observations about the map of Africa before Stanley are widely supported by African maps produced in the eighteenth and early nineteenth centuries. Henry Schenck Tanner, for example, mapped Africa successively beginning in the 1820s; his earlier maps mark the center of Africa as "UNKNOWN PARTS."[25] One of his more interesting maps is

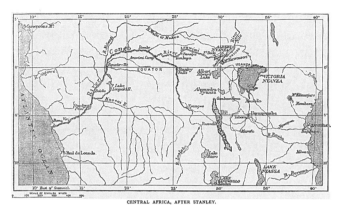

J. Scott Keltie. *Central Africa after Stanley*

dated 1830, and includes European colonies established at the coasts and offshore islands as European and American colonizing began to gain control of the continent.[26] Before Tanner, several notable eighteenth century cartographers had already begun to indicate the commercial interest that the continent held for European powers; Herman Moll's map dated 1710 identified the grain, ivory, gold, and slave coasts but listed the vast interior as "Unknown to the Europeans."[27] Moll's map is also worthy of note for locating both the Greenwich Prime Meridian, as many mapmakers of the day had begun to do, as well as the older location of the Meridian through the Canary Islands. In fact, it was not until 1884 that more than twenty countries agreed to adopt Greenwich as the location of the Prime Meridian. Conrad even reflects on the difficulty for navigators like Tasman plotting longitude in "Geography and Some Explorers," "They could calculate their latitudes but the problem of longitude was a matter which bewildered their minds and often falsified their judgment" (GSE 7).

An eighteenth-century map by Johann Hase (1737) displays a fascinating example of transculturation in a cartouche of what appears to be an interview between European traders with a local chief. Elephant tusks decorating the title box and oil palms add further detail to the image indicating both ivory

Chapter Two: Spectral Sightings, Mapping, and Exploration... 87

and palm oil as desirable commodities. Both early maps—Moll's and Hase's—reproduce only a small portion of the trajectory of the Congo River, consistent with the fact that the vast interior was unknown, but both also represent evolving cartographic illustrations of possession and trade.

Johann Hase. *1737 Map. Evolution of the Map of Africa*

John Tallis's *Illustrated Atlas,* intended to coincide with the Great Exhibition of 1851, included a map entitled "Africa" which displays the characteristics that made Tallis's atlas one of the most decorative of the nineteenth century. The illustrations include insets of St. Helena, Algerian and Bedouin Arabs, and two tribes of Hottentots, but like the others, the map also displays its blank spots with just the legendary Mountains of the Moon in the center of the continent and the incredibly short trajectory of the Congo River.[28]

Two decades later, Stanford's Geographical Establishment in London published a map entitled "A Map of the Forest Plateau of Africa Shewing the Great Rivers and Lakes

Discovered and Explored by Dr. Livingstone" (1874), based on information Livingstone obtained from both "Natives and Arabs." The map tracks Livingstone's journeys from 1851-1873 across the continent below the equator in search of the source of the Nile River, crossing over what he thought was the southward trajectory of the Congo, then along the course of the Zambesi and around the circumference of Lake Tanganyika. Livingstone's focus was always on the Nile, though, and he missed making important connections to the Congo River.[29]

In 1873, Winwood Reade produced an interesting map entitled "A Map of African Literature," in which he coded the map by marking the names of the explorers who had contributed to expanding geographical knowledge of and appropriation of the continent, several of those names appear in Conrad's essay. Among the names, of course, are Livingstone, writ large across the center of the map, Burton, Speke, Du Chaillu, and numerous others – with Stanley in smaller print on the eastern edge of Lake Tanganyika – at this point Stanley had only explored that region with Livingstone. The trajectory of the Congo River remains incredibly short with dotted lines suggesting where its course might flow, but incorrectly connecting it to the south with the Zambesi and failing to plot its course ascending above the equator and then back to the south of the equator. The great value of this map, though, lies in the details of names and locations of African explorers to 1873.

In "Appendix IV" to his *The African Sketch Book*, Reade offers explanatory details for the map and includes a history lesson on African exploration going back to Herodotus on Egypt as well as comments on many of the listed explorers by region (524-29).

Reade's volumes were published just before Stanley's breakthrough expedition from 1874-1877, which resulted, most importantly, in tracing the course of the Lualaba River north to its conjunction with the Congo River and the entire downstream course of the Congo to its mouth in the Atlantic Ocean, a journey of over 7000 miles. Later, after his fourth and

Chapter Two: Spectral Sightings, Mapping, and Exploration...

William Winwood Reade. *Map of African Literature*

final African expedition, Stanley reflected on the necessity of maps in his "books of travel," insisting upon their importance and the labor expended on their production:

> Critics are in the habit of omitting almost all mention of maps when attached to books of travel. This is not quite fair. Mine have cost me more labour than the note-taking, literary work, sketching, and photographing combined. In the aggregate, the winding of the three chronometers daily for nearly three years, the 300 sets of observations, the calculation of all these observations, the mapping of the positions, tracing of rivers, and shading of mountain ranges, the number of compass-bearings taken, the boiling of the thermometers, the records of the varying of the aneroids, the computing of heights, and the notes of temperature, all of which are necessary for a good map, have cost me no less than 780 hours of honest work [...]. If there were no maps accompanying books of this kind it would scarcely be

possible to comprehend what was described, and the narrative would become intolerably dry. (*In Darkest Africa* 2: 334-35)

The payoff, of course is a spectacular map Stanley produced to accompany his two-volume *In Darkest Africa*, a palimpsest of his successive maps beginning with his discoveries in the 1870s and a clear demonstration of the African map as a process. Altic comments that Stanley was an excellent cartographer, despite his lack of training, and that the first accurate maps of the interior of Africa were based on his field maps ("Henry Morton Stanley").

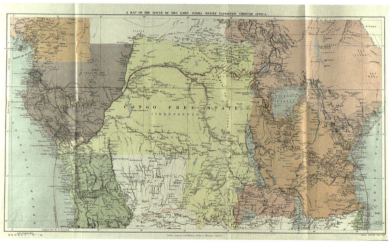

Henry Morton Stanley. *A Map of the Route of the Emin Pasha Relief Expedition through Africa*

Dominating the center of Stanley's map, in yellow, is the Congo Free State, immediately reminding Conrad's readers of Marlow's recognition: "I was going into the yellow" (HD 51). Symbolically, the choice of yellow to symbolize the Congo Free State could suggest the light of civilization promised by Leopold II when he established it as his own private colony. Stanley's map reproduced above was produced by Stanford's Geographical Establishment and included in the back pocket of

Chapter Two: Spectral Sightings, Mapping, and Exploration... 91

In Darkest Africa. The map offers incredibly rich details, vastly expanding European knowledge of central Africa. Stanley's route on the expedition is traced in red, from his departure from Zanzibar to round the Cape of Good Hope, then north to the mouth of the Congo, following its course east to the Aruwimi, and finally overland heading south past Lake Victoria Nyanza and ending in Zanzibar. The trajectory of Stanley's expedition provides important coding, with Stanley making his indelible mark on the map as its most significant explorer. Further coding reveals the Congo Free State, dominating the center of the map, as now open to the European gaze. Identified by Stanley as "Independent," the colony was hardly independent but privately owned by Leopold II from 1885-1908. Leopold promised free trade to European traders but never meant it; thus, one purpose of the map was to designate the boundaries of the zone of so-called free trade marked by broken lines. To the west, the Congo Free State is bordered by the French and Portuguese colonies, while to the east, its borders are with British and German colonies; but Stanley has not named the bordering colonies, indicating thereby the centrality and importance of the Congo Free State – the only named colony. Other than color coding to reflect areas of European possession based on the colors adopted by each country, font size also suggests both size of the area named as well as its importance. For example, Victoria N'Yanza appears to be larger in area than Lake Tanganyika, so the font size is proportionately larger, and for each of the lakes, Stanley has plotted the height above sea level. Note too that the map includes a legend clearly based on Greenwich as the Prime Meridian, indicated in the left lower corner, and below that, the scale is based on English miles, so measurement based on the European center of empire has been stamped on this map. A legend personally important to Stanley appears at latitude 12 degrees by longitude 30 degrees: "here Livingstone died / 4 May 1873."

On his four journeys through central Africa, Stanley accumulated information from African natives, including names of rivers, lakes, villages, etc. The majority of named spaces on this map are native, but Stanley has also made his mark and included marks made by Speke and other explorers as well: Stanley Pool is prominently named several hundred miles from the mouth of the river, while Leopoldville appears in slightly smaller font just across the river. Lake Leopold II appears prominently below the word "Congo," and Stanley Falls Station is located just above the equator. Stanley has also designated one commodity on the map, locating copper mines at Mirambo in the rich copper deposits of Katanga Province. By co-opting indigenous names, stamping a European presence, and locating the Congo Free State at the center of the map, Stanley establishes a map space that does much more than follow the route of his expedition to relieve Emin Pasha, this map proclaims the power of Leopold II. The Congo Free State is open for business.

Stanley's earlier maps included in *Through the Dark Continent* were produced by following the entire course of the Congo River in 1874-1877, providing an intriguing complement to the later version just discussed. The later version displays Stanley stamping his identity on the territory he has mapped, sure of the revelations he makes. The earlier map shown below suggests a younger Stanley full of the excitement of discovery.

Of course, this is prior to Stanley's employment by Leopold II, and this map is all his – the primary marker is his route, marked in red along the entire course of the Congo River. We know that Stanley used James Wyld's *Map of Central Africa* (1874) as he traveled along the course of the Congo, marking in pencil its trajectory, place names, dates of passage, compass points, and calculations of dead reckonings; using these methods, Stanley fills in almost 1000 miles of unknown territory, all faintly visible on the map shown below, the only copy bearing Stanley's annotations.

Stanley's map of 1877-1878 added important details to the personal copy of the Wyld map he used in the Anglo-American expedition, and he filled the map he drew with fascinating textual entries providing valuable topographical and ethnographic descriptions. It is very clear on the Stanley

Chapter Two: Spectral Sightings, Mapping, and Exploration... 93

Henry Morton Stanley. *Map Showing the Western Half of Equatorial Africa*

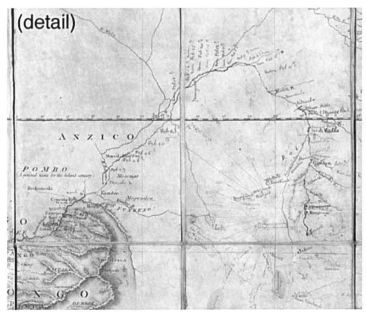

James Wyld. *Map of Central Africa*[30]

map that he wanted to name the Congo the Livingstone River in homage to his mentor, and he named the Edwin Arnold River for the editor of *The Daily Telegraph* who supported his expedition. The dominating icon in Stanley's 1877-1878 map is the river, named by Stanley "The Livingstone" at the point where it rises to the 2nd degree latitude north of the equator. Stanley includes a note on the river: "This great river bears different names between one bank and the other. It is sometimes called after villages by which it flows, but the word 'Ibari' or 'River' is sufficiently comprehensive between Longitude 15° and 21° E."

Stanley offers additional details, drawing the numerous islands in the river, identifying them as covered with dense woods, he marks the locations of villages, and offers warnings such as "Tribe armed with muskets," and identifies the "Land of the Dwarf Immigrants," writing further on the map: "Dwarfs are variously called Watwa, Wakwanga, Wakuma, and Wakumu. They are said to be vicious and most murderous. Their range is believed to be extensive." Stanley's language suggests that this is information he has gathered from more peaceful, friendly, and informative natives.

Stanley's identity becomes entwined with the Congo as he names both the Pool and the Falls after himself at this early date, 1877-1878 – both names appear on maps for the first time following the Anglo-American Expedition—but native names still predominate indicating territories of various tribes whose names Stanley has learned from the inhabitants along the banks of the river. Thus, Stanley's earlier maps are exceptionally valuable documents for recording original local toponyms before these names disappeared with the intrusion of colonial naming. Overall, there still appears to be a vast amount of blank space but the great river has been found and mapped. Stanley's map illustrated above, *Map Showing the Western Half of Equatorial Africa*, is half of the total, the other part consists of the eastern half and tracks Stanley's overland journey from Zanzibar and the Indian Ocean as he circumnavigated Lake Victoria Nyanza and Lake Tanganyika

Chapter Two: Spectral Sightings, Mapping, and Exploration...

and indicates the place where Livingstone died; Stanley marks a spot near Chitambo's Village just south of Lake Bangweolo, writing: "Dr. Livingstone is supposed to have died here."[31]

Clearly by 1890, the blank spaces of the map of central Africa had been filled in primarily by Stanley.

Harry H. Johnston. *The Colonizability of Africa*

Naturally the possession of Africa through evolving mapmaking was crucial to its partition among European nations, but one map reveals in chilling detail just what Africa had to offer the colonizer. This map, dated 1899 by

J. G. Bartholomew, created for Harry Hamilton Johnston's *A History of the Colonization of Africa by Alien Races*, shows the callousness with which Europe viewed the African continent as territory to be appropriated for settlement and exploitation, revealed in the explanatory note below the map. The vast center of the continent is described as "Unhealthy but exploitable Africa; impossible for European colonization, but for the most part of great commercial value and inhabited by fairly docile, governable races; the Africa of the trader and planter and of despotic European control." The exception lies with those areas deemed extremely unhealthy, including the banks of the entire course of the Congo River.

Geography and *Some* Explorers

Conrad's passion for maps suggests a desire to have filled in blank spaces himself and his revulsion at the scramble for loot that mapping the interior of Africa allowed. As the prime suspect in lifting the veil of mystery from central Africa and opening it to European trade, Stanley must have earned Conrad's unremitting disgust. In this light, Conrad's final title for his geographical essay is revealing, only *some* explorers are named as icons who have earned his reverence. Notably, Stanley is not among them, but his specter rises in the essay, nonetheless. As Conrad reminisces about his voyage on the Congo, he can't avoid naming "Stanley Falls"; the site of that remembrance will summon his attack on the anonymous perpetrator of a newspaper stunt; surely pointing to the media sensation which accompanied each of Stanley's four expeditions to the continent.

Among *some* explorers Conrad does name as role models for geographical exploration the following: James Cook, Abel Tasman, John Franklin, Leopold McClintock, Mungo Park, Richard Burton, and David Livingstone. Conrad's reverence for Cook, particularly, will resurface near the end of the essay as he sails through the Torres Strait, ending the essay at the

Chapter Two: Spectral Sightings, Mapping, and Exploration... 97

point of Cook's exit through Endeavour Strait. Cook's own motivation for exploration is famously quoted as "[he] had the ambition not only to go farther than any other man had been before; but as far as it was possible for man to go" (qtd. in Lack 10). But Cook was far from the flawless explorer Conrad imagined him to be. For Conrad, Cook is an example of an explorer whose aims were pure, free from "the desire of loot" (GSE 9). One of the last "Fathers of Militant Geography," Cook is exemplary as one whose "only object was the search for truth" (9). Pairing his voyage through the Torres Strait with Cook's, Conrad sailed into the Torres Strait through Bligh's Entrance in August one hundred and eighteen years after Cook's voyage, following navigational charts identified by his wife Jessie Conrad as the ones used for his voyage through the straits.[32] Reflecting later in his essay that Cook may have gone ashore on an unnamed island outward bound from the Strait "to be alone with his thoughts for a moment" (17), Conrad misidentifies the year of Cook's voyage as 1762. Cook, however, did not sail to Australia and the Torres Strait until 1768-1770; his primary mission was to observe the Transit of Venus from the island of Tahiti in June 1769 (as Mason and Dixon had done eight years prior at the African cape). Furthermore, if Conrad is imagining Cook's landing at an unnamed island upon exiting the Strait, is he referring to Booby Island named by Cook for the huge number of booby birds there or Possession Island, just off the tip of the northern coast of Australia, as the Strait exits into the Arafura Sea? Cook did land on both, but on Possession, as Brendan Casey points out, he went ashore with a company of men, was spotted by a group of Torres Islanders who fled from sight, and hoisted "English Coulers and in the name of His Majesty King George the Third took possession of the whole Eastern Coast [...] together with all the Bays, Harbours Rivers and Islands situate on the said coast" (qtd. in Casey 8). Rather than going ashore "to be alone with his thoughts," it appears that Cook was instead claiming already indigenously inhabited territory in the name of the King of England. But by choosing not to name the island and to portray Cook absorbed in reverie there, Conrad successfully mutes Cook's act of possession.

Conrad also maintains high regard for the Arctic explorers Franklin and McClintock, adding the importance of their land explorations to those of the ocean voyagers. Franklin's fate and the mystery of the *Erebus* and *Terror* intrigued Conrad, who read McClintock's account of his discovery of the fate of John Franklin and his crew in *The Voyage of the Fox in the Arctic Seas*. From the northern pole, Conrad turns his attention to equatorial Africa, recalling Mungo Park's tale of the kindly African woman who gave him a restorative drink of water (GSE 13). Park had so indelibly stamped the image of the western Sudan in his mind that Conrad reflected "I could draw the rivers and principal features from memory even now" (13). He aligns his infancy with the discovery of the African Great Lakes by Burton and Speke, reproducing their explorations by tracing the outline of Lake Tanganyika in his out-of-date atlas in the late 1860s. In fact, Burton and Speke performed their own filling in of "blank" spaces, but beneath those "blanks" lay accumulated evidence of an earlier knowledge derived from African, Arab, and Indian sources represented in earlier nineteenth century maps but later repudiated by Burton and Speke in the maps drawn from their East African Expedition (1856-1859). Operating within a well-developed Arab-African trading network which facilitated the expedition's surveys, Burton and Speke's four published maps "represent an attempt by both explorers to erase the Arab-African basis of their cartographical statements [...] and showcase the early development of an imperial cartographical strategy" (Wisnicki 106). Within twenty-five years, European powers could redraw the African map "with little thought either for existing cultural and material realities in Africa or for the long-term impact European partitioning would have on Africa's many ethnic groups" (106).

The African explorer and missionary for whom Conrad holds the highest regard is David Livingstone. Central Africa evokes Livingstone's name; for Conrad he is "a notable European figure and the most venerated perhaps of all objects of [his] early geographical enthusiasm" (GSE 14). Yet there is no mention of his "finding" by Stanley in July 1872, other than perhaps the thinly veiled reference to the newspaper stunt later in the essay, instead Conrad remarks on Livingstone's death in the "dark native hut on the Congo headwaters in which he died clinging in his very last hour to his heart's unappeased desire for the sources of the Nile" (13). In this highly romanticized version of Livingstone's death there appears a very important detail that Conrad seems to have overlooked – the headwaters of the Congo River, actually the Lualaba springing from Lake Bangweolo, were not known until after Livingstone died in 1873, when Stanley traced its course in his 1874-1877 Anglo-American expedition. Livingstone's heart is buried at the site Conrad mentions and indicated on Stanley's map above, but his body was returned to England to be buried in Westminster Abbey with Stanley as one of the pallbearers. Livingstone's last days in Africa are entwined with Stanley in important ways; as Matthew Rubery remarks, Stanley's finding Livingstone "was one of the most sensational news stories of the nineteenth century" ("On Henry Morton Stanley's Search for Dr. Livingstone"). Conrad's reverence for Livingstone and the purity of his mission was matched by Stanley's reverence for the man whose passion to abolish slavery Stanley adopted as his own. Stanley remained with Livingstone for four months, exploring the northern coast of Lake Tanganyika with him in that unrelenting search for the source of the Nile, then Stanley returned to Great Britain to glory in his newfound notoriety.

Certainly by 1924 when Conrad began "Geography and Some Explorers," and long before, Stanley's image had been tarnished, and Conrad diminishes Stanley's achievement by refusing to acknowledge him other than in the name of the falls which Stanley named for himself. Yet Stanley's achievement as the "greatest" and most controversial of African explorers is difficult to deny even by Conrad whose oversights allow Stanley to appear more eloquently in the muting and silences of the text. If Stanley's finding Livingstone serves as Conrad's "newspaper stunt" in "Geography and Some Explorers," there are several anomalies in Conrad's remembrance to unpack. As Stephen Donovan observes, Conrad's spot of reminiscence is more than five hundred miles from the location in the village of Ujiji where Stanley found Livingstone ("Conrad's Unholy Recollection" 83), so hardly the exact spot where the newspaper stunt occurred. It is unlikely, Donovan adds, that Conrad at thirteen would have known anything about what was in Europe the "scoop of the century" (84). Of course, Conrad could hardly have avoided knowing about it later, especially given his reverence for Livingstone's missionary work and exploratory travels in central Africa.

Resurrecting Stanley:
Finding Dr. Livingstone, 1871-1872

On Stanley's first foray into central Africa searching for Livingstone, hoping for that scoop of the century, he arrived in Zanzibar, the center for the African slave trade on the eastern coast. With America recovering from civil war and the opening of the Suez Canal, Europe had become the major trading partner to the east coast of Africa. Stanley began his expedition to find Livingstone in Zanzibar, getting far more valuable information from Arab slave traders about how to outfit his expedition than he could glean from combing Burton's and Speke's narratives for details about how much and what to buy to feed his bearers and trade with the natives. What Stanley had to rely on, as Burton and Speke did before him, was a caravan system that was well established. "A transregional and multiethnic culture," Stephen Rockel writes, "had long facilitated trade, communication, and the movement of people, commodities, and ideas" ("Decentering Exploration" 172). Africans and Asians had penetrated the interior carrying trading goods and ivory long before European explorers arrived, yet Europeans, even while relying on this knowledge, persisted in ignoring the precedents established by these prior travelers. Livingstone was well aware of the

Chapter Two: Spectral Sightings, Mapping, and Exploration...   101

networks of trade and the caravan system which supported them, commenting on the professionalism and strength of the porters (Rockel, "Decentering Exploration" 176). Stanley came into this culture as a neophyte, but he quickly learned how to adapt the system to his own aims and manage his porters, even with brutality if he had to. As Stanley set out, Livingstone had not been heard from officially in more than two years; John Kirk, the British consul in Zanzibar, told Stanley that Livingstone might be in the vicinity of Ujiji, but that more than likely, he was dead. Livingstone had gained international fame by tracing the course of the Zambezi River and discovering Victoria Falls as well as for his vigorous anti-slavery campaign; in his last expedition in 1866, Livingstone estimated the slave trade at as many as 100,000 slaves captured and sold each year (Bierman 95). Ill and aging as he waited to be resupplied in Ujiji, Livingstone learned of Stanley's approach with relief, while Stanley, dressed to kill, marched on, confident in the belief that he had indeed found Livingstone. In anticipation of his meeting with Livingstone and determined to maintain the *sang froid* and superiority of the white explorer surrounded by Arab and native onlookers, Stanley wrote:

> And I – what would I have not given for a bit of friendly wilderness, where, unseen, I might vent my joy in some mad freak, such as idiotically biting my hand, turning a somersault, or slashing at trees, in order to allay those exciting feelings that were well-nigh uncontrollable. My heart beats fast, but I must not let my face betray my emotions, lest it shall detract from the dignity of a white man appearing under such extraordinary circumstances. (*How I Found Livingstone* 411)

Overwhelmed with emotion, Stanley pronounced those infamous words for which he will be forever remembered: "Dr. Livingstone, I presume?" (412). Pressed later in life, Stanley admitted "I couldn't think what else to say" (Bierman 114). But Stanley quickly eased into a conversation in which he revealed many events of the past two years that Livingstone had missed by having no access to newspapers: completion of the Pacific Railroad, the election of President Grant, the opening of the Suez Canal, and more. "There we sat," Stanley would later claim, "the man, the myth, and I" (qtd. in Bierman 115). There was no need, Stanley wrote, to embellish; "no need of exaggeration – of any penny-a-line news, or of sensationalism. The world had witnessed and experienced much the last few years" (*How I Found Livingstone* 415). Those comments appear rather disingenuous and ironic considering Stanley's clear choice of sensationalism in his narrative style. After traveling with Livingstone to the northern coast of Lake Tanganyika, Stanley received his journals and his letters to take back to London – proof he would need later that he had actually found Livingstone. While Stanley would face criticism, skepticism, and scorn in the press after his return, he had outfoxed the geographical establishment by finding Livingstone before the Royal Geographical Society expedition could get to him and his *How I Found Livingstone,* a runaway bestseller, made him a wealthy man. But Stanley would not escape British elitist attacks and disbelief that an *American* (Stanley was not American, he was Welsh), who was no scientist and no *gentleman*, could act as the personal representative of the revered Dr. Livingstone (Riffenburgh 60). While on the other hand, papers like the *London Daily News* reveled in the discovery, regardless of the social class of the discoverer, gushing "Stanley […] *is like a man returning with the story of another universe*" (qtd. in Berenson 42). Newspapers, with the immediacy of reporting through telegraphs, the proliferation of readership, and widespread circulation, not only had the power to overcome class barriers but also the power to reveal what had once been mysterious and obscure to the West.

Stanley's Anglo-American Expedition, 1874-1877

By 1873 Livingstone was dead; once Stanley learned of his death, he forged a new determination, transforming his

Chapter Two: Spectral Sightings, Mapping, and Exploration...   103

career path from journalist to explorer and writing in his diary: "May I be selected to succeed him in opening up Africa to the shining light of Christianity!" (qtd. in Bierman 146). In 1874 Stanley got his chance, embarking on what was arguably his most important expedition to fill in the blanks of the vast center of the African continent, and he did fill in those blanks. Charged with the mission to continue Livingstone's efforts to explore and map the center of the continent, Stanley set out once more, funded by *The New York Herald* and *The Daily Telegraph* on the biggest and costliest expedition thus far mounted from Zanzibar, waving American and British flags. In 999 days, Stanley proved that Lake Victoria Nyanza is one body of water, and that Lake Tanganyika is not the source of the Nile; but most importantly, he charted the entire course of the Congo River.

Extraordinary for the advancement of knowledge of Africa as he suffered from fevers and fell under constant attack, Stanley's newest expedition was also infamous for the violence against natives in which Stanley himself seemed to revel. Stanley used slave chains to punish deserters who were found and returned, but a prime example of the lengths to which he could go is the attack on the natives of Bumbireh island in Lake Victoria, recounted in Stanley's letters published in *The Daily Telegraph* and later in *Through the Dark Continent* (1878). As his boat was surrounded by natives brandishing spears and arrows, Stanley attempted to placate them with offers of cloth and beads, but the natives seized the oars, assuming this would keep Stanley and his crew as their captives. However, Stanley and the crew cobbled together oars from the boat's seats and footboards and launched, firing at the attacking natives with an elephant gun and a double-barreled shotgun. Later, without their proper oars, Stanley and his men nearly died in the lake when a furious storm capsized their boat and left them stranded, starving, on an uninhabited island.

Stanley was not done with Bumbireh and its inhabitants. He decided to take revenge on the "savages" blocking his progress to Uganda:

> We then moved to within 50 yards of the shore, to fire at close quarters, and each man was permitted to exercise himself as he best could. The savages gallantly held the water-line for an hour, and slung their stones with better effect than they shot their arrows. The spirit which animated them proved what they might have done had they succeeded in effecting a landing at Mahyiga at night, but here, however, the spear, with which they generally fight, was quite useless. (*Through the Dark Continent* 1: 292)

In the later published volume, indicated by the quote above, Stanley has muffled the extremity of the attack reported earlier in *The Daily Telegraph*, which when it was made available to readers in Britain and America a year after the attack, caused enormous outcry. For example, in *The New York Herald* dispatch,[33] Stanley adds to his description,

> I then ordered the canoes to advance within fifty yards of the shore, and to fire as if they were shooting birds [...]. When they were close to the water's edge the bugle sounded a halt and another volley was fired into the dense crowd, which had such a disastrous effect on them that they retired far up the hill, and our work of punishment was consummated. (*Stanley's Despatches* 260)

This is what European and American newspapers readers would have read first; and in the report filed several days before, Stanley fired off the following recording his escape from Bumbireh,

> Twice in succession I succeeded in dropping men determined on launching the canoes, and seeing the sub-chief who had commanded the party that took the drum I took deliberate aim with my elephant rifle at him. That bullet, as I have since been told, killed the chief and his wife and infant, who happened to be standing a few paces behind him, and the extraordinary result had more effect on the superstitious minds of the natives than all previous or subsequent shots. (247)

The most incendiary of these remarks are not repeated in *Through the Dark Continent*; the reference to shooting the natives like birds and the killing of the chief, his wife, and infant had disappeared.

The toll on the natives included thirty-three dead and approximately one hundred wounded, amazingly low considering Stanley was firing an elephant gun, while Stanley's crew suffered only two injuries (Bierman 181). Even Richard Burton, an inveterate racist, was appalled; he (Stanley) "'still shoots negroes as if they were monkeys,'" he wrote in a letter to John Kirk in Zanzibar (qtd. in Bierman 182). But in New York, Bennett reveled in the notoriety of his newspaper caused by this sensational attack and defended his reporter vigorously. On February 9, 1878, the following appeared in *The Standard* in opposition to the honors awarded by the Royal Geographical Society:

> It cannot be seriously contended that in judging an explorer's achievements in geographical discovery no account should be taken of his acts from a moral point of view [...]. The line must be drawn somewhere. We allow explorers a large latitude; but there are some extravagances of zeal against which a protest ought to be made. (qtd. in Riffenburgh 66)

As Stephen Donovan points out, by July 1878, Conrad was learning English and began reading *The Standard* while on the *Skimmer of the Sea* ("Conrad's Unholy Recollection" 84). *The Standard* was one of the papers that objected to the Royal Geographical Society honoring Stanley and to the "controversial reception given earlier that year to *Through the Dark Continent*" (84). If the attacks on Stanley in the *Standard* earlier in the year persisted into late summer of 1878, Conrad may have puzzled them out.

But the power of Stanley's discoveries in this expedition, despite the public outcry against his tactics and the jealousy his work inspired in the geographical establishment, could not be denied. In the two volumes of *Through the Dark Continent*, consisting of approximately twelve hundred pages, Stanley records in sensationalist prose his adventures through the Congo, indicating but not forefronting his collection of geographical data throughout. Stanley's methods of geographical exploration had advanced beyond his abilities to measure his path in the expedition to find Livingstone. Where in 1871-1872, Stanley used a watch and a compass to measure distance traveled through the method of "dead reckoning,"[34] by 1874, Stanley's methods had become more sophisticated, not only using a pedometer to measure distance traveled, but also measuring latitude and longitude by chronometer and sextant, altitude by the boiling point of water, air pressure with an aneroid barometer, and a theodolite to measure height of inaccessible points on mountains. According to Peter Daerden, this expedition was Stanley's most successful for the geographical information and mathematical data he accumulated (13). Stanley began trying the "artificial horizon & chronometer" in October 1874 on a small island near Zanzibar, then took his first measurement of latitude and longitude on November 19, 1874 (12). Using a chronometer set to Greenwich Mean Time, Stanley calculated the scale of distance between local time of his position and local time in Greenwich by taking every four minutes as one degree. Thus in 1874 Stanley had begun to map Africa's longitudinal position based on Greenwich as the center point of measurement of the world.

Bula Matari and the Founding of the Congo State, 1879-1884

As a conquering hero in 1878, Stanley delivered lectures in front of a huge painted map of Africa created by four bedsheets sewn together. His achievements were so widely publicized that one person in particular couldn't fail to pay attention – King Leopold II of Belgium. In *The Daily Telegraph* of November 12, 1877, Stanley wrote the following about the Congo: "This river is and will be the grand highway of commerce to West Central Africa" (Preface, *The Congo* 1: vi). In his previous expedition, he had even recorded offering "some of Huntley and Palmer's best and sweetest biscuits" to the "great magic doctor of Vinyata" (*Through the Dark Continent* 1: 122). So, by the 1870s the globally traded biscuit, a marker of the

Chapter Two: Spectral Sightings, Mapping, and Exploration...

commodity transcendent, had come with Stanley to the center of Africa. Later, when asked by a reporter from the *New York Herald* about commercial prospects in the Congo, Stanley replied:

> They are boundless. There is no part of the world with such chances unworked. Before my arrival there these chances were entirely in the trading ring at the mouth of the Congo, and naturally the gentlemen there are deeply annoyed at our work of endeavoring to keep the commercial highway to Central Africa open to all the world. The interests of the entire world in central Africa are too great to permit its great water highway to be annexed for the benefit of any one selfish nation. ("On the Congo," Newspaper Cutting from the *New York Herald*, 30 Oct. 1882)

By 1882, however, while declaring that his aim was to open the center of the continent to global trade, Stanley would, on the contrary, render it hostage to the greed of one selfish king, Leopold II.

In his third major expedition, Stanley bulldozed through the continent, his mission to "'strike a white line across the Dark Continent'" (qtd. in Driver, *Geography Militant* 120). From 1879–1884, with a brief return to Europe to recover from serious illness, Stanley earned his favorite African name, "Bula Matari," breaker of rocks, for his work on building roads. He began establishing trading stations on the banks of the Congo River, under constant pressure from Leopold II and his deputy, Colonel Strauch, to make haste in claiming the vast Congo basin. In addition to road building, Stanley brought steamers to the navigable reaches of the river, portaging them in sections along the coast of the unnavigable portions. Beginning in late 1879, Stanley began founding stations with the construction of Vivi, continuing upriver to Isangila, Lukungu, Manyanga, of Leopoldville at the Stanley Pool, which Stanley had discovered in 1877. The key to the Congo, Thomas Pakenham argues, was the Pool – "that great lake which formed the gateway to 5000 miles of navigable waterways" (150). Furthermore, the road Stanley built from Manyanga to Leopoldville on the south bank of the river forms one of the great ivory routes to the coast (Johnston, "A Visit to Mr. Stanley's Stations" 574). Stanley would forge ahead to establish the station at Stanley Falls by December 1883. By the time he left the Congo in June 1884, the race for control of the entire continent had begun – the *scramble* was on.

The book that would follow this expedition, Stanley's *The Congo and the Founding of Its Free State,* panned by some scholars as his dullest – but in my view, his most fascinating – could only be published with Leopold's consent. Leopold could have prevented publication if he found the manuscript unacceptable for achieving his own ends; he retained the right to make editorial changes and had final approval of the text (Jeal 286). A copy of the manuscript that was known to have been cut and altered by Leopold then disappeared, most likely destroyed by him. As Tim Jeal argues, Stanley allowed editing that suggested he had negotiated hundreds of treaties that he never did so that Leopold could strengthen a legal case for international recognition of the Congo as a state (286). For Jeal, study of the existing manuscript pages indicates tampering by Leopold and refutes the claims by Adam Hochschild and others that Stanley alone robbed African chiefs of their sovereignty and land for "a few bales of cloth and some trinkets" (286). Jeal writes compellingly in a general note: "Most of the key documents in the early history of the Congo Free State were destroyed on Leopold II's orders in the opening years of the twentieth century" (523). As disenchanted with Leopold as Stanley might have been at this stage, he was the one who enabled Leopold to make "the big swallow possible" (Hochschild 74).

Africa Dismembered: The Vilest Scramble for Loot

> Leopold II [...] has knit adventurers, traders and missionaries of many races into one band of men, under the most illustrious of modern travellers [H. M. Stanley] to carry into the interior of Africa new ideas of law, order, humanity, and protection of the natives. (*The Daily Telegraph,* 22 Oct. 1884, qtd. in Pakenham 239)

Chapter Two: Spectral Sightings, Mapping, and Exploration...

Before ascending to the throne, Leopold had a marble plaque from the Acropolis engraved with the words: "*Il faut à la Belgique une Colonie*" ("Belgium requires a colony," qtd. in Bierman 217). Leopold had convened the Brussels Geographic Conference in 1876 under the guise of pursuing geographical exploration during which the AIA, International African Association, later to become the AIC, Association Internationale du Congo, was formed. The goal was really to coordinate European exploration into Africa; it was here that Leopold advanced the notion of establishing stations across central Africa along with the development of roads and telegraph lines. The more important conference, though, the Berlin (West Africa) Conference, would follow in 1884-1885.

The countries represented in the illustration from *Illustrierte Zeitung* depicting the partitioning of Africa include Great Britain, France, Germany, Italy, Portugal, Russia, Prussia, the US, Hungary, Sweden-Norway, Germany, and of course Belgium. Notice the huge map of Africa hanging on the wall as the delegates negotiate to carve the continent into colonies. Count Bismarck is portrayed as the convener

Illustration of the Conference of Berlin

seated at the center of the image; his aim was to ensure that the continent of Africa would be "carved up in an orderly and peaceful fashion" (Bierman 244). Even though his AIC was not fully recognized by all the delegations and therefore could not be represented, Leopold II had the cards stacked in his favor with US support for his position, delegates from other countries who were his friends, and Stanley sitting in with the American delegation. The stated aims of the conference were, of course, to bring civilization to the benighted natives, secure free trade in the region, and end slavery. When the conference was over and the Berlin Act of 1885 signed, Leopold II held personal dominion over 900,000 square miles of the Congo basin, declaring himself on May 29, 1885, *le Roi-Souverain* of the Congo Free State. A catastrophic blow had been struck, sealing the fate of the Congo.

Stanley's Last Hurrah: The Emin Pasha Relief Expedition, 1887-1889

> Whatever happens we have got
> the Maxim gun and they have not.
> (Belloc and Blackwood 62)

In 1887 Stanley embarked on the most controversial, most disorganized, and least successful of his four expeditions, "an abject failure" (Berenson 123) – the Expedition for the Relief of Emin Pasha. The irony of the title of the expedition is the first fact to consider; Emin Pasha, actually a German also known as Eduard Schnitzer, was appointed governor of the Equatoria Province by General Charles Gordon, the governor-general of the Sudan. Following Gordon's assassination during the Mahdist Rebellion in Khartoum and the uproar about it in the British press, Emin Pasha's position in Equatoria seemed perilous, but he does not appear to have asked directly for help. The British government declined to sponsor the expedition but John Kirk, British Consul in Zanzibar, and William Mackinnon, a Scottish tycoon, conspired to promote the expedition with

Chapter Two: Spectral Sightings, Mapping, and Exploration... 111

Stanley as its leader. Since Leopold II was technically still Stanley's employer, the mission could only be arranged with his consent, and to get that, the financiers had to agree to a much longer route, traveling from west to east, so that Leopold could try to annex Equatoria to his Congo territory and Stanley could break new ground in discoveries. Kirk and Mackinnon, however, had underlying reasons; Emin Pasha was known to be sitting on a huge stock of ivory worth approximately 60,000 British pounds sterling, so there was enormous potential for commercial gain not only in acquiring that stash but also in the accumulation of land through treaties that Stanley would make with African chiefs (Youngs 114).

Stanley set sail from Zanzibar, circling the Cape to the mouth of the Congo River in February 1887. With him he carried an extraordinary amount of firepower including the infamous Maxim gun – a machine gun invented in 1881. When he reached the mouth of the Congo, Stanley discovered that the Congo Free State steamers were not waiting for him as Leopold II had promised; in fact, only the *Stanley* was in good repair and the others were in various stages of disrepair. Thus, the mission began under inauspicious circumstances as Stanley commandeered steamers from very reluctant missionaries; but even with those steamers, there was insufficient capacity to transport all the mission's supplies. Stanley made a difficult and fateful decision to split the expedition into two groups – the Advance Column and the Rear Column, leaving the sick and disabled behind at Yambuya in the Rear Column to await the assistance of Tippu Tib, the slave and ivory trader Stanley engaged to bring porters with reinforcement supplies which never arrived. Meanwhile Stanley made a grueling trek through the Ituri rainforest, struggling for ten months to reach Lake Albert and find Emin Pasha. By the time he reached the lake, Stanley had lost more than one half of his forces through death or desertion. Along the way, Stanley encountered the forest pigmies and engaged in slaving tactics to force the natives to provide food. Finally, when Stanley reached Emin Pasha in April 1888, it was questionable who was rescuing whom. Emin

Pasha seemed in rather better shape than Stanley's motley crew (Berenson 137).

On the way back to the Rear Column, Stanley saw the Ruwenzori Mountains, usually cloaked in mist most of the year – no European had ever seen them or perhaps recognized them before Stanley[35]; now Stanley could confirm these snowcapped peaks as the source of the Nile River (Berenson 138). But when he arrived at the Rear Column camp at Banalya, he found devastation.

> Pen cannot picture nor tongue relate the full horrors witnessed within that dreadful pest-hold. The nameless scourge of barbarians was visible in the faces and bodies of many a hideous-looking human being, who, disfigured, bloated, marred and scarred, came, impelled by curiosity, to hear and see us who had come from the forest land east [...]. There were six dead bodies lying unburied, and the smitten living with their festers lounged in front of us by the dozen [...]. I heard of murder and death, of sickness and sorrow, anguish and grief, and wherever I looked the hollow eyes of dying men met my own with such trusting, pleading regard, such far-away yearning looks [...]. I sat stupefied under a suffocating sense of despondency. (Stanley, *In Darkest Africa* 1: 521)

This quotation bears repeating at length for the echoes it suggests with Conrad's grove of dying Africans in "Heart of Darkness." Here, too, more than half of the expedition members left behind died, including the leader Major Edmund Barttelot, shot to death for threatening to kill an African woman, James Jameson had died of fever, and John Troup was sent home seriously ill. Stanley had to face the dangerous trek through the rainforest for a third time, dangerously ill himself for most of the trek, and when he finally reached Lake Albert after almost three years on the mission to relieve Emin Pasha, he found that Emin had been taken captive and Equatoria seized by the Mahdists (Berenson 139). Emin's huge stock of ivory was gone. Even though he released Emin and persuaded him to come to the coast, Stanley failed in bringing him to England in triumph. Instead, the near-sighted and possibly inebriated Emin suffered a bad fall from a window at a welcoming banquet

Chapter Two: Spectral Sightings, Mapping, and Exploration... 113

in Bagamoyo, and once recovered, chose to work for a German charter company rather than align himself with Stanley (140). Stanley, however, survived howls of criticism, rising above the initial outrage expressed in the British press, to become a national hero, the "man who embodied Britain at its best" (141). Stanley, the editor of *The Morning Post* wrote, was "the best embodiment of qualities which, while they exist in every race, are, as we hope and as we believe, more distinctive of the Anglo-Saxon strain than of any other" (qtd. in Berenson 141). In the view of *The Morning Post* writer at least, Stanley was the shining example of manliness, and, added a writer for *The Leeds Mercury,* an example as well for "undaunted, indomitable courage" (qtd. in Berenson 141).

In three months, writing at a furious pace in Cairo, Stanley produced the two-volume *In Darkest Africa,* whose first 150,000 copies sold out within a few weeks. Feted everywhere and delivering numerous addresses to sellout crowds, Stanley focused on the positives: measuring the extent of the Ituri rainforest at 224 million acres, seeing the forest pigmies for the first time, tracing the length of the Aruwimi River, and locating the Mountains of the Moon, the Ruwenzori range, the "Cloud King" ("Geographical Results" 317, 325, 327). In an address to the Royal Geographical Society, Stanley claimed:

> The most glorious portions of Inner Africa have been traversed and described for the first time; and we know that there is scarcely an acre throughout the area but is a decided gain to our earth; and I assert that every mile of new lands traversed by us will serve in the coming time to expand British commerce, and stimulate civilized industry. And, finally, we have extended British possessions to the eastern limits of the Congo Free State, having acquired many a thousand square miles of territory [...] *by force of arms.* (328, emphasis added)

The New Journalism:
"The unholy recollection of a prosaic newspaper stunt"

Conrad's disgust with journalists and journalism in general has been frequently commented upon and is adequately displayed in his essay "Autocracy and War"; his salient comments from this essay, quoted in the last chapter but worth repeating here, could easily apply to Stanley's journalism:

> [T]here must be something subtly noxious to the human brain in the composition of newspaper ink; or else it is that the large page, the columns of words, the leaded headings exalt the mind into a state of feverish credulity. The printed voice of the press makes a sort of still uproar taking from men both the power to reflect and the faculty of genuine feeling; leaving them only the artificially created need of having something exciting to talk about. (AW 76)

Where Conrad is clearly writing about news coverage of the Russo-Japanese war in these lines, and I've quoted them in that context in the previous chapter, his words take on new meaning when applied to the rise of the New Journalism and Stanley's participation in that rise. First, though, I should unpack the famous allusion to that "prosaic newspaper stunt." While it's widely assumed that Conrad is, in fact, referring to Stanley's "scoop" at finding Livingstone, Stephen Donovan convincingly argues that Conrad is more likely referring to Stanley's Anglo-American Expedition, as Conrad, a keen reader of *The Standard* beginning in 1878, might have read about Stanley's brutality there ("Conrad's Unholy Recollection" 84). Helen Chambers, on the other hand, (as well as Zdzisław Najder) remarks that as a boy Conrad read *Wędrowiec,* a periodical in Polish devoted to publishing reports of expeditions not only of Polish explorers but also those of Cook, Stanley, Samuel Baker, Mungo Park, and Livingstone ("'A Sort of Still Uproar'"; Najder, *Joseph Conrad: A Life* 42). Thus, Chambers counters Donovan's claim, suggesting that it is possible Conrad read about the Stanley-Livingstone expedition as a boy. Regardless of whether Conrad is referring to either of Stanley's first two expeditions, or even to the later Emin Pasha Relief Expedition, his comment does, in Donovan's view, indicate his "hardening prejudice against journalism" ("Conrad's Unholy Recollection" 84).

As I observed in the previous chapter, the second half of the nineteenth century witnessed the novelty of immediacy in newsprint; with the invention of the telegraph and railroad, news accounts could reach millions within reach of telegraph cable in a few days – the age of the world's first mass medium had arrived, especially in the United States (Berenson 25). *The New York Herald,* under the guidance of James Gordon Bennett, Jr., maintained the largest circulation in the US for almost two decades despite fierce competition from *The Sun.* Bennett employed extraordinarily talented journalists – Mark Twain, Walt Whitman, and Charles Nordhoff, to name a few, along with an equally talented staff of foreign correspondents (Riffenburgh 53). Furthermore, Bennett was especially interested in covering exploration, devoting more coverage to it than any other paper, and in demonstrating his talent for creating the news by sending reporters to events in exotic places to cover the very place itself, embedding correspondents as members of expeditions as well as organizing and sending expeditions himself (57).

The penny press became a formidable cultural, economic, and political power in its own right, in fact as British papers began to follow the American lead in sensationalist journalism, *The Daily Telegraph* would trumpet on July 3, 1872: "Nothing can be hid long in this age from the researches of enterprise and science. The burning equator and frozen poles alike must give up their secrets" (qtd. in Berenson 42). It was the penny press that made Stanley's laughable greeting to Livingstone famous and later Stanley's rhetorical power heralded a new journalistic form; Stanley was the first overseas correspondent to adopt a specialized form of delivering the news: *reportage*, "imaginative" nonfiction. Making himself the center and hero of his narratives while even creating some of the events he reported, Stanley could emphasize danger as he battled his way through uncharted and often hostile territory. Stanley effectively invented the sensation of finding Livingstone, launching that expedition on his own without being ordered to do so by Bennett (Berenson 33). His newspaper audiences were left anticipating each new sensationalist dispatch to *The New*

York Herald and later to *The Daily Telegraph*. Looking at the July 2, 1872, issue of *The New York Herald,* Edward Berenson emphasizes the space allotted to the Stanley-Livingstone story – while nearly half the paper consisted of advertisements, the news coverage included a map of east-central Africa, summaries of Stanley's dispatch, and columns of editorials and comments praising *The New York Herald* itself for its scoop, Stanley's bravery, and Livingstone's discoveries (45). Most importantly, the articles emphasized a sensationalist approach with florid headlines and romanticized accounts of encounters with the natives.

To give some of the flavor of Stanley's extraordinarily lengthy dispatches, I'll include the following from November 1872, just before Stanley reaches Livingstone:

> Well, we are but a mile from Ujiji now, and it is high time we should let them know a caravan is coming: so "Commence firing" is the word passed along the length of the column, and gladly do they begin [...]. Down go the ramrods, sending huge charges home to the breech, and volley after volley is fired. The flags are fluttered; the banner of America is in front waving joyfully; the guide is in the zenith of his glory [...]. Never were the Stars and Stripes so beautiful to my mind – the breeze of the Tanganyika has such an effect on them [...] delighted Arabs have run up breathlessly to shake my hands and ask anxiously where I came from. But I have no patience with them. The expedition goes far too slow. I should like to settle the vexed question by one personal view. Where is he? Has he fled? (*Stanley's Despatches* 89)

Just after this gushing account filled with anticipation and patriotism, Stanley finds Livingstone:

> I see the white face of an old man among them. He has a cap with a gold band around it, his dress is a short jacket of red blanket cloth, and his pants – well, I didn't observe. I am shaking hands with him. We raise our hats, and I say: "Dr. Livingstone, I presume?" And he says, "Yes." *Finis coronat opus.* ("The end crowns the work," *Stanley's Despatches* 89)

Notice the breathless present tense with which Stanley draws us, his readers, into his moment of glory, but also notice the

Chapter Two: Spectral Sightings, Mapping, and Exploration...

manner in which he holds us at bay, heightening our tension and anticipation as his own was heightened. Claire Pettitt suggests that the use of the historic present tense, with its power to dramatize the present while narrating past events, invites the reader as witness to the immediacy of the log books and journals Stanley kept in the moment of the journey ("Exploration in Print" 90). Stanley, Pettitt argues, becomes the intermediary between the known and the unknown (97). While Stanley's "reportage" makes us witnesses to the event, except, of course, when, like Stanley, we don't observe Livingstone's pants, the absence of that description lends humanity and a wry comic touch to Stanley's narrative.

Most ironic of all is the fact that, of course, Livingstone knew where he was and the British government had some idea, provided with reports by its consul in Zanzibar John Kirk; so Livingstone was only lost in a Western world awash with newsprint creating the primal moment (Berenson 34). Even though much of the Western world and some of the non-Western were interconnected through the immediacy of the telegraph cable, Stanley's first encounter with Livingstone took place in a region of Africa outside of that rapidly expanding network of global communication. The encounter, therefore, did not surface in print until months after, in July 1872, Bennett crowed to Stanley: "'You are now as famous as Livingstone, having discovered the discoverer'" (qtd. in Berenson 40). Berenson muses at some length about why the phrase "Dr. Livingstone, I presume?" has lingered so long in the consciousness of the West. Certainly, some of the fame should be attributed to Stanley's own charisma, but more importantly, once the news reached readers in the West, it cannot be emphasized enough that the Stanley-Livingstone story "marked the ascendancy of the world's first mass medium, the industrially produced penny press" (24).

As the rising momentum of Stanley's fame grew over the course of the next two decades, W. T. Stead, who fifteen years later would pen a scathing review of Conrad's "Autocracy and War," wrote an eight-page sketch of Stanley in the very first issue of *The Review of Reviews*. In it, he claimed that because of the attention Stanley drew to central Africa *through the press*, he had set in motion the scramble for Africa "'which is the most conspicuous feature of our day'" (qtd. in Murray 9). Further, in his editorials in *The Pall Mall Gazette,* Stead claimed:

> Though Mr. Stanley's strength of purpose and devotion to duty have been the main factors in his success, he nevertheless owes much to an agency which is one of the peculiar forces of the present age. Mr. Stanley is essentially a newspaper man. He is a hero in his own right; but he is also a celebrity *by grace of the newspapers*. (qtd. in Berenson 160, emphasis added)

Not only did Stanley in some way create the news events that he reported, he himself became commoditized, an embodied news event.

Stead had done much to bring the "new journalism" to Britain, as Conrad was quick to attack; but Conrad was hardly alone in viewing sensationalist journalism as dangerous. Matthew Arnold wrote an opinion piece in 1887, coining the term "new journalism" and calling out W. T. Stead as its inventor:

> We have had opportunities of observing a new journalism which a clever and energetic man has lately invented. It has much to recommend it; it is full of ability, novelty, variety, sensation, sympathy, generous instincts; its one great fault is that it is *feather-brained*. It throws out assertions at a venture because it wishes them true; does not correct either them or itself, if they are false; and to get at the state of things as they truly are seems to feel no concern whatever. (qtd. in Riffenburgh 99).

Arnold's remarks could apply just as easily to Bennett and to Stanley.

Once back from his expeditions, Stanley would turn his dispatches into volumes of print, writing hundreds of pages to recreate and capture the essence of his past experiences in the present. Drawing his readers into the moment, Stanley both heightens their anticipation through delaying the climax

Chapter Two: Spectral Sightings, Mapping, and Exploration...   119

as well as bringing his sensationalist prose to a fever pitch. The following quotation from *Through the Dark Continent* narrating Stanley's departure from Zanzibar on his way to the "Dark Continent" amply demonstrates these features:

> The parting is over! We have said our last words for years, perhaps forever, to kindly men! The sun sinks fast to the western horizon, and gloomy is the twilight that now deepens and darkens. Thick shadows fall upon the distant land and over the silent sea, and oppress our throbbing, regretful hearts, as we glide away through the dying light towards The Dark Continent. (*Through the Dark Continent* 1: 69)

Stanley's incorporation of his expedition team in his use of plural first person, his imagery invoking the darkness into which he sails, his use of illustration, and his deployment of emotion capture a reader eager to continue to the next chapter. By means of his prose, Stanley's texts bear witness to a two-decades long spectacle; both textual and visual, his wordy volumes recounting his exploits are best sellers, and by 1890, he had helped to turn Africa into a global marketplace.

"The newspaper," Berenson claims, "would provide the road map to Africa's unexploited wealth" (41-42). In a speech to the Manchester Chamber of Commerce in 1884, Stanley speculated on the millions of yards of Manchester cloth to provide Sunday dresses for the inhabitants of the Congo basin, imagining the Congo as a "limitless market for the commodities of Manchester" (Murray 13). And Stanley insisted on tapping into this reservoir of African wealth over and over. In *How I Found Livingstone,* for example, Stanley's faith in African progress was unbounded:

> It is simply a question of money, which is the sinew of all enterprises. With a sufficient supply of it all Africa can be explored easily. Not only explored, but conquered and civilized. Not only civilized, but intersected by railroads from one end to the other, through and through. (681-82)

"Oh for the hour," Stanley imagines, "when a band of philanthropic *capitalists* shall vow to rescue these beautiful lands" (*Through the Dark Continent* 1: 223, emphasis added). Entrepreneurs were thrilled to learn that, according to Stanley, Africa contained "43,000,000 people ready and eager to pay for manufactured goods with Africa's fabulous raw materials" (Jeal 233).

By 1890 Stanley himself, like the continent he opened up for sale, had become a commodity. His books, functioning as commodities, even became the subject of the process of their writing and publication – for example, Edward Marston, Stanley's publisher, capitalized on the Stanley craze in the aftermath of *In Darkest Africa* to examine Stanley's "method of writing, and the daily life" (qtd. in Youngs 145). This revelation, Youngs argues, stamps the book with the "mark of its producer" (145), and Stanley was in huge demand on the lecture circuit, performing his explorations in person as his books perform them in print. His fame as a marketable personality was promoted in a special journal, *"The Graphic" Stanley Number,* published April 30, 1890.

Appearing as it did just before Conrad's departure for the Congo, it's appealing to imagine that he might have looked at this issue; Helen Chambers remarks that Conrad even mentions *The Graphic* by name in "The End of the Tether" ("'A Sort of Still Uproar'"). But despite his knowledge of and occasional reading of the illustrated weekly, the pressure of time as he prepared to depart for the Congo in early May might not have given him any opportunity for casual reading, even of a periodical filled with information about his destination. In the early months of 1890, the weekly *The Graphic* provided substantial reading material, usually running close to thirty pages with text and illustrations; the *Stanley Number* ran a bit longer at thirty-two pages including maps, illustrations, extensive text, and advertising. Additionally, the Stanley issue offered a history lesson on ancient knowledge of Africa along with a three-hundred-year-old map, but quickly moved to describe the Emin Pasha Relief Expedition, background on Emin Pasha and Stanley, information on Stanley's previous expeditions and David Livingstone, all richly illustrated

Chapter Two: Spectral Sightings, Mapping, and Exploration... 121

by reproductions of Stanley's sketches, among others. The focus throughout is on Stanley's heroism and conquest of the interior of the continent. Even the slaughter at Bumbireh is depicted from Stanley's point of view as the attacked rather than the attacker, only taking revenge when fired upon. Near the end of the issue, an illustration portrays Stanley triumphant as he emerges from the Ituri rainforest. Not only is Stanley the conquering hero, the commodity to sell out this issue of the *Graphic*, but he is also the promoter of commodities, appearing at the end of the issue in a Bovril advertisement.

Perhaps fame hung heavy on Stanley; his posthumously published *Autobiography* suggests that he struggled with the notoriety.

> In Africa, where I am free of newspapers, the mind has scope in which to revolve, virtuously content. Civilisation never looks more lovely than when surrounded by barbarism; and yet, strange to say, barbarism never looks so inviting to me as when I am surrounded by civilisation. (Stanley, *Autobiography* 527)

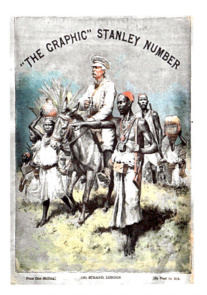

Cover Page. 30 April 1890. *"The Graphic" Stanley Number*

Mr. H. M. Stanley's Anglo-American Expedition for the Exploration of Central Africa – Bumbireh Hospitality

In these remarks, Stanley appears to exist between two spaces, longing for a return to the "barbarism" of the Congo to escape a civilization that had turned him into an embodied commodity, even to be free of the constant barrage of newsprint. Having become a brand name, his fame commodified and his days of exploration over, Stanley, in addition to playing a major role in establishing the *Stanley and African Exhibition* in 1890, was himself a frequent visitor at other African exhibitions, notably the earlier *Antwerp Universal Exhibition* of 1885. Stanley visited the exhibition, writing to his future wife, Dorothy Tennant: "The flag of the Congo Free State on its tall staff waved proudly side by side with other national emblems. For a moment a glow of pride filled me. But shortly a sense of something like guilt filled me" (qtd. in Murray 14). Why guilt? Does Stanley feel shame at the possibility of being exposed at an exhibition touting his own fame or does he look back

Chapter Two: Spectral Sightings, Mapping, and Exploration...   123

Daylight at Last!

Stanley Recruits His Strength with Bovril

on atrocities in the Congo and feel remorse? Stanley was, in his own words, *"incog"* and reluctant to be recognized, "how I would blush to be caught," and to be subjected to the "prurient Belgian Press minutely describing me, how I looked [...] &c. So I reconnoitred the building with furtive glances [...] and by & bye [sic] joined with the crowd and went in" (qtd. in Murray 14). Once in the crowd of spectators, Stanley mounted the stairs and experienced an extraordinary moment of self-recognition: "[As] I ascended the topmost step leading in I saw a full length picture of myself regarding me with a good natured humorous glance" (qtd. in Murray 15). In addition to his own image, Stanley views his trophies and objects reminiscent of his battles with the Basoko on the Aruwimi River – a spear, a drum, bows and arrows – and admits once more to feeling a sense of guilt. Brought back for a moment to the "forests of Stanley Falls in 1877" (qtd. in Murray 15), Stanley may have been forced to face that moment of *anagnorisis*, to the recognition of self as complicit in the commodification of the continent and the murder of its natives who would have little chance of becoming the longed-for new consumers for European goods. Stanley faces his own image as a "commodity transcendent," an icon of European colonialism, in danger of losing his personhood, and yet still, in my view, so poignantly human.[36]

Slavery in the Congo:
"The yet unbroken power of the Congo Arabs"

With the rise of ivory as the most sought after African commodity to be exploited and shipped to Europe, the human commodity which bore it from the African interior to the coast was most often the African slave. Conrad's veiled acknowledgment of Arab slavery in the Congo in "Geography and Some Explorers" points to a fact witnessed by every African explorer in the late nineteenth century and before. Conrad writes: "no more than ten miles away in Reshid's camp just above the Falls the yet unbroken power of the

Chapter Two: Spectral Sightings, Mapping, and Exploration... 125

Congo Arabs slumbered uneasily" (GSE 14). "Reshid," Rashid ben Mohammed had taken over as Governor of Stanley Falls after his uncle Tippu Tib retired to Zanzibar in 1890 – both were notorious slavers. Earlier, in 1886, Rashid had attacked the station and burned it over a slave woman he wanted to capture, but Stanley proposed to calm the volatile situation at the station by installing Tippu Tib as Governor of the Falls, assuring Leopold that Tippu would behave himself. Control of that station was crucial to the Congo Free State as a depot for most of the world's supply of ivory arriving from the Congolese interior. And buying off Tippu Tib, by now the "uncrowned king of the Arabs in Central Africa," (Pakenham 318) was vital for Leopold's ivory trade. But by 1924, and even before in 1899 when he wrote "Heart of Darkness," Conrad would have known that with Tippu Tib out of the picture, the Arab hold on the Falls was destined to be challenged in the ongoing struggle for control over slaves and ivory.

Zanzibar, from 1832, was the "headquarters of the Central African slave trade" (Bierman 81). By 1874, when Stanley arrived there for his second expedition, slavery had been "officially" abolished but it was hardly ended. In fact, slaves continued to be brought to the coast from the interior, their value even higher because of the so-called ban (Meredith 282). Livingstone had worked hard in the service of abolition, but how far into the interior that prohibition extended is another story. When Livingstone reached Zanzibar in 1866, between 80,000 and 100,000 slaves were being marketed per year and he witnessed firsthand the degradation of the slave market (Bierman 95). Often Livingstone passed deserted villages whose inhabitants had fled, mistaking Livingstone's caravan for Arab slavers.

Stanley's contact with Arab slavers was continuous throughout his expeditions; feeling, for example, that he had insufficient information on how to outfit his first expedition to find Livingstone, Stanley turned to Arab slave traders in Zanzibar, who had extensive knowledge of the African interior, for advice. Later, on the trail, Stanley faced the constant threat of bearers' desertion, even employing a long slave chain to threaten deserters into submission. In one of his dispatches to *The New York Herald,* Stanley bragged that this was the best method of dealing with deserters and claimed that "he would 'never travel again in Africa without a good long chain'" (qtd. in Bierman 107). Despite seeing appalling evidence of the

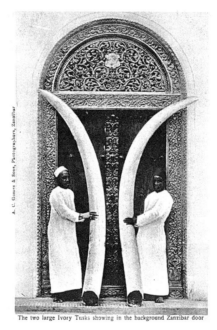

The Two Large IvoryTusks Showing in the Background Zanzibar Door[37]

slave trade, a caravan of over a thousand slaves, mostly women and children, as he camped alongside Lake Tanganyika, Stanley still committed to slave chains for deserters. Yet he could rage at the cruelty of this trade in human flesh: "'Yet I may say that all the Satanic host protects them, for it must be assuredly owing to the deep wiles of hell and its inhabitants that the people of a small island like Zanzibar are permitted to commit crimes such as no European State understands'"

Chapter Two: Spectral Sightings, Mapping, and Exploration...

Chained prisoners in Zanzibar, photo taken by J. Sturtz 1888-1890

Chained Prisoners in Zanzibar

(*Stanley's Despatches* 319). Later, in his third expedition as he established stations along the Congo and reached the Falls he'd named for himself, Stanley saw firsthand the continuing devastation wrought by Arab slavers – burned and abandoned villages and ruined crops with not a soul in sight. From an interpreter, Stanley learned that the Arabs had attacked only a few nights before, massacring the men and carrying off the women and children into slavery (Bierman 239).

But Stanley seemed to forget those earlier passionate and pious outbursts against slavery when he, in the desperation and near starvation of the Advance Column of the Emin Pasha Expedition, ordered the women and children captured in villages and held captive to force the men to provide the column with food (Berenson 136). Of course, in his earlier expeditions Stanley had enlisted the help of the notorious slaver Tippu Tib to provide him with bearers – some of whom would have been free – but it is more likely that most were slave porters. Stanley himself acknowledges that in mustering his bearers early in the Emin Pasha Relief Expedition, he found that of 737 men only about 150 of them "were free men, and that the remainder were either slaves or convicts" (*In Darkest Africa* 1: 95). The ambivalence in Stanley's attitudes was not lost on critics back in Europe. Stanley was defiant in defending his tactics while insisting on his status as the heir of Livingstone and appearing at anti-slavery meetings in 1884-1885 in Manchester and London (Driver 139). Members of the Anti-Slavery Society in Britain supported Stanley's Emin Pasha Relief Expedition, but as more facts emerged about Stanley's use of "unfree labourers," Stanley's association with the infamous Tippu Tib, and the flogging and slaughter of natives on the expedition, Stanley's reputation as a philanthropist slipped considerably (140-41).

Following Stanley's final departure from the Congo, E. J. Glave, one of his former officers, wrote about the state of the Congo River in February 1890. In his comments, Glave reported on the trade in ivory by the French, the Dutch, and the Congo Free State: "The lucrativeness of this trade is apparent from the several hundred tons of ivory exported by these companies during the past two years" ("The Congo River" 620). Glave adds that in competing against the French and Dutch companies, the Congo Free State purchases regularly from the Arab slave raiders at Stanley Falls; that, in fact, the "only product on the upper river profitable to export is ivory" (620), but that with the coming of the railway, more native products can be profitably exported. Glave's conclusion, though, is on the African as emerging consumer: "The natives of central Africa are continually having their wonder aroused by the innovations of the white men. The opera-glass, rifle, and steamboat have all played their part in exciting their wonderment, but the mysterious railway locomotive is yet in store for them" (620). Glave's cheery predictions seem utterly blind to the realities, his opinion typically orientalist, to assume that the natives could be overwhelmed with awe at the inventiveness of the "white men." Indeed, his flawed perspective is belied by the fact that at that very moment of his writing in 1890, Zanzibar was supplying three-quarters of the world's trade in ivory, carried on the back of slaves, and decimating the elephant population by approximately 60,000 elephants per year (Meredith 289). Horace Waller, friend of David Livingstone, missionary, and anti-slavery activist, provides a corrective to Glave's comments, writing in 1891:

> You may say that by our commercial relations with African tribes we must surely have let in light. I reply, if it be so, it is the blaze of the burning village, or the flash of the Winchester rifle – at best it is the glare from the smoke-stack of the Congo steamer bearing away tons upon tons of ivory. (Waller 88)

Stanley preceded Conrad in the Congo, subduing it to his indomitable will, shaping its image for the western gaze with his incredibly detailed maps, and wreaking havoc in his wake, leaving the remnants of a ravaged continent for Korzeniowski the steamboat captain to bear witness with incomparable artistry as Stanley never could. In that key reference to the Congo in "Geography and Some Explorers," Conrad indicts Stanley as the anonymous journalist whose newspaper stunt is nothing more than an attempt to sell the Congo and whose "geography triumphant" is no geography at all. Conrad turns his back on that ghost of Stanley he allowed to briefly peep out in the pages of the text and turns in the end to his own geographical accomplishment, following that geographer "militant," Captain Cook, in his passage through the Torres Strait, "commanding very likely the first and certainly the last merchant ship that carried a cargo that way" (GSE 16). Conrad's *Otago* may have been the last sailing ship to take this dangerous route, but even Conrad could not escape his own complicity in trade and commerce as he carried a mixed cargo to Mauritius. Left out of the published version, Conrad's thoughts about his own role as explorer are more extensive in the manuscript and predominate over any other he might have had about carrying cargo and his role in global trade:

And I have been lucky, because neither explorer or navigator, it has been given to me also to pass through a central place in the history of sea exploration which has been for long a place of mystery to the civilised world, and even in my time was very imperfectly charted and very lonely. ("Geography," Original Manuscript 50-51; "Geography," Stevens and Stape 389).

Chapter Three:
A Witness in the Congo:
Conrad's "The Congo Diary" and "Up-river Book"

Stanley's Africa: A Utopian Vision

What Conrad would become most known for, despite his wish to be remembered as a sea explorer through the Torres Strait, are the accumulative reminiscences that built up over time to stamp his presence in the African Congo on the imagination of the West. Scant attention has been paid, for example, to Conrad's Congo notebooks,[38] yet their study yields rich geographical information about the terrain and much more as Conrad traveled overland along the lower Congo from Matadi to Stanley Pool and by steamer on the upper Congo from Stanley Pool to Stanley Falls. Here, however, Conrad could not blaze a trail through blank spaces on the map; Stanley had already created the government stations and built the roads along which Conrad would travel. As a witness to history in the making, Conrad's journals provide a valuable window into the Congo Free State at the fin de siècle, but they reveal the impact of this experience as well on the evolution of Conrad the writer. What I propose to do here is not to match the details of the journals to "An Outpost of Progress" or "Heart of Darkness," but rather to analyze the intersections and implications of geographical exploration, mapping/cartographic practices, and the commodification of space in the light of intertextual dialogue with Africanist discourses penned by Stanley and others.

In counterpoise to the foregoing chapter, Stanley doesn't float in these Conradian manuscripts as a spectral presence to be repressed, because his actual presence created the change that allowed Conrad to follow his tracks; even though Conrad will make no mention of that. Stanley departed central Africa for the last time just six months before Conrad's arrival, so the palimpsestic layering of both his material presence in and discourses about the Congo create a rich context for Conrad's own eyewitness account and later reminiscence of moving through African space.

For Stanley the white spaces in the heart of Africa were not there simply to be dreamt over, but rather to be filled by civilization, commerce, and Christianity. Recording a conversation with Frank Pocock in *Through the Dark Continent,* Stanley wrote:

> I assure you, Frank, this enormous void is about to be filled up. Blank as it is, it has a singular fascination for me. Never has *white paper* possessed such a charm for me as this has, and I have already mentally peopled it, filled it with most wonderful pictures of towns, villages, rivers, countries, and tribes – all in the imagination – and I am burning to see whether I am correct or not. *Believe?* I see us gliding down by tower and town, and my mind will not permit a shadow of doubt. (2: 195, emphasis added)

This is Stanley's Utopian dream; not just to change the material reality of central Africa but also to fill the "white paper" maps with a visual text as a guide to creating European empires in the heart of Africa. And as I shall note later in the chapter, this is far from the only time that Stanley waxed eloquent about the possession of African material space and the wealth and civilizing influence that exploration into the unknown interior could produce. From January 1877 in the Anglo-American Expedition, when he first "heard the roar of the First Cataract of the Stanley Falls series" (221), through August of the same year, Stanley and his followers, not knowing what they would find as they descended the Congo, tried to navigate past the dangerous cataracts and fend off hostile tribes from the Falls down to Stanley Pool both in canoe and on land, often pulling the canoes by ropes along the banks of the river. The detailed map entitled *Map Showing the Western Half of Equatorial Africa,* illustrated in the previous chapter, depicts Stanley's route through the western half of equatorial Africa in the

Chapter Three: A Witness in the Congo: Conrad's „The Congo Diary"... 133

second volume of *Through the Dark Continent*, and provides a visual text, offering the most accurate geographical mapping of the river up to that time. But the visual map text will change, indigenous names of villages, river tributaries, and cataracts on this early map that Stanley drafted would begin vanishing in less than two decades, replaced with names Conrad would recognize in witnessing the process of colonization. Stanley's path appears on the map in red, stamping Anglo-American possession through the effort to name the great river the Livingstone, which didn't stick, and Stanley Pool (now Malebo Pool), which did, at least until decolonization.

In recognition of African presence on his map, Stanley notates a native road traveled by the Babwende tribe between the Atlantic coast and their lands on the south and north shores of the Congo below Stanley Pool. This notation becomes important because Stanley is mapping the movement of commodities and writes approvingly of the Babwende, revealing that they were engaged in lively trading with other tribes, many of them traveling to the coast as shown on his map, and even displaying "Delft ware and British crockery" as well as "Birmingham cutlery, and other articles of European manufacture obtained through the native markets" (358). In 1877 Stanley witnessed thriving mobile markets that reached all the way above the equator along the shores of the Congo River and thrust European commodities deep into the heart of Africa:

> From district to district, market to market, and hand to hand, European fabrics and wares are conveyed along both sides of the rivers and along the paths of traffic, until finally the districts of Ntamo, Nkunda, and Nshasa obtain them. These then man their large canoes and transfer them to Ibaka, Misongo, Chumbiri, and Bolobo, and purchase ivory, and now and then a slave […] and finally to Upoto – the present reach of anything arriving from the west coast. (359)

Indeed, Stanley's push will be to expand European commerce along the entire trajectory of the Congo River and its tributaries all the way to the east coast – and Stanley's maps increasingly became justification for the explosion of commerce and trade to follow in his wake.

Breaking Rocks:
Stanley's Creation of the Congo Free State

Following Stanley's Anglo-American Expedition, much of the interior along the Congo River was now mapped territory being viewed for the first time by European eyes. While hints of the potential for commercialization appear in Stanley's mention of indigenous trading for European goods near the coast, geographical features which will dictate how that trading can be further accomplished predominate on Stanley's 1877 map as noted in the last chapter. Labelling rolling table land, high rolling grassy plains, unnamed villages, islands in the river, many covered with dense woods, the number of cataracts, and elevation above sea level – Stanley's map marks terrain to be further explored and exploited. Such geographical features serve as a manual for how and where Europeans can invade the interior. But he also indicates threats to beware among certain tribes located on the map – the Mangala (also referred to as the "fierce Bangala") (359), are described as a "Ferocious Tribe," another tribe is described as "armed with muskets." By printing the name "Livingstone River" in place of the Congo boldly across the top of the map as the river arcs north of the equator, Stanley seeks to naturalize an "alien" space through the imposition of the beloved missionary's name on a mighty river. Stanley's notations are a compelling view of the Congo environment before the onset of the Scramble, and it bears repeating that they preserve indigenous names and mark locations that would have otherwise been lost to history once colonization effaced much of the pre-existing indigenous presence.

When he reached Boma (also known then as Embomma) on foot, starving and exhausted, Stanley had traced the full course of the Congo River.

Stanley's march downstream in the Anglo-American expedition moved in a reverse direction to the path Conrad

Chapter Three: A Witness in the Congo: Conrad's „The Congo Diary"... 135

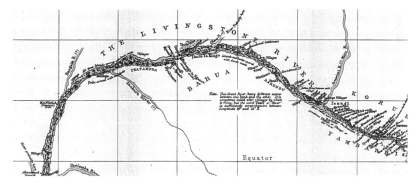

Section of Stanley's *Map Showing the Western Half of Equatorial Africa*

would later take on his own overland Congo journey; but from 1878-1883, Stanley built wagon roads and founded stations along both banks of the lower and the upper Congo, opening wider passageways for large caravans and steamer portaging. In his preface to *The Congo and the Founding of Its Free State,* Stanley continued to promote the commercialization of the Congo, writing to a European audience: "I could prove to you that the Power possessing the Congo, despite the cataracts, would absorb to itself the trade of the whole of the enormous basin behind. This river is and will be the *grand highway of commerce* to West Central Africa" (1: vi, emphasis added).[39] For just such bombast Stanley would earn attention and high praise from Léon Gambetta, "the great French statesman" whom Stanley proudly quoted in his Preface.[40]

> You have thrown the light of knowledge on what you have well described as the Dark Continent. Not only, sir, have you opened up a new Continent to our view, but you have given an impulse to scientific and philanthropic enterprise which will have a material effect on the progress of the world [...]. What you have done has influenced Governments. (*The Congo* 1: vi)

The influence on European governments had just begun in the 1870s. In 1879, on his third expedition, Stanley searched for appropriate sites to build the Congo government stations, beginning with Vivi on the north bank of the Congo, then adding the stations at Isangila and Manyanga in 1880-1881. But Stanley also needed wagon roads, again, constructing on the north bank of the Congo from Vivi to Isangila and then from Manyanga to Stanley Pool, earning along the way his favorite African name, Bula Matari, "Breaker of Rocks."[41]

But early in Stanley's exuberant march in possession of the Congo, he looks upland from the thriving station at Boma in 1879 and stops for a moment; while positioning himself as the "first" explorer, he seems to take sweeping command in possession of all he sees:

> There is a grand sweep of massive hills lifting and falling to the north; a long undulating line of hilly land is visible across the river, stretching away into the grey distance [...]. Over all the vast area of land, visible upland and plain, I see no aspiring tower or dome, or chimney, or even the likeness of a human structure [...] not even a column of smoke threads through the silent air to suggest the thought that I am not alone. All is nature, *large, ample, untouched and apparently unvisited by man*. From all I can see I may have been the *first man*, black or white who has ever stood on the ungrateful soil under my feet. (*The Congo* 1: 93, emphasis added)

But despite this display of hubris, a hubris that suggests Africa could only be possessed or known by a white man, Stanley's Congo was not untouched for long. By this time, numerous Christian missions had been founded in Stanley's wake and he expresses delight that his work has moved these missionaries to carry "the banner of peace up the Congo beyond the Equator" (vii); he is also gratified that other explorers he has inspired are bringing European nations into the "field of colonial enterprise" (vii). The true nature of the enterprise, though, becomes more evident as Stanley notes trading and commerce in Banana Point – the presence of casks of palm oil, a major African export of the time, and in warehouses "bales and bales, a *million* yards of cotton," "enough to make a Manchester cotton manufacturer weep with pleasure" (74, emphasis added). In Boma, Stanley writes that it is the "principal emporium of trade on the Congo," it sports "congeries of factories," that is, a number of detached buildings used as stores or sheds, or workshops (91). Europe has sent her agents "to scatter these trading stations at every available point along both banks of the river (91). And there are more now, in 1885, than there were in 1879. But there is also a dark side to this thriving port: Boma's history of slavery. As Stanley tells it: "a cruel blood-curdling history, fraught with horror, and woe, and suffering. Inhumanity of man to man has been exemplified here for over two centuries by the pitiless persecution of black men, by sordid whites" (96). The result is that the native population has fled to the upper Congo to escape the incessant slaving between the sea and Stanley Pool.

Further upriver, Stanley describes a thriving market near Manyanga, where he will build another station. Everything from slaves and ivory to sheep and goats is for sale, with trading caravans moving toward Stanley Pool exchanging cloth and beads for copper and wire in "enormous quantities" (282). As he begins to draw the first volume of *The Congo and the Founding of Its Free State* to a close, Stanley continues to prioritize the potential for commerce and trade:

> We had discovered that *no native is averse to* trade – that the very name of barter actively excites the aborigines. Unless we are prepared to relinquish our discoveries, and the moral success we have gained, we had to secure all the rights that the native chiefs could endow us with, that we might exercise the political power necessary for guaranteeing the permanency of the benefits we had sought to obtain. (463, emphasis added)

Later, Stanley writes of the vast territory along the Congo past Stanley Pool to Chumbiri, the "real heart of equatorial Africa" yet to be opened up to European trade:

> it was this million square miles of almost level area, which we may call the kernel, that was worth the trouble of piercing the 235 miles of thick rude mountain husk which separates it from the energies of Europeans, who, could they but reach it, would soon teach the world what good might come *out of Africa*. (514, emphasis added)

Stanley's determination for European control and possession of territory and trade contrasts markedly with Conrad's disgust in 1905 at competitors in Africa "flying at each other's throats" at the chance to turn the black African into a "buying machine" (AW 88).

The second volume of *The Congo and the Founding of Its Free State* finds Stanley moving upriver in a small flotilla of steamers to Stanley Falls, and his dismissal of the Africans lining the banks of the Congo is quite evident as he describes the "stupid wonder" with which the natives viewed him (2: 11). Believing himself to be the arbiter of massive change, Stanley imagines what the natives must think as he and his three steamers, the symbols of civilization mentioned below, the *En Avant,* the *A.I.A.,* and the *Royal,* pass by; and he writes with his customary hubris:

> And we, looking out from under our awnings, appear to say, "Ay, gaze, oh men and women, upon these three symbols of civilisation. Ye see things to-day which the oldest and wisest inhabitant of your land never heard or dreamed of, and yet they are but tiny types of self-moving leviathans that plough the raging sea by night as well as by day!" (12)

Returning from his voyage on the upper Congo to Stanley Pool in 1884, Stanley traveled on foot, leading a large caravan downriver along much of the same path Conrad would travel in a few years' time going upriver. As he marched south to Inkissi, Stanley's caravan moved along "an elevated and grassy table-land, with the Congo a few miles to our right tearing down over its successive terraces" (192). Stanley writes romantically of "pleasant people" and "happy villages" passed on his way to ferry across the Inkissi, then he notes the "neat and happy station" at Lutete (193, 208). Stanley is now in Bakongo territory, remarking on scenes common to both banks of the river, ridges, hilltops, and crevasses near the public path as he approaches the station at South Manyanga (209, 211). Traveling along steep slopes, Stanley arrived at the well-kept Livingstone Mission in the valley of Lukunga, then another day's march takes him through the valley of the Luima and on to the valley of Lunionzo. All the while, Stanley is thinking of railroads. He next stops at Banza Manteka station where another Livingstone mission has been established and pauses a moment to consider Europeans who have struggled over

> heart-breaking hills, with the endless ascents and descents, through winding labyrinths of suffocatingly tall grass, and each time they emerge into light and glare [...]. Some of them, under the fiery impulses of getting on, on, and on, will march their fifteen miles per day, and on arriving at the Pool at the end of their journey, they will turn round and deliberately curse the land, the climate, and the people but never their own idiotic frenzy. (216)

Ah, but Stanley concludes, "if I could take them through such a land as this in twenty-four hours, they might live as long in Africa as in moist England" (216). With the railroad, Africa can become Europeanized. Stanley's journey concludes, after marching through Congo la Lemba, past Pallaballa [sic] mountain, at Vivi.

Stanley's narrative of this overland journey, while reversing Conrad's route, not only matches so many of the named places on Conrad's map of his overland journey but also provides additional geographical detail that helps illuminate Conrad's sketches and narrative in "The Congo Diary" and suggests the sources of frustration and disgust that Conrad described as he passed through the same terrain.

Stanley's Last March

Stanley's last overland journey along the south bank of the Congo, beginning in March 1887, most closely matches the path Conrad would take in summer 1890. Stanley's narrative of the overland journey in *In Darkest Africa* is covered in one chapter, Chapter IV; by Chapter V, he's moved beyond Stanley Pool onto the upper Congo. Beginning its march along the south bank of the Congo River, Stanley's massive caravan started out on March 25, 1887, from Mataddi [sic] on the way to Stanley

Pool, carrying 420 pounds of biscuits as well as thousands of pounds of additional provisions, amounting to 466 loads (*In Darkest Africa* 1: 80). Stanley typically liked to emphasize the excitement of the beginning of an expedition, making sure to include the sounding of the trumpets and organization of the carriers, but once underway, he arrived at the Mposo River with an expedition that was already lagging. The next day, he made camp on the grounds of the Livingstone Inland Mission at Palaballa, as he calculated the toll of the sick and dying. In Congo la Lemba, where before he saw a flourishing camp, he found instead that the "village site is now covered with tall grass, and its guava, palm, and lemon-trees are choked with weeds" (84). According to Stanley, an insolent chief there had been beheaded by the State using a force of Bangalas – most likely members of the Force Publique[42]; the village had been burned and the inhabitants fled.

After he made his way to the Lufu River, forcing a fatiguing march, his bearers streamed into camp until midnight, exhausted. There was a fair amount of traffic on this road – Stanley comments on a German caravan whose bearers are hauling the *Florida*'s shaft and a French trader "with a fine lot of ivory tusks" (84). Stanley jokes about the slow rate of speed the German party is making, observing they'd probably arrive at the Pool by August – five months for a march that should take about a month. This offers another possible explanation for why, several years later, the *Florida* remained disabled when Conrad arrived in the Congo, presumably to command her. At Banza Manteka Stanley received bad news from his officers further upstream about the state of repair of the Congo steamers at Stanley Pool but forged on, passing the Lunionzo River and camping at the abandoned village of Kilolo. Another three-hour march took the expedition to the Kwilu River, a march up and down hills increasingly demoralizing his caravan. While waiting to cross the Kwilu, Stanley wrote letters, including one to Reverend Bentley at his Baptist Mission, requesting the use of the steamer *Peace*. Proud of his management so far of an 800-person expedition,

Stanley reached the Lukungu Station by April 8, welcomed by "hospitable Belgians," Messrs. Francqui and Dessauer (87). But by the time he reached Lutete's on April 12, his caravan was in disarray with many bearers ill or deserting and stealing provisions as they sneaked away.

On the 16th of April, Stanley ferried his massive expedition across the Inkissi, and at the next camp learned from a letter by Reverend Bentley that the Baptist mission would loan him the steamer *Peace*, but only if Stanley's Zanzibaris behaved themselves; Stanley, annoyed by this disparagement of his bearers, felt that Reverend Bentley had forgotten that Zanzibaris helped build his missions. Finally arriving at Leopoldville on April 21, 1887, Stanley found only a handful of steamers available to him for the upriver journey. In Kinshassa, Stanley visited the manager of the "Sanford Exploring Company," who offered him the hull of the *Florida* to be pulled by the *Stanley*. In this iteration of his overland march along the Congo, Stanley seemed more preoccupied by his troubles with bearers and steamers and the exhausting nature of the path than with a description of geographical features of the landscape, but he did take time to notice the sharp ascents and descents of hills on the path to the Kwilu, the suffocating high grass, and the terrible heat. More in tune with the status of the expedition, Stanley had little compunction in describing the methods he used to keep his men in line:

> An unreflecting spectator hovering near our line of march might think we were unnecessarily cruel; but the application of a few cuts to the confirmed stragglers secure eighteen hours' rest to about 800 people and their officers, save the goods from being robbed – for frequently these dawdlers lag behind purposely for such intentions. (87)

The cuts, of course, could have been made by rattan canes or even worse by "chicottes," whips made of sun-dried hippotamus hide which sent those beaten into unconsciousness after twenty strokes and left permanent scars on the back. Despite the stringent methods used to keep the caravan moving, by the end of April 1887, Stanley had managed to lead it over

200 miles in less than a month; of course, his journey upriver on broken down steamers, the abandonment of the Rear Guard, and his criss-crossing through the nightmare of the Ituri forest followed this overland march, not only putting the fate of the entire expedition in jeopardy but also causing the uproar which seriously damaged Stanley's reputation.

"Getting jolly well sick of this fun"

"I am surprised, to say the least, how these apparently minor details might perhaps help us to find out more about the precise chronology of Conrad's sojourn in the Congo" (Hans van Marle on the value of the Congo notebooks, "Letters" 60).

Three years after Stanley's last overland march along the lower Congo, Conrad arrived at Boma on June 12, 1890, and left the next day for Matadi, where he wrote his first pencil entry in the journal entitled by his literary executor, Richard Curle, *Conrad's Diary*.[43] The provenance and history of the diary and its companion piece, the "Up-river Book," have been documented not only by Richard Curle, but also in Zdzisław Najder's edition, and in Ray Stevens and J. H. Stape's Cambridge edition of *Last Essays*. It is remarkable, as I mentioned before, if Curle's version is accurate, that Jessie Conrad retrieved both journals from the "waste-paper basket" twice (Introduction, *CD*, Strangeways 10). If that was so, I can only wonder why and when Conrad chose to throw these documents away – was he finished rereading as he worked on, perhaps, "An Outpost of Progress" and later "Heart of Darkness"?

Additionally, these journals apparently turned up in a trunk of effects shipped to him from the Congo while he was honeymooning on the Ile-Grand in Brittany (Jean-Aubry 220), suggesting that he would have had them available for use in the future. There is some dispute, too, if this was the only journal Conrad ever kept – Curle asserts that it was because there is no other diary extant, "He was not at all that type of man, and his piercing memory for essentials was quite sufficient for him to recreate powerfully vanished scenes

Chapter Three: A Witness in the Congo: Conrad's „The Congo Diary"... 143

and figures for the purposes of his work" (Introduction, *CD*, Strangeways 12). Najder, however, rejects Curle's assertion, claiming instead that he thought it "highly probable that the Congo diary was not the only one Conrad ever kept," insisting that Conrad "used to make extensive notes when preparing for and writing his books" (Najder, *Congo Diary* 4). Nevertheless, no others have been found and the unique interest in the ones we do have lies in their revelations of Conrad working as a navigator and cartographer on land and water. Early in 1925, following Conrad's death on August 3, 1924, Curle began negotiations to get the journal into print; Curle's edition of just the first notebook made its appearance in the *Blue Peter* in October, 1925, followed by publication in the *Yale Review* in January 1926, a privately printed edition by Strangeways that same month, then finally in *Last Essays* (1926); however, the manuscripts in the Harvard Houghton collection are my base for detailed study of both journals and the sketches which accompany the texts.

    Clearly, Conrad kept the two journals of his Congo journey for personal reasons and not with an eye to publication. They differ, therefore, sharply, from Stanley's journals which were always meant to support subsequent publication; in fact, Stanley occasionally refers to and quotes from his journals to add immediacy to the published versions of his expeditions. There is, then, no published filter between the reader and Conrad's fragmented remarks, leaving out, of course "An Outpost of Progress" and "Heart of Darkness" as fictional rather than purely nonfictional accounts.[44]

    Conrad entered the Congo River at Banana Point, traveling by the steamship *Ville de Maceio,* carrying cargo that included rails and equipment for the Congo railway, which began construction at Matadi (Stape, "Conrad's Voyage to Africa" 109). Matadi, upstream from Boma, the capital of the Congo Free State, was a hub for Belgian enterprise with multiple international trading companies and the location of the Congo Railway Company that would make overland journeys like Stanley's and Conrad's unnecessary in the future (Stevens and

Stape, "Explanatory Notes" 453). The view below indicates a thriving port with a lively market in the 1890s.

The Market in Matadi

From the state of the first manuscript journal, which I will refer to as "The Congo Diary," it is difficult to tell if Conrad's first entry is on the 13th of June 1890 when he arrives in Matadi, because what appears to be the first page is torn in half. That torn page may have been a title page – the first part of the word *Jour* appears above the "N° I" with some indecipherable scribbling on the right side. If Conrad meant to entitle this notebook, then he also intended to write more than one journal – perhaps the "Up-river Book," the second manuscript journal to which Conrad gave that name – was already on his mind. The first full page of decipherable text in "The Congo Diary" does begin with the arrival at Matadi. Conrad's initial observations are supported by the historical context of the port – he's met by the manager of the Belgian trading post, Mr. Gosse, thus becoming personally aware of the nature of the ivory trade as well as being introduced to Mr. Underwood, the manager of the English factory (trading company) Hatton and Cookson, by Roger Casement, who, like Conrad, was employed by the *Société Anonyme Belge pour le Commerce du Haut Congo*. Casement, no stranger to the Congo, was arranging transportation for trading caravans and engaged in working on the Congo railway. Conrad's initial pages register his impressions from approximately the 13th until he begins his overland march on Saturday, June 29.

By 1890, trading on the Congo had exploded, especially in Matadi, but England had the largest share of European trade in the Congo region to the tune of about two million pounds sterling between 1883-1884 (Anstey 50-51). As far back as 1845-1850, British factories like the Liverpool based Hatton and Cookson traded mostly textiles for ivory, copper, and malachite (51). Even more to the point for tracing the intersecting paths of Stanley and Conrad is the fact that carriers from Hatton and Cookson in Boma arrived with food and supplies just in time to save Stanley's caravan from starving to death in August 1877:

> By this time the procession of carriers from Messrs. Hatton and Cookson's factory had approached, and all eyes were directed at the pompous old "capitan" and the relief caravan behind him. Several of the Wangwana officiously stepped forward to relieve the fatigued and perspiring men, and with an extraordinary vigour tossed the provisions – rice, fish, and tobacco bundles on the ground, except the demijohn of rum, which they [...] handled more carefully. (*Through the Dark Continent 2*: 456-57)

In 1877 the firm of Hatton and Cookson was a major player in trade with the natives at the bustling port of Boma, increasing its factories (trading company warehouses) upriver in the wake of Stanley's establishment of trading stations, but Conrad's observation is that this factory appears to be only an "av^{ge} com^{al}" [sic] (average commercial) establishment. Under the date of June 13th, Conrad continues his remarks, approving of Underwood and praising Casement eloquently, while Gosse is only "(o.k.)," for keeping Conrad at the station for two weeks for "some reason of his own" (CD MS). In sharp contrast to Underwood and Casement are those whites whom Conrad intends to avoid – shortly he'll mention how the "Prominent characteristic of social life" is people "speaking ill of each other." Gosse's reasons for keeping Conrad at the Matadi station become clear when Conrad writes that Gosse and

Casement have gone upriver to transport "a large lot of ivory down to Boma" while Conrad has been kept busy "packing ivory in casks. Idiotic employement [sic]." Conrad's brief eyewitness account and dismissive repugnance to personal involvement in the handling of ivory suggests a sharp contradiction to Stanley's utopian vision of European trade and advancement into the heart of the Congo. Rather than celebrate the commodity in the Congo, as Stanley does so effusively, Conrad focuses on keeping a record more purely geographical and navigational in nature – a journal where mapping takes precedence over much else.

Beginning the Overland Journey

Finally, Conrad departed on his African journey on June 28, saddled with Prosper Harou, a sick Belgian, as a traveling companion, whose brother Victor had worked with Stanley to establish the Vivi station (Stevens and Stape, "Explanatory Notes" 455). Harou is dead weight, almost literally, a heavy man who had to be carried by reluctant bearers. However, while Conrad continues to notice and remark upon characters he meets along the road, it is at this point in the narrative that his interest in noting and sketching the geographical details of the terrain begins to take shape.

Conrad's rather small caravan, consisting of 31 men, made its first halt, like Stanley's less than three years earlier, at "M'poso." In March 1887, Stanley set out from "Mataddi" (sic), with a huge caravan that straggled across the "Mpozo" river and camped (*In Darkest Africa* 1: 80). This was the second time that Stanley traveled along the south bank of the Congo; in his earlier overland journey in 1884, he stopped at "Mpozo" station to lament the lack of progress on building the station at Vivi as he surveyed the scene with his binoculars: "But so far as I can see, not even a hut has been thatched. What a poor result after the passage of 260 Europeans of all nationalities through the station! Grieving and sad at heart, I continue my descent to Mpozo Station" (*The Congo* 2: 219). Progress does follow in Stanley's wake, however, and Conrad traveled on the government roads and stopped at the government stations Stanley built.

View of Mpozo Station and River from Vivi

Mapping the Overland Journey

To track Conrad's path on the overland journey, Richard Curle produced identical maps for two editions of Conrad's diary: first, in *The Blue Peter* in October 1925, and second, his privately printed pamphlet in January 1926; both appear to match many of the places Conrad names in his journal.

But Curle's map published in *The Yale Review,* January 1926, displays several variations from the other two: first, the orientation is different, rather than appearing horizontally, this map is displayed vertically with the place names printed to conform with the vertical orientation. Additionally, Curle's legend "Rough Map" has disappeared. The printing has changed as well: all place names are printed in approximately the same size block print, with the following transcribing errors:

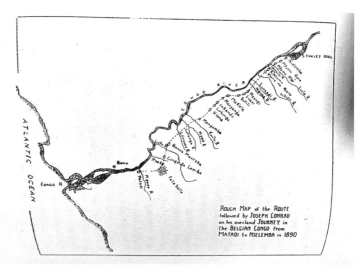

Rough Map of the Route Followed by Joseph Conrad on His Overland Journey in the Belgian Congo from Matadi to Nselemba[45]

"Patabella" for "Pataballa," "Congo de Kemba" for "Congo da Lemba," "Nsona lan Sefe," for "Nsona na Miefe."

These are interesting variations that Curle seems not to have corrected or changed. Note, too, the discrepancies in titles for these two versions of the diary: the first, wordy *Joseph Conrad's Diary (hitherto unpublished of his Journey up the Valley of the Congo in 1890)* in *The Blue Peter* and the shorter, to the point, *Conrad's Diary* in *The Yale Review*. The title *The Congo Diary* appears for the first time in the first editions of *Last Essays*, the British edition published by J. M. Dent and the American published by Doubleday, both in 1926.

Neither version of Curle's map, however, is identical with Conrad's own map of his overland journey, which, as a point of reference, bears repeating below. Note that there are fewer place names on Conrad's map but a more detailed drawing of the river's course with extended tributaries, suggesting as I observed in the last chapter that Conrad was consulting other maps as he drew this one. Furthermore, place names appear on this map that do

Chapter Three: A Witness in the Congo: Conrad's „The Congo Diary"... 149

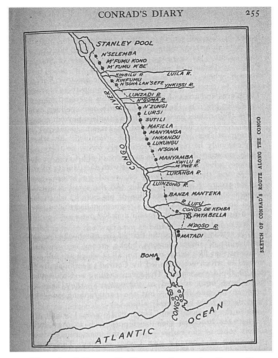

Sketch of Conrad's Route along the Congo[46]

not appear on Curle's, indicating that Curle did not have access to this map when he drew his own. It is questionable whether Conrad had access to his journal as he composed this map, since it's unclear when he drew it, but it is clear from the legend that he meant to leave his mark of his own journey on the south bank of the Congo River. There are so many fascinating anomalies among the maps and descriptions – Conrad's, Curle's, and Stanley's – that they warrant investigating in detail. Curle's map locates Boma, Matadi, and the Mposo River, showing the starting point at Matadi. Conrad's map also marks Boma and Matadi in larger block print than other place names and shows his path crossing the "Pozo" river; however, while the name of the river "Pozo" is marked in green, the map does not indicate a camping spot with a small circle, the symbol he used

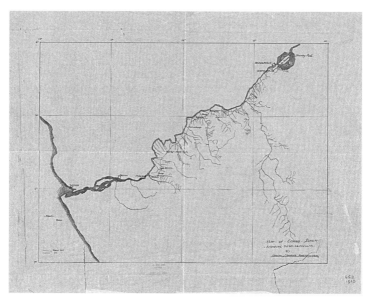

*Map of Congo Basin: Showing Path Traveled
by Joseph Conrad Korzeniowski*

to mark other camps. Additionally, Stanley's map published with his 1885 edition of *The Congo and the Founding of Its Free State* does not list Matadi but does include Mpozo in larger print, shown on the map section below across from Vivi, indicating a fairly large settlement, close in size to Vivi. Also notable in Conrad's map of the Congo Basin is the location of "Mukumbungu," with a small circle indicating a mission or a station. The image below displays the mission church three decades after Conrad was in the Congo, but John Myers, of the Baptist Missionary Society, identifies Mukimbungu as a mission established by the Swedish Missionary Alliance in 1886 (161). Conrad does not refer to this as a stop in his diary nor does it appear on Curle's map. So why is it on his map of the Congo Basin? It seems that at some point between crossing the Kwilu River and camping at Nsona on the 5th and the 6th of July, Conrad must have passed this mission and perhaps even a market nearby – he does remark on passing a large marketplace at 10 a.m.

Chapter Three: A Witness in the Congo: Conrad's „The Congo Diary"... 151

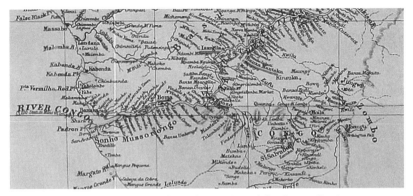
Mpozo in section of Stanley's *Map of the Congo Basin*

Mission Church, Congo

on the 6th of July. "Mukumbungu" is also on Stanley's map shown below as "Mukimbungu," clearly marked above the Kwilu River, but Stanley makes no mention of this mission either in his *The Congo and the Founding of Its Free State*.

In his diary for Sunday, June 29th, Conrad mentions the ascent of "Palaballa," "sufficiently fatiguing," – written on his map as "Palabala" – followed by camp made at the Nsoke River (CD MS). Curle notes topographical details to indicate the mountain, but mis-transcribes it as "Pataballa" – upon closer inspection of Conrad's map, it appears that he had written track marks in pencil before he inked in Palabala, so it almost looks like he crossed the *t*, but he didn't. Palaballa Mountain, on the south shore of the Congo 5 miles upriver

Mukimbungu in section of Stanley's *Map of the Congo Basin*

from Vivi rises to 1700 feet above sea level (Stanley, *The Congo* 2: 217). No mention of Nsoke appears on Conrad's map nor is another river marked near Palaballa, but it is on Curle's and appears as "Nseke" on Stanley's. Curle also fails to note the almost due east orientation of Nsoke from Palaballa, but both Conrad and Stanley clearly indicate that direction before the path turns north. Instead of Nsoke, what appears on Conrad's map is the mysterious "Tombagadio" – marked as a camping place in approximately the same location at the Nsoke River on both Curle's and Stanley's maps – perhaps the name of a native village that Conrad learned but he doesn't mark a river there. In fact, Tombagadio still exists as a town in present day Democratic Republic of Congo in approximately the same location east and slightly north of Palaballa.

On Monday, June 30, Conrad and company were climbing again on the way to "Congo da Lemba" – this camp was bad

Chapter Three: A Witness in the Congo: Conrad's „The Congo Diary"...   153

with water, "far" and "dirty," but on his map, he's named it "Congo da Gamba" (CD MS). For Stanley, in sharp contrast, "Congo la Lemba" is a "pleasant village" above the "Luizi valley and river. Yellala mountain is in view on our right and Pallaballa mountain is in our front" (217). Stanley, of course, is marching south heading downriver to Vivi.

Conrad left the next day, July 1, to march north toward the Lufu River – following Stanley's cart route "through forest on the sharp slope of a high mountain. Very long descent. Then marketplace, from where short walk to the bridge (good) and camp. V. G. Bath. Clear river" (CD MS).

Stanley's photograph showing the bridge just a few years before Conrad crossed it creates a visual presence while his description adds considerably more detail:

> The next valley we meet westward of the Ntombo Lukuti is that of the Lufû, a considerable stream with a rapid current, from whose woody fringes we rise to breast rock-strewn slopes and cross pebble-sown hill-summits, until after a short series of these we thread the twilight aisles of a forest-covered mountain side. (*The Congo* 2: 215)

Aside from Stanley's purple prose, there are similarities in both descriptions of the terrain viewed as Conrad and Stanley traversed it in opposite directions. Conrad's map of the Congo Basin indicates his crossing the Lufu River but doesn't pinpoint the location of the camp nor does Curle.

As he writes, Conrad pays increasing attention to landscape; on July 2, for example, despite feeling unwell, he describes marching through "Country more open – gently undulating hills. Road good in perfect order – (District of Lukungu)" (CD MS). He's on the way to Banza Manteka, marked on all three maps, camping at the marketplace where "Water scarce and bad – Camp^g place dirty" (CD MS). Both he and Stanley mention the mission – Conrad feels too unwell to visit the missionary there but doesn't identify the missionary or the mission, while Stanley identifies the mission as the Livingstone Inland Congo Mission but also omits the names of the resident missionaries (*The Congo* 2: 214).

Bridge over Lufu River. Cataract Region.[47] Stanley Archives, Coll. King Baudouin Foundation, entrusted to the AfricaMuseum, Brussels, Belgium

On the road early on the 3rd of July leaving his camp at Banza Manteka, Conrad continues navigating the land, where he "crossed a low range of hills and entered a broad valley or rather plain with a break in the middle" (CD MS). Stanley too notes a "grassy expanse" just north of Banza Manteka, situating the station itself on "a continuous plateau," whence, looking south, he can see the "groves of many villages" (*The Congo* 2: 214-15).

What Conrad sees next is an extraordinary window into the workings of the Congo Free State; he meets an officer of the State on an inspection tour and sees a dead Bakongo just minutes later at a camping place. Whatever caravan the dead man may have been a part of just left him where he dropped, perhaps shot for stealing, and apparently dead Bakongos were too unimportant for the State inspector to notice or bury. It also appears, though, that such sights were far from uncommon at this time. Conrad is in the vicinity of Bakongo territory, as

Chapter Three: A Witness in the Congo: Conrad's „The Congo Diary"... 155

Stanley has noted in commenting that the "delicious bits of domestic life among the Bakongo, and Iyenzi, with very tall palms, which promise gifts of their effervescing juice, will not soon be forgotten by men who have seen their open spaces shaded by the glorious leafy trees" (209). Clearly Stanley is seeing the terrain and the communities of the Bakongo in a very different light than Conrad's later repulsive discovery. Stanley mentions the Bakongo in several places in *The Congo and the Founding of Its Free State*, referring to their prowess as traders to and from the western coast of Africa. William Samarin adds important details to the history of Bakongo as bearers on caravans. "In taking possession of the heart of Africa in the last quarter of the nineteenth century," Samarin writes, "Belgians used Bangalas to carry their guns and Bakongos to bear their burdens" (269). The name *Bakongo* represents an ethnic designation more broadly known as the Kongo peoples – usually referred to by Europeans as natives of the lower Congo (271). Between 1884 and 1887, Belgian officers of the Congo Free State recruited thousands of local porters to carry tens of thousands of loads between the mouth of the river and Stanley Pool, and as construction of the railroad to Leopoldville began in 1889, thousands more porters were required. As I've already observed, the land route along the cataracts of the Congo was difficult and challenging for porterage. "Portering was a task that tested the mettle of the strongest of men," Samarin writes, "many of whom died on the path, leaving by 1898 'thousands of skeletons' along the way" (qtd. in Samarin 277). Samarin's claim suggests that Conrad's dead Bakongo may have been just an unpleasant but ordinary sight on the caravan roads.

    Once away from the sight and the smell, Conrad notes his passage through mountains "running NW – SE," by a "low pass." He notes a valley and ravine as well as another range of mountains running parallel with a chain of "low foothills running close to it," and stops to camp on the banks of the "Luinzono" River (CD MS). While Curle's map reproduces Conrad's spelling for the river where Conrad camps, Conrad's map identifies the river as "Unionzo" – again implying that

Conrad may have drawn the map for some later purpose without necessarily referring to his diary and for some unexplained reason misidentified the Luinzono and included the names "Tombagadio" and "Mukumbungu." In contrast, when Stanley crossed the "Lunionzo" [sic] River he was thinking of its valley and its great potential for a railway (*The Congo* 2: 214).

Porters Stop to Rest[48]

While camping on July 3, Conrad drops another titillating detail: "Govt. Zanzibari with register – Canoe" (CD MS). As Najder duly notes, Zanzibaris were employed by the Congo Free State as soldiers or police (*Congo Diary* 16). And Stanley depended on Zanzibaris for all his expeditions, especially appreciative of their work with him founding stations for the Congo Free State in 1882 (*The Congo* 1: 462). Sadly, Zanzibaris later in service to the Congo Free State engaged in violent abuses against the local tribes, resulting in the depopulation of the very trade route that Conrad would follow. For example, missionary John Weeks reported that

> In the early eighties the road from Matadi to Stanley Pool was thickly populated, and every hour or two brought the traveller to a large,

Chapter Three: A Witness in the Congo: Conrad's „The Congo Diary"... 157

decently-kept town; but in 1890 the people were mostly gone, and the few villages left on that long stretch of road were small and neglected, and the few remaining people had a wretched, poverty-stricken appearance. Why this change? (*Among Congo Cannibals* 20)

Because, Weeks continued, "Zanzibaris were imported during this period, armed with rifles, and sent up-country to help found and occupy the State stations on the Upper Congo" (20). Naturally, an unarmed populace was no match for Zanzibari soldiers, nor did they have protection against the constant raiding and looting. "Hence," Weeks concludes,

> what was once a populous trade route, humming with life in the early eighties, had become by 1890 a desolate track […]. "Where are the people?" a newcomer might ask. "They have left the trade route, and have rebuilt their towns and villages in the woods, the valleys, and the bush lands for peace and security." "Why" – the answer was always: "Because the land was cursed by a plague of rascally Zanzibaris, and irresponsible white men who feared their soldiers more than they feared God, and who acted unjustly in their dealings with the people." (21)

Even though many of the villagers had disappeared into the interior, trading had not stopped. Weeks's observations, though, give additional context to the function of the Zanzibari in Conrad's diary whose task it was to record and track the locals for enforced labor. On the next page of his diary for July 3, Conrad seems to confirm what Weeks would later write: "Villages quite invisible. Infer their existence from calbashes [sic] suspended to palm trees for the 'malafu'[49] – *good many caravans and travellers*" (CD MS, emphasis added). This is the only moment when Conrad mentions that there are numerous caravans passing, but it is a very important indication of the amount of traffic on the march, underscoring the high volume of trade. However, contradictory to Weeks's observations, the villages and the markets are still there, for Conrad makes note of the villages he passes on July 6th, 8th, and on the 26th, when he passes more villages and writes that the area is "thickly inhabited." The last village he records seeing appears on a "hill to the right" on the 28th. While his path doesn't seem to take him into the villages, Conrad does pass through markets – some of them quite large with hundreds of people – on an almost daily basis, clearly indicating lively activity, so necessary not only for the locals to trade for food but essential for the caravans as well on this overland route.

Conrad's Sketches of the Overland Journey

A remarkable dimension of geographical navigation emerges in the sketches scattered throughout the two volumes of Conrad's diary, sketches that are, in my view, the most exciting and overlooked elements in these manuscript journals. On July 3, Conrad began to sketch maps of the day's journey. It is curious that Curle chose to leave out these sketches in his edition, and that both Najder and Stevens and Stape add the written text in the sketches but not the drawings. I include and discuss several here because I believe that the sketches are not only an extraordinary window into Conrad's gifted imagination and his "passion for maps" but also they act as integral companions to the text, enhancing the visuality of Conrad's fragmentary descriptions. The first drawing on July 3 shows a "Section of today's road." The narrative on the pages leading up to the first sketch depicts detailed description of what Conrad will draw, thus setting a scene for the visual rendering of the path. "Crossed a range of mountains running NW-SE by a low pass. Another broad flat valley with a deep ravine through the center [...]. Another range parallel to the first-mentioned with a chain of low foothills running close to it." Before he reaches the end of his record for the day, a record which concludes with the sketch, he writes his impressions of what he's seen and felt: "Up to 9am – sky clouded and calm – Afterwards gentle breeze from the Nth generally and sky clearing. [...] White mists on the hills about halfway. Water effects, very beautiful this morning. Mists generally raising before sky clears." The narrative forefronts Conrad as the camera's eye traveling through his surroundings while the sketch adds details measuring

Chapter Three: A Witness in the Congo: Conrad's „The Congo Diary"... 159

Section of To Day's Road. 3 July 1890

distance, displaying topography through an approximation of elevation, and tracking his path with solid and faintly visible dotted lines. Conrad has taken some time at the end of the march to develop this sketch of his path from Banza Manteka, marked on the far right to the Luinzono River on the far left. Furthermore, counter to most if not all his other geographical sketches, this one and all the others in this diary, are cross-sectional, or profile maps, not bird's eye views. Mirela Altic, an expert in the history of cartography, notes in an email to me that cross section maps like these require less skill than a bird's eye view map, and without instruments to measure the height of hills and mountains, Conrad is simply drafting what he both sees and imagines he could see from a more distant on-the-ground perspective ("Pondering a Sketch by Conrad"). Altic also suggests that cross sections are often used in maritime cartography to draft views of the coast from the ship, which makes sense given Conrad's experience at sea. Without the instruments needed to calculate heights, like the theodolites Stanley used, Conrad would not have been able to sketch a topographical map with any accuracy. But he had a compass, a 32-wind compass rose to use for taking bearings as well as the method of dead reckoning to measure distance traveled. In his profile sketches he could indicate, as the mapmaker standing on the earth's surface and looking toward the horizon, a side view of the jagged peaks and approximate highs and lows of mountains he'd actually climbed and crossed. What is very striking in all these sketches is the double vision of Conrad's perspective – his power to envision his path, sketching from a distance, as though he can see his path on the horizon while sketching miles away from his actual location – like being in two places at once. For example, note the faint dotted line that marks his path along the flank of the tall mountain in the midsection of the drawing. Altic's observation is particularly pertinent here: Conrad may be sketching a "coast," but distinct from the usual profile map where the mapmaker or sketch artist draws what he or she looks at; this is a section over which Conrad actually walked. Perhaps to help him navigate the land, the *Société Anonyme Belge* had provided Conrad with a map like A. J. Wauters' *"Carte de l'État independent du Congo dressée d'après les derniers renseignements,"*[50] which includes coded sketching indicating mountainous ranges and some elevations. However, by now Stanley had left lots of signposts for Conrad to follow.

Note in the sketch the broad plain Conrad traverses as he leaves Banza Manteka, the descent, the track of the low pass, and parallel ranges of mountains with foothills he's referred to earlier. Also important is the orientation – the direction of the path, clearly marked by an arrow, moves from right to left across the page; Conrad is using his compass to note the direction traveling NNE from SSW. In each sketch, beginning with this one, Conrad draws an arrow pointing in the direction of the path, always from right to left – the reverse of what we might expect as readers of print on a page that moves from left to right. But if we swivel Conrad's section sketch 90° clockwise, the path points in a northerly direction, which is where he's going. Furthermore, he's measured the distance of the day's travel at 15 miles, most likely using dead reckoning as his methodology. From this point on in the diary, Conrad includes eleven more sketches with varying levels of detail, all of them cross sections of a day's journey, most with distances indicated; all of them except the last indicating direction with

Chapter Three: A Witness in the Congo: Conrad's „The Congo Diary"... 161

arrows pointing from right to left, and all of them – except the last – including points of the compass for direction. We can only infer why on the sixth day on his march, Conrad started sketching his route, but he did, adding profile maps for twelve days out of the seventeen he was on the march – navigating the land.

On July 4, Conrad added another sketch which tracks his path with a dotted line and shows more detail of direction, a clear indication that he's using a 32-point compass with no degrees marked – NNE ½ N, measuring a distance of thirteen miles from the Luinzono to the camp reached at the end of the day.

NNE is two clicks over from due N – thus NNE ½ N is one-half click back toward N from NNE. Conrad, in this journal, reckoned direction by points, not by degrees, and was well familiar with "boxing the compass," naming all thirty-two directional points in order clockwise. The narrative leading up to the sketch on July 4th indicates "[m]arching across a chain of hills and then in a maze of hills" followed by "an undulating plain," all of which appears along with the plotted path in the middle of the drawing.

To Day's March. July 4, 1890

Conrad notes that he took bearings and records ascent up steep hills but doesn't mark the river passed or the Mpwe River where he makes camp – only the word "camp" is marked below.

As he records the march on July 5th, Conrad adds another drawing, showing his direction has shifted back to NNE:

Section of To Day's Road. July 5, 1890

Marching twelve miles on this day's journey, Conrad has left the camp marked on the far right to travel to Manyamba indicated on the far left. He passes a "narrow plain," reaching the Kwilu River, "Swift flowing and deep 50 yds wide – Passed in canoes." As shown on the left side of the map, Conrad notes marching "up and down very steep hills intersected by deep ravines."

There are sketches for the marches on July 6th and 7th, but Conrad's march on July 8th is notable for the first glimpse of the Congo River on the path; and the strenuous terrain partly accounts for the fact that the caravan only accomplished nine and one-half miles that day. The line of mountains/hills is accentuated to show the path, with two lines of hills in the background to the right and an indication of a hill just before the camp at Manyanga on the left. With a direction of N by E, the direction of travel is just one click away from due north. This is Conrad's first sighting of the Congo on the overland trek – even though the road parallels the river, it is actually several miles away, rendering it invisible for a number of days. In his text, Conrad writes that he's left the main government path for the Manyanga track, "Road up and down all the time." Also note the description of "a confused wilderness of hills" as "land slips on their sides showing red. Fine effect of red hill covered in places by dark green vegetation." Recording the first sight of the river, Conrad writes, "1/2 hour before beginning the descent got a glimpse of the Congo." We can almost mark on his sketch where he is when he first sees the river, and if we return to his map of the Congo Basin, he has marked how close his path took him to the south bank of the river. There

Chapter Three: A Witness in the Congo: Conrad's „The Congo Diary"... 163

appears to be another river, not named here in his sketch, but marked on his "Congo Basin" map as the "Pioka," which would appear to his right as the Congo River is on his left.

To Day's March. July 8, 1890

Following a lengthy stay in Manyanga, Conrad's caravan has made good time on the 26th after leaving the camp at Mafiela, traveling 18 miles, crossing a crocodile pond and marching on the government path. His detailed direction indicates that he's traveling E ½ N from W ½ S. On the points of the compass, he's traveling almost due east, just ½ tick above east to the north, and if we look at his map of the Congo Basin, we see that he has indeed turned east from Manyanga. We should note again that Curle's map does not show the easterly trajectory of the path from Manyanga to the Ngoma River.
This route takes him to a large marketplace that appears "thickly inhabited." Conrad's sketch indicates that "a white man died here" but his text makes no mention of that, so it's an interesting mystery that he marks that annotation on the sketch. Other than remarking that the road is "ascending all the time," the narrative adds little detail to the sketch, which in fact offers a bit more information.
  On the 27th, Conrad writes that he's taken a detour, so "this being off the road no section given"; which does suggest he's drawing his section sketches with the help of a map.

Sketch on July 26, 1890

He includes distance and direction in his narrative, continuing ENE for 15 miles. He's gone off the government road to visit the mission at Lutété – Curle, Najder, and Stevens and Stape all mistakenly transcribe this location as "Sutili," and it's easy to see why when we examine Conrad's handwriting. The L could easily be mistaken for an S, but the mission was definitely located at Gomba Lutété, or simply Lutété as noted on numerous maps of the lower Congo, including Stanley's.

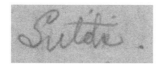

Excerpt from Narrative. July 27, 1890

Indeed, "Gomba Lutete" is clearly marked on Conrad's map of the Congo Basin, and the map shows the detour to the mission, where he's departed from the government path which does continue its ENE trajectory. Once he's back on the government road at "Luasi," he travels toward the Ngoma River. It's not clear from Conrad's narrative if Luasi is a village or another river he crosses – he does cross the "Luaza" marked on his Congo Basin map, but that's some miles from the juncture with the government road, so the next unmarked river on his map may be the "Luasi."

Conrad continues to travel ENE on the 28th to camp on the right bank of the Ngoma River. He's sketched details of the

Chapter Three: A Witness in the Congo: Conrad's „The Congo Diary"... 165

wooded valleys on either side of the ridge which is his path. "Then walking along the ridges of hill chains with valleys on both sides – The country more open and there is [sic] much more trees growing large clumps in the ravines." Conrad marks Nzungi with a flag in his sketch and notes passing it in his narrative but doesn't explain what it is; however, both Stanley and Herbert Ward do. For Stanley, Nzungi is "a village of carriers" (*The Congo* 2: 207), while Ward (214) identifies Nzungi as a marketplace; in his sketch, Conrad has flagged it but passed by without comment.

Sketch on July 28, 1890

While Conrad includes another sketch on the 29th, I will conclude by focusing on the sketches dated July 30 and July 31. On the 30th, Conrad indicates "A remarkable conical mountain visible from here," but he makes no mention of this sighting in his narrative. Stanley's map of the Congo Basin which accompanies *The Congo and the Founding of Its Free State* does identify "Nsenge Mt" in the vicinity Conrad

Sketch on July 30, 1890

was traveling, just past the Inkissi River, but Stanley makes no mention of it in his narrative either. Other observations which appear in this sketch are two notations for wood – one near the Lulufu River and another near a stream – he'd written on the day before as he crossed the Inkissi, "Banks wooded very densely and valley of the river rather deep but very narrow." At the two ends of the sketch, he's drawn what appear to be tents to show his camping places. The flag accompanying Nsona a Nsefe shows that Conrad is also noting the market day.

Earlier in his narrative, upon leaving Manyanga on July 25, Conrad made a list of the Congolese days of the week:

List of Congolese Days of the Week

On Wednesday, July 30, he's reached the market which coincides with the dates in his list. Curle ignores the list of market days in his edition of the diary and Najder mistakenly identifies these names as the names of chief carriers of the day (*Congo Diary* 16n21). However, Stevens and Stape find

Chapter Three: A Witness in the Congo: Conrad's „The Congo Diary"...   167

corroboration in Bentley's *Pioneering on the Congo* for this list: "Markets in these parts are held once in every four days; the names of the days being *Nsona, Nkandu, Konzo [Nkonzo], Nkenge*" (Bentley 1: 358; Stevens and Stape, "Explanatory Notes" 458). Furthermore, markets rotated not only every four days but also larger trade markets where several thousand could congregate occurred every eight days, and Conrad continuously refers to the markets he encounters, clear evidence of lively African native trade. There's an interesting blurring of the names of the days and villages or camps and even the names of chiefs of the villages; for example, Conrad has camped at a place named Nsona on Sunday, July 6, having just passed a large marketplace, and if we calculate backwards from Conrad's list of market days, Nsona market would have occurred on that day as well.

On the penultimate day of his march, July 31, Conrad neared the Congo River once more, describing beforehand "sharp ascents," with wooded valleys and ridges. At this point in the march, the Congo was "very narrow and rapid Kinzilu rushing in. A short distance up from the mouth fine waterfall." His direction since leaving the Ngoma River on the 29th has turned more NE by E ½ E and NE ½ E from ENE as he nears Stanley Pool and his destination point southeast of it at Nselemba (also known as Lemba). Conrad continues to track the Congolese market days of the week, but he's made an error on the sketch if his list of the market days with European dates is accurate.

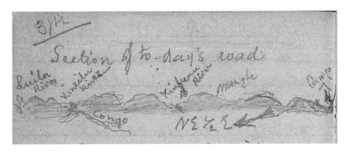

Section of To Day's Road. 31 July 1890

He's noted "Nkenghe" to the right of the Kinfumu River, but the correct day for Nkenghe would be Saturday, August 2, according to his list, and by then he's stopped recording his daily travel on the overland path. Conrad leaves one last sketch in the journal marking his last day's journey with arrival at Nselemba (Lemba), just east of Kinshasa; his narrative makes clear that he's had enough: "Glad to see the end of this stupid tramp." He's feeling "rather seedy," so for him, apparently, land navigating has not been much fun.

Populating Conrad's Congo Journey

While I have focused on the sketches and descriptions of terrain traveled through in the preceding section, Conrad's descriptions sketch the people he encounters as well, and his contacts with Europeans take up more space in his narrative than his encounters with the native population. His very warm comments about Casement show that he was able to find at least one kindred spirit in the Congo, but other "whites" in Matadi make him uncomfortable so he intends to keep to himself. These comments suggest that at a very early stage he's already seeing the ugly reality of Belgian administration in the Congo. Once on the march, his Belgian traveling companion Harou is a source of irritation because he's constantly ill, and the two Danes in Conrad's caravan receive only scanty attention and keep to themselves. Later in his march, Conrad warms up to other Europeans, for example, the government agents Heyn and Jaeger are good hosts for the duration of his stay at the Manyanga station from the 8th-25th of July. In addition to the representatives of the Congo state that Conrad has met, there are also Baptist missionaries who cross, or fail to cross his path. At Lutete, Conrad spends time in the Wathen missionary station, welcomed by Mrs. Comber – the only member of the mission there at the time. Conrad is duly impressed by the condition of this mission establishment "eminently civilized and very refreshing to see" which he contrasts with "the lot of tumble down hovels in which the state company agents are content to live" (July 27, 1890)

Chapter Three: A Witness in the Congo: Conrad's „The Congo Diary"...

In his *Congo for Christ,* John Myers includes a map indicating the position of the Wathen (Lutete) Baptist mission station, which coincides with the location on Conrad's map of the Congo Basin; this mission was managed by Reverend and Mrs. Bentley, both of whom Conrad missed meeting as they were away on a preaching tour. Sadly, Conrad's hostess for the day, Annie Comber, would die of fever in December 1890 on her way out of the Congo at about the same time as Conrad's departure.

Conrad comments rarely on the native population, but when he does, his remarks are revealing. On July 3, as I noted earlier, Conrad sees the dead "Backongo" or Bakongo at a camping place and the very next day he encounters another body "lying by the path in an attitude of meditative repose." Then, on July 26th, he notes on his sketch that a "a white man died here," begging the question why the death of an unnamed white man is significant enough to appear on his sketch. On the 29th, he sees a skeleton tied to a post as well as a "white man's grave – no name. Heap of stones in the form of a cross." The contrast is striking – the anonymous white man is worthy of burial while the native's skeleton has been left to decompose in plain sight. And there's just a hint of danger lingering in the distance "when the moon rose heard shouts and drumming in distant villages." Conrad doesn't mention encountering natives in their villages, but in the markets he does; yet he writes little of those encounters nor does he dwell on what's being traded. However, there is one important encounter that occurs near the end of this journal when Conrad tends to a chief's son suffering from a gunshot wound; but Conrad offers no information about how or why the boy was shot – so we can only surmise that he may have been a victim of a government agent, a Zanzibari, or a hostile tribe.

Of course, Conrad is in the constant company of Africans, his bearers in the caravan, but they receive limited attention, even serving as almost comic relief from the exhaustive nature of the trek. It's not until July 5 that Conrad records "To day fell into a muddy puddle. Beastly.

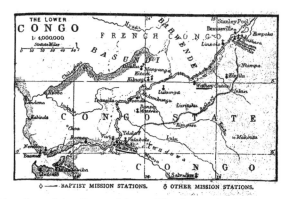

Illustration from John Brown Myers. *The Congo for Christ: The Story of the Congo Mission*

The fault of the man that carried me." It's notable that he's being carried when most of the time he is on foot with Harou being carried. On the 7th of July, there's a "[r]ow with the carriers," a sign of more trouble to come. Once he leaves Manyanga on the 25th, there are "plenty of hammock carriers" – Harou is lame but Conrad is on foot. On the 30th, "Row with carriers all the way. Harou suffering much through the jerks of the hammock." I wonder if the jerks are deliberate. Conrad adds a scene of comic relief on the 30th: "Expect lots of bother with carriers to-morrow. Had them all called and made a speech which they did not understand. They promise good behaviour." We're left to question how they can promise anything if they didn't understand the speech. It's no wonder the carriers are rebelling: "Great difficulty in carrying Harou. Too heavy. Bother! Made two long halts to rest the carriers." The carriers reappear on the last day of the march, "Row between carriers and a man stating himself in govt employ, about a mat. Blows and sticks raining hard. Stopped it."

While serving as a measure of comic relief, the porters in Conrad's caravan have become, as Stephen Rockel argues about porterage in general, "almost invisible – part of the scenery" (qtd. in Rockel, *Carriers of Culture* 5). Yet, Rockel continues, there is a long history of Europeans' complaints about porters, creating a "*Leifmotiv*" in their narratives (5). Conrad appears to have some measure of authority over the unruly carriers, but we're left only to guess at what other loads they carried in addition to the heavy Harou to trade for food like chickens, eggs, and pineapple at the local markets. Surely, they would have borne the tents that Conrad refers to as well as cooking supplies and very likely the "holy trinity" of cloth, beads, and brass wire for trade at each of the marketplaces where they stop – but Conrad makes no mention of anything other than tents and hammocks. Further, if some of these carriers were in fact slaves for hire, I would expect Conrad to make note of that fact; however, in writing about East Africa, Rockel argues that some "domestic slaves or freed slaves, the Waungwana" were regular carriers, could earn their pay in serving on a caravan, and could ultimately buy their freedom (21). Without these carriers, Rockel insists

> nothing would have moved [...] economic development would have been impossible; no Muslims or Christians would have traveled up country, and no converts would have been made in the interior; European exploration, conquest, and colonization would have been infeasible. The historic importance of caravan porters is therefore obvious. (4)

Rockel adds that African women often traveled along with male caravan porters, working alongside the men ("Enterprising Partners" 751).

Conrad, however, must have had no women in his caravan; he even comments on July 3 that he's seen "No women unless on the market place." Yet the very next day he sees three women passing his camp, one of whom is albino, "Horrid chalky white with pink blotches. Red eyes. Red hair. Features very negroid and ugly."[51] The comment is shocking to the contemporary reader for its matching color and race with ugliness, but such sentiments were hardly uncommon. And just as shocking is the entanglement of gender with this observation of ugliness.

Curle's notes on Conrad's diary in the pamphlet edition include a remarkable discussion, quoting a friend's opinion of Conrad's observation:

> Here we have in a few words, from the pen of a keen observer and a master of descriptive writing, a woman with complete albinism of skin and eye [...]. Conrad notices the repulsive appearance which all albino negroes present to us, and the fact that negroid facial characters appear more marked in a white-skinned native. (*CD,* Strangeways 23-24n2)

For the missionary William Bentley, albino girls are "strange freaks of nature,"

> An albino African has a skin like an Englishman, with a tendency to pink; the frizzy hair is white or slightly yellow; the eyes are pink, and more or less intolerant of light. They often suffer from some skin disease. The African features, hair, and dress, seem strangely out of place with the white skin. It is *rather a shock* to come upon one suddenly. (1: 200, emphasis added)

The remarks from these white men uncover a dis-case with the notion of white skin associated with the negroid race complicated by gender – the appearance of the uncanny, which unsettles each writer's sense of racial, gendered superiority. But this repulsion toward the albino extends to Africans as well; David Livingstone includes a story of a mother of an albino son who killed him to satisfy the father's wish to get rid of him (*Missionary Travels* 576). On the other hand, what Stanley witnessed in *Through the Dark Continent* provides a contrast to Livingstone's account; in one African monarch's court, "albinoes" were entertainment as part of his entourage, while another chief displayed pride in his pure albino son for his whiteness: "as he said he was also a little Mundelé" – the African term for white people (1: 408; 2: 440-41).

Writing and sketching briefly on an almost daily basis in a journal, though, leaves Conrad little room or perhaps time for speculating on the nature of race and skin color in his journey along the lower Congo. When he does comment, the whites

Chapter Three: A Witness in the Congo: Conrad's „The Congo Diary"... 173

he encounters fare little better in his opinion than the unruly carriers, the albino woman, or the dead bodies that litter the path. His Congo diary notebook is the only record of Conrad's march on the banks of the Congo; he does not record the trip back downriver in his return to Matadi in October-December 1890. As Najder points out, he was too ill (*Joseph Conrad: A Life* 162).[52] At least so it appears.

"The Congo Diary," continued ...

The second notebook, "Up-river Book" is clearly marked on its title page, "Commenced / 3. Augst 1890 – / S. S. 'Roi des Belges'"; Conrad starts his navigational notes two days after apparently ending the diary of his overland journey. However, at some indeterminate point in time Conrad returned to the notebook containing the first diary, leaving twenty-six blank pages before beginning to write and draw again. These later entries are partly unrelated to the record of his overland journey and Conrad makes no indication of the date when they were written. Furthermore, Curle omits these additional pages in his edition as does Najder – both end the journal with Conrad's last dated entry, August 1 (1890). Stevens and Stape, though, transcribe these pages and offer explanatory notes identifying some of the items; but they offer no explanation when or where these notes might have been written. Conrad resumes the diary with a sketch that appears undefinable – a structure on wheels – after another blank page there is a list of numbers added up to a total with a doodle at the top of the page marked "Cape Town." Hans van Marle, in a lengthy letter to Ian Watt in 1980, insists that this doodle "can therefore be dated to 1892 or 1893" – during Conrad's return voyages from Adelaide to London on *The Torrens* ("Letters" 73). He adds further that a later page including a list including oil cans and drums, "mast" color tins and paint tins must refer to the *Torrens* episode (73) because the *Roi des Belges* had no mast; I thought the same, but I also think this list of supplies might refer to those needed to transport palm oil on river steamers.[53] More blank pages follow, then Conrad records two pages of calculations which are very interesting because, as Stevens and Stape suggest, at least one calculation at the bottom of the second page appears to be the latitude and longitude of a point off the southwestern tip of Australia, possibly referring to the London-Australia route of several of Conrad's ships before he traveled the Congo River and his last post on *The Torrens* after the Congo ("The Congo Diary," Stevens and Stape, *Last Essays* 135). The pages contain calculations of distance and time as well as GPS coordinates, for example, the 40th parallel south which appears in these notes runs through the Atlantic, Pacific, and Indian Oceans south of the equator – where Conrad would have sailed in the South Seas. On the next page he lists several titles, all identified by Stevens and Stape, none of them referring to the Congo. Woodford's *A Naturalist Among the Headhunters*, published in January 1890, describes expeditions to the Solomon Islands – which Conrad would have sailed past or through on his way to the Torres Strait as captain of the Otago in 1888, as well as earlier voyages through the South Seas. The next, published in 1889, is Clements Markham's *A Life of John Davis, the Navigator*, who, in the seventeenth century, discovered the Davis Straits between Greenland and Baffin Island. James Grant's *The Newspaper Press*, 1871, the next title, tracks the evolution of newspapers from the earliest gazettes to the present metropolitan daily news. Last is an article in *The Nineteenth Century*, March 1890, on the battle at Tel-El-Kebir in 1882 during the Anglo-Egyptian War (Stevens and Stape, "Explanatory Notes" 459-60). These titles reflect an eclectic mix that suggests Conrad's wide-ranging interests in geography, exploration, battles, and the newspaper – but could he have obtained these in the Congo? That seems highly unlikely just as it seems unlikely that he carried them with him on his journey. What strikes me as more likely is that these are references he's picked up in conversations with someone – possibly W. H. Jacques or John Galsworthy on board *The Torrens*.

Chapter Three: A Witness in the Congo: Conrad's „The Congo Diary"... 175

After another blank page, Conrad returns to Kikongo vocabulary, writing phrases in ink[54]; after another blank page, Conrad continues noting Kikongo words and phrases both in ink and in pencil. On the next page, Conrad returns to Kikongo, this time translating into French, followed by market days, perhaps names of towns where the markets occur, and a doodle of a bunch of bananas and a seed pod.

Then Conrad changes course, heading up the next page with the name "Kodak Camera," the address of the Eastman Company and the cost of the camera; there's no explanation why Conrad's thinking about a camera at this point, however, the first Kodak camera went on the market in 1888, a game changer in the development of photography for the amateur. On the same page, Conrad lists the missionaries at two missionary stations: Mr. Hoste at Lukunga and Mr. Ingham at Banza Manteka; this is interesting because in 1884 Stanley identified Mr. and Mrs. Ingham as the resident missionaries at the Livingstone Mission in Lukunga not Banza Manteka (*The Congo* 2: 212). "G. Stern. Gray's Inn," refers to the makers of "Pepsalia" – a digestive table salt, overlaid with some doodling that resembles directions including an image of a house in a circle, leading up to a point of intersection with the name "Nzenghe," where two lines head up, forking to the left and to the right toward end points with indistinguishable doodles and on the left, the underlined name "Lankonzo [?]." Written diagonally at the bottom are the words: "Hierarchy / Anarchy." Was Conrad thinking about the nature of the administration in the Belgian Congo? The next pages return to matters which must refer to his activities in the Congo – the market days with their translations in French, calculations with the initials SAB repeated – most likely *Société Anonyme Belge*, then finally a listing of casks with weights which may refer to the packing of ivory – at the top Conrad has written "Matadi. 23rd 6th 90"—surely referring to June 23, 1890, when he packed casks with ivory, with the weights packed into four casks. These scribbled pages leave so much unexplained, but if, as van Marle suggests, Conrad began writing this addition after his stint in the Congo, then it becomes clear that Conrad wasn't done with the journals when he left the Congo but put them to use at a later date. Or, as Jean-Aubry suggests (220), retrieved them from the trunk which arrived on the Ile-Grande, just in time to rescue him from trying to write what would much later become *The Rescue* (1920).

"The Up-river Book," Navigating the Upper Congo

Conrad mentions disturbing news in his "Congo Diary" – on July 29 he learns "very bad news from up the rivers. All the steamers disabled. One wrecked" (UB MS). His purpose of course in traveling to Stanley Pool was, so he thought, to take command of the *Florida,* but that was rendered impossible by the condition of the seriously damaged steamer which had been towed to Kinshasa for repair (Najder, *Joseph Conrad: A Life* 154). But one steamer at Stanley Pool was still serviceable, so on August 3, Conrad embarked on the *Roi des Belges* for Stanley Falls traveling as supernumerary to its Captain Koch. In a second notebook, Conrad kept a record of navigational instructions, including navigational symbols for triangulation points and fixed points to identify location, symbols for islands, Roman numeral indicators for each chart, and capital letters for positions on the charts. There are sketches, but this time, Conrad draws bird's eye views of the course to be taken along the river, possibly copying from navigational charts supplied by the *Société Anonyme Belge*. Two blank pages precede the first page on which Conrad begins taking notes; but exactly where he is on the river, or if he's just exiting Stanley Pool, is unclear. The narrative, with a few sketches, consists of two parts of which Conrad only entitles the second part as he crosses the equator into the northern hemisphere. Part I is not marked as such, beginning abruptly with the words "on leaving – from A." this section continues for thirty-six pages, followed by two blank pages, then picks up again on Thursday, August 14, when Conrad

Chapter Three: A Witness in the Congo: Conrad's „The Congo Diary"... 177

continues the running narrative with instructions for when and if he gets his own command. His Part II begins in the northern latitude "from Equator to Bangala," continuing to chart the trajectory for thirty-six recto and verso pages interspersed with largely blank verso pages and a few versos containing sketches of sections of the river.

Conrad is annotating presumably using the navigational charts supplied by Captain Koch as he makes detailed notes and instructions for charting this dangerous river. The early pages of the journal indicate the prevalence of islands, sandbanks, clumps of trees, as he notes to pass close to the sands "<u>Cautiously!</u>" At one point Conrad even references Captain Koch "(Capt Coch" [sic]) in parentheses as his source for steering past a dangerous sandbank. His directions for steering are given both by the sun and by the compass; the compass he's using now measures the 32 points and degrees. The contents of this journal are highly technical and don't offer much in the way of personal observation of life along the shore, rather they attend much more to the course to follow to avoid danger as well as the notations for wooding places so necessary to keep the paddle steamer running. But there are a few details besides the purely technical, for example, "over pt XVI curious yellow path on a hill" and "On the other side villages on slope of hill." While Conrad records passing villages and missions, he does so without adding details.

The second part of the journal tracks the journey into the northern latitude, and here Conrad clearly references that he's following navigational charts. In this portion, Conrad is writing on the recto pages and tends to leave the versos blank except for an occasional sketch. The sketches have less detail than those in the first overland Congo diary and are all bird's eye views of the bends in the river. As an example, the dotted path below marks the trajectory of the steamer tracking NNW on a section of the river.

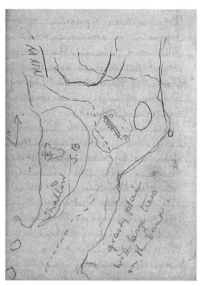

Drawing on verso of page marked at the top VI N.

While Conrad doesn't provide detail about the nature of the villages, the villagers, mission and government stations and employees, or even details about camping places, we can expand our knowledge of his journey by examining other sources. In April 1885, Reverend Thomas Comber gave a talk to the Royal Geographical Society on the explorations he and George Grenfell made of the upper Congo on the Baptist missionary steamer *Peace* in 1884 – the same steamer Stanley would commandeer during the Emin Pasha expedition in just three years. In the jointly authored paper, entitled "Explorations by the Revs. George Grenfell and T. J. Comber," from which Comber read, he included valuable details about what Conrad may have seen but didn't record five years later.[55] Aside from a brief detour on the Bochini River, Comber and Grenfell traveled along the southeast bank of the Congo all the way up to Bangala – the same point at which Conrad's "Up-river Book" ends. A detailed map entitled "The Congo River from Stanley Pool to Bangala Surveyed by George Grenfell and

Chapter Three: A Witness in the Congo: Conrad's „The Congo Diary"... 179

T. J. Comber 1884" appears at the end of the publication of the talk and offers a powerful visual to the details in paper's narrative. The Grenfell-Comber map adds details to Conrad's path, and while some of the place names do not appear in Conrad's narrative, there are important correspondences with Conrad's navigational directions, with the addition of the location of missions, and the locations and names of numerous villages along both banks of the river extant at that time.

Grenfell and Comber note that the current of the river from Stanley Pool is "swift and strong, and twists and turns considerably. Navigators need to take great care to avoid occasional feldspathic rocks, sometimes isolated and cropping up almost in mid-stream" (354). Comber adds that the country between Stanley Pool and the Bochini River is largely uninhabited but does note a town at Ganchu (354), which Conrad passes on his manuscript page marked XI (also in Najder, *Congo Diary* 22). Comber accounts for the lack of human habitation in this district by "the barren and uninviting character of the country" (Grenfell and Comber 354); Conrad mentions the point and another close by, Bankab Point, but not the town. Conrad also notes numerous wooding places but not the amount of time devoted to gathering wood for fueling, while Comber adds the detail that "a third of a day needed to be devoted to fueling, for us to run the remaining two-thirds" (355). But on the same page, Comber adds that "[w]ood for fuel we found to be easily attainable in most places."

Conrad hasn't noted the date when he passed the entrance to the Kassai River – Comber calls this the Bochini, but it's the same river which joins the Congo at Kwamouth as shown on the Grenfell-Comber map. Using information from Reverends Bentley and Grenfell, Harry Johnston adds visual details to the flow of the Kassai into the Congo. "At a point eighty-five miles east of Stanley Pool the Kasai joins the Congo, pouring its immense volume into it at a right angle through a deeply cut chasm in the rocky hills some seven hundred yards in width" (Johnston, *George Grenfell and the Congo* 1: 287). Conrad passes a Catholic mission at this point where the steamer stops

The Congo River from Stanley Pool to Bangala

for an hour and a half, and identifies passing the Lawson River, also known as the Alima, located on Comber's map. Comber writes of the Lawson that "its mouth," on entering the Congo, is "distinguished by great sandbanks, and its waters of a pale steely color" (Grenfell and Comber 359), and Conrad notices the opening of the "Lawson river with sandbank across the mouth and rocks stretching off." There are hills and forests Conrad mentions as they steam along, adding caution about snags and stones, but he doesn't name Chumbiri, which is odd because Comber refers to it as one of the largest of the very numerous towns in this region – but that was in 1884, and perhaps by 1890, the status of Chumbiri might have changed. "Some of these points," according to Grenfell and Comber, "are extremely picturesque, and run out far into the water that the towns built on them front the river both up and down" (359). Najder disputes the notion of population density on the upper Congo by the time Conrad was there; he offers powerful corrections to earlier accounts of prosperous villages by citing the account of traders on the *Roi des Belges* just six months after Conrad. "'The country is ruined. Passengers in the steamer *Roi des Belges* have been able to see for themselves'" that along a 200 mile stretch of the river "'there is not an inhabited village left – that is to say four days' steaming through a country formerly so rich, today entirely ruined'" (qtd. in *Joseph Conrad, A Life* 157). These were eyewitnesses, Najder concludes, to the devastation caused by Belgian colonization.

Conrad's next named point of reference is Grenfell Point and the English mission, which may refer to the Baptist Missionary Society mission at Bolobo. Here again Comber, but not Conrad, remarks on the dense population of towns, "Bolobo […] is a town composed of about two miles of villages" (Grenfell and Comber 360). The character of the population, however, is far from attractive; Comber insists: "the main characteristics of the Bolobo people appear to be drunkenness, immorality, out of each of which vices springs almost too fearful to describe" (360). Comber continues describing the density of population and the number of towns along with added descriptions of the "ingeniously cruel" practices of the people, writing "Indeed, interior Congo is one of the 'dark places of the earth, full of habitations of cruelty'"(365). "A few of the houses are ornamented with human skulls," Comber adds, "one having as many as thirteen" (361). Later in his narrative Comber describes one horrid method of execution practiced by the natives in the vicinity of the Equatorville station where victims are forced to run for their lives while being chased and finally brought down with spears, bows and arrows (364). But when Conrad passes Bolobo village, he is focused squarely on navigational instructions.

After two blank pages, Conrad takes up writing once more, recording the date Thursday, August 14th. One curious item in this part of the narrative is the mention of "Vllge of Ikongo – Bad." But why? Comber doesn't note a village named Ikongo on his map or in his narrative but given his descriptions of the Bolobo towns in the near vicinity, the reason Conrad made this note should be apparent. Just before reaching the equator Conrad mentions passing the American mission, which was established at the Equator station by 1885. From this point forward in his narrative, Conrad remains in the northern hemisphere until he ends his journal as he reaches Bangala. He'll pass the "Loulanga R." noted on Comber's map as the "Mai Lulongo," which gives us a visual of how close Conrad is now to Bangala. Conrad also notes the French Factory near this position, a clear reference to trading on the upper reaches of the river. The narrative ends abruptly after pages of navigational instructions about where to steer and warnings about islands, snags, and sandbanks to avoid.

Grenfell and Comber's paper closes with suggestions about increasing white settlement on the upper Congo; the people "are a little wild and want managing, but at no place did they attempt to molest us" (368). Comber adds that, as Stanley observed, navigation on the upper Congo is free of the difficulty created by the cataracts of the lower Congo, making it "a highway into the interior" (368). For Comber, the upper Congo also seems to be healthier for Europeans, offers much in the way of products to export – palm oil, coffee, and rubber – and land suitable for towns. Of great importance, of course, is the construction of a railway (368-69).

Comber and Grenfell were not alone traveling the Congo River in the mid 1880s – the U.S. Navy sent an expedition led by Lieutenant E. H. Taunt which lasted six months and resulted in a lengthy report that adds valuable information to both Conrad's navigational narrative and Comber's descriptive paper to the RGS. A year after Comber and Grenfell traveled the upper reaches of the Congo, Taunt made the same journey, finding it more difficult to obtain wood for fuel than Comber had. What Taunt adds is a description of the river from Bangala to Stanley Falls which neither Conrad nor Comber includes,

Chapter Three: A Witness in the Congo: Conrad's „The Congo Diary"... 183

and what he experienced from this point forward may well have been a prelude to Conrad's experiences, not to be recorded in his navigational journal but to become the stuff of fiction. Where Taunt saw no hostility among the natives below Bangala, now, he writes, "we met an entirely different race of people, suspicious, savage, and hostile" ("Report"). He had reached cannibal country. From this point he faced constant danger, "[t]he din of the yells, mingled with the drums and horns, was something terrific, for each village in turn had contributed to the number of yelling savages that followed us" ("Report").

In further corroboration, Comber refers to Stanley's great battle with the natives in this region in 1877, so apparently the natives had hardly calmed down in the interim (Grenfell and Comber 365). On this stretch, the natives had no firearms, only arrows and spears; so, despite being greatly outnumbered, Taunt and his company were able to keep moving. Nearing Stanley Falls, Taunt found that the natives were living in canoes because the Arabs had burned the villages on both banks – this was when the infamous Tippu Tib was manager of the Stanley Falls station. Steaming downriver was easier, as Taunt kept to the south bank of the river and did not encounter the ferocious attacks of the cannibal tribes on the north bank.

Writing just at the time that Conrad was traveling in the Congo, Reverend W. H. Bentley confirms what Taunt had found earlier:

> The whole wide country from the Mubangi to Stanley Falls for six hundred miles on both sides of the main river, and up the Mubangi as well, is given up to cannibalism. This is a bad habit, but it does not necessarily mark out the natives as being of a lower type than others who do not eat human flesh [...]. The natives of Manyanga and elsewhere in the cataract region are far more degraded and no less cruel and wicked than the wild cannibals of the Upper Congo, but they would scorn the idea of eating human flesh as much as we should do. (qtd. in Johnston, *George Grenfell and the Congo* 1: 399)

However, Taunt's report also offers a description of views of the upper Congo, including the "hundreds of beautiful islands," the dense forests and the richness of the soil near the banks; yet as we also saw in Conrad's account, the river contains "[s]trong currents, and in many cases, outlying reefs from the rocky points" ("Report"). After Bolobo, Taunt continues, "the river widens very rapidly, the islands of the Congo commence, and sand-banks and snags are met with." "At or near Bolobo the river is from 8 to 10 miles in width [...]. The river at this point has the appearance of a vast lake interspersed with many beautiful islands." "From Bolobo to Bangala," Taunt writes, "the character of the river is much the same – an immense sheet of water, full of islands, large and small, and sandbanks and snags in abundance" ("Report").

Lieutenant Taunt's extensive account is filled with much more information about government in the Congo state, including the locations of government stations, station agents, housing, availability of food, state garrisons, Protestant and Catholic missions, the hazards of navigating the Congo, and a great deal about cannibalism and slavery among the natives. Many of his comments confirm what Comber and Grenfell reported as well as observations found in Conrad's overland "The Congo Diary" manuscript. Of note is Taunt's observation that on the lower Congo the "market place, which usually covers some acres of ground, is used as the place of execution, and it is not an unusual sight to meet a skeleton hanging and bleaching in the sun on the outskirts of the market" ("Report"). His observation underscores Conrad's remarks about encountering dead bodies on his path. Another sad fact Taunt adds is that without question slavery exists "among the natives of the entire Congo Valley," but, he adds, while the men have more freedom to work, the "women are slaves in every sense of the word." "The most cruel phase of the native slavery is the right of the owner to put to death any slave at will, and this frequently exercised, especially in the case of the women" ("Report"). Toward this fact, if true, Conrad seems to have cast a blind eye both in the diary and the resultant fictions set in the Congo. But what Conrad does justly attack is the greed exhibited by all the European powers in the Congo, surely enhanced by Taunt's conclusions that "the reported wealth of the Upper Congo Valley has not been exaggerated" ("Report").

Peter Firchow's study of "Heart of Darkness" adds additional valuable information about the traffic on the upper Congo and its wealth in natural resources in the late 1880s-1890s. "River traffic on the Congo increased enormously" by 1889, Firchow writes, with "some twenty-three steam-powered vessels of various sizes on the upper reaches of the Congo [...] the largest, the *Ville de Bruxelles*, able to transport three hundred people in 'comfort'" (189). Dragutin Lerman, the resident officer in charge of the Falls when Conrad was there, wrote of the steamers carrying "'the torch of progress into the remotest parts of the Congo and its confluents'" (qtd. in Firchow 189). The reason for that was because Stanley Falls had become "the greatest trading center in Central Africa, largely because the transport of goods (especially ivory) by steamboat up and down the Congo River had rendered the old and very time-consuming caravan routes to and from Zanzibar superfluous" (Firchow 188). However, these facts are in dispute as Najder argues with Norman Sherry's claims that "the passage up the Congo was 'a routine, highly organised venture along a fairly frequented river-way linking quite numerous settlements of trading posts and factories'" (qtd. in *Joseph Conrad: A Life* 156). Sherry's account, though, conforms to Firchow's, indicating relatively heavy river traffic and extensive trading on the river by 1890. Indeed, the Congo was miles wide at places in its upper reaches, perhaps making some vessels invisible to others. Taunt's eyewitness account in 1885 highlights the great revolution in ivory transport and trade effected by the establishment of a new caravan route from Stanley Pool to Vivi, allowing more direct contact between the ivory traders and the factories below Vivi. "The bulk of the ivory on the Congo," he adds, "comes from the Upper River and its affluents. The ivory wealth of the latter has been little drawn on, and there must be considerable yet in store. The elephants are reported to be in large numbers" ("Report"). Taunt continues that between May and October of 1885, there was an enormous increase in the number of ivory caravans traveling this new caravan route.

Conrad, as we have seen, did refer to the large number of caravans on the overland route, but on the upriver journey, he's navigating. Even though steamers are carrying ivory from the Stanley Falls region to the western coast, Conrad pays no attention to that, his immediate need was to keep his steamer from running aground and sinking. We must remember, though, that the very reason for Conrad being there in the first place was to captain a steamer employed in the ivory trade.

Chapter Four:
"An Outpost of Progress": "The lightest part of the loot I carried off from Central Africa"

"It is a story of the Congo" (CL 1: 294)

Through his own account and those of his biographers, Conrad was well aware of and involved in the ivory trade on the Congo River during his brief presence there. But the depth of the impressions made on him during those few months cannot be denied and would erupt in the fictionalized outbursts of both the "lightest" and the heaviest loot he brought out in print in the last decade of the nineteenth century.

Conrad mentions in his Author's Note to *Tales of Unrest* that "An Outpost of Progress" was a sharp departure from the two Malayan stories included in this volume; he had "stepped into the very different atmosphere of 'An Outpost of Progress,'" one in which he "fancied [himself] a new man – a most exciting illusion" and yet of a piece with an evolving but consistent writerly presence, "[w]e cannot escape from ourselves" (6). Conrad's "plunder," rather than ivory, was just that which "could go into one's breast pocket when folded neatly," the story itself "true enough in its essentials." (6). Conrad's opinion of this story, written, it appears, in a white-hot heat, wavered over the course of time. Upon completion, he wrote confidently to Fisher Unwin of his "indignation at masquerading philanthropy," so many emotions boiling to the surface to spill out on the page. "Upon my word," he added, "I think it is a good story" (CL 1: 294). But shortly afterward, Conrad recoiled from Edward Garnett's negative comments, writing "The construction is bad [...]. It's very evident that the first 3 pages kill all the interest [...]. I thought I was achieving artistic simplicity!!!!!! [sic]" (qtd. in Hamner 173). In abasing himself to Garnett's editorial opinion, Conrad even went so far as to refer to the story, already sold to *Cosmopolis* for £50, as "that ghastly masterfolly" (*CL* 1: 301). Yet in just ten years, in a series for *The Grand Magazine* entitled "My Best Short Story and Why I Think So," Conrad would "confess a preference" for this story insisting that he had "aimed at a scrupulous unity of tone, and it seems to [him] that [he has] attained it there" (qtd. in Hamner 173).

One explanation for both the change of course from writing about the Malayan Archipelago to the Congo and Conrad's ambivalent feelings about the story could have been the arrival of his metal trunk containing his effects from the Congo expedition at the Ile-Grand in Brittany. He may have found therein, as Jean-Aubry suggests, his two Congo notebooks – the "The Congo Diary" and "Up-river Book" – and so, Jean-Aubry concludes, Conrad wrote "An Outpost of Progress" in five days, using as its base "a ghastly adventure which he had been told about in the heart of Africa" (220).[56] Conrad may have needed, however, no more ghastly adventures than his own to spin this tale.

"that ghastly masterfolly"

The manuscript for "An Outpost of Progress" in the Yale University Joseph Conrad Collection reveals on its title page written after completion, the number of pages (36), words (9500), the dates of composition or completed revision (17th-21st July, 1896), and the place (Ile-Grande). Having dedicated the story to Edward Garnett, Conrad must have been especially stung by Garnett's negative reaction. Simmons and Stape reveal that the typescript has been lost, so we are especially fortunate that the manuscript has survived intact. They also dispute Conrad's dating of the composition, suggesting instead that the story may have been written in a three-week period rather than in five days ("The Texts" 198). The manuscript does display what Simmons and Stape describe as a story written "in extreme fluidity" (198). Conrad's wife Jessie mentioned his "somewhat savage mood" (199) while writing and his insistence on not giving the story to her to type until he was completely done. During composition, the story was entitled "A Victim of Progress," so it appears that Conrad chose to change the title when he completed the manuscript and inscribed the title page, but why was the change made? The first manuscript page indicates a title that Conrad has decorated with double lines on *A, Victim,* and *Progress*, suggesting that he's toying with the idea of the title as he begins to compose.

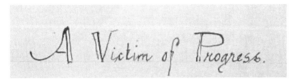

Page One. "An Outpost of Progress." GEN MSS 1207

The change in title is significant; for example, Andrea White calls attention to the irony embedded in the final title through the clash between "outpost" and "progress" (158), and Robert Hobson in his textual history of the tale suggests that Conrad may have decided on the final title as he prepared and revised the manuscript for typing, aiming for a "greater ironic impact" ("A Textual History" 151). By choosing "A Victim" as his initial title, why wouldn't Conrad employ the plural form *if* he meant the two apparent "victims" in the story, Kayerts and Carlier? One answer lies, I believe in the end of the story where the focus rests on Kayerts: "Progress was calling to Kayerts from the river" (OP 98).

However, Conrad may also have intended a broader view of the Congo itself as the victim of colonial "progress." By revising the title to "An Outpost," Conrad changes the direction of the title from an individual character or a broader view of African space to the more narrow designation of a specific place in the farthest reaches of that space. This deepens in my view, and as White argues (158), the ironic clash between a European construct of an outpost on the outer edge of colonial space and the attempt to force progress, impossible to achieve in that imaginary space or in the space of the story.

Unlike the African notebooks, "The Congo Diary" and the "Up-river Book" which Conrad wrote in pencil, the "Outpost" manuscript is handwritten in ink; in fact, Conrad adds a charming anecdote about pens in his "Author's Note" to *Tales of Unrest,* remarking on the affection he had for a common steel pen which he used as he began "The Lagoon" (5). The pen seemed to turn up everywhere until finally he put it in a bowl with other odds and ends. Somehow another old pen made its way to join the first in the wooden bowl, and since he could no longer distinguish between them or feel sentimental about both, he "threw them both out of the window into a flower bed – which strikes [him] now as a poetical grave for the remnants of one's past" (6).

In discarding the pens, though, Conrad could hardly dismiss the past which had affected him so deeply, erupting in the lava flow of the "Outpost" manuscript, written perhaps with that very same common steel pen. In drafting the manuscript, Conrad seems to have had the characters, plotting, theme, and point of view firmly in hand, and the numerous revisions in the manuscript text mostly reflect Conrad's changes in syntax and tone (Hobson, "A Textual History" 149).

From the Manuscript to *Cosmopolis*: Mapping the Textual Evolution

In the Cambridge edition of *Tales of Unrest,* Simmons and Stape carefully detail the evolution of "Outpost," listing the variants that occur between the manuscript and the two-part *Cosmopolis* printing, as well as others, but noting as well that the typescript from which the *Cosmopolis* publication and the later versions must have been set has not survived.[57] Macmillan reset the story in October 1896 to gain an American copyright (Hobson, "A Textual History" 144), and while it does help to resolve some issues about the lost typescript; it is extremely rare, was not widely distributed at the time, and is now only available to view in digitized form at the Indiana University Digital Library. This document is significant, however, for appearing to be the closest to Conrad's missing typescript. Simmons and Stape have thoroughly listed the variants among the three versions: manuscript, Macmillan pamphlet, and *Cosmopolis,* and while there are more substantive variants between the Macmillan pamphlet and the manuscript than there are between the Macmillan pamphlet and the *Cosmopolis* version, I plan to focus my remarks on changes I believe are significant between the autograph manuscript and the tale as it appears in *Cosmopolis,* adding relevant information from the Macmillan pamphlet where indicated.[58]

During its short life, *Cosmopolis* was an extraordinary international monthly, publishing first rank authors like Tolstoy, Yeats, Mallarme, and Bernard Shaw, among others. Laurence Davies labels *Cosmopolis* as "the most remarkable of the magazines that carried Conrad's early short fiction" for its international audience and for the timeliness of the appearance of Conrad's story in the midst of the magazine's debate about European imperialism in Africa ("Don't You think"18). One year before the appearance of the first part of "An Outpost of Progress," *Cosmopolis* printed Charles Dilke's searing critique of Leopold's Belgian Congo "Civilisation in Africa." Coincidentally, Dilke's piece appeared in the same month that Conrad completed "Outpost," July 1896. Dilke famously cited Charles Gordon railing against European colonizers: "'I am sick of these people; it is *they*, and not the blacks, who need civilisation'" (qtd. in Davies, "'Don't You think'" 21). As Davies observes, this outburst could as easily have come from Conrad himself (21). Indeed, the quotation seems to correspond perfectly with the narrator's assessment of his colonialist characters Kayerts and Carlier. Davies concludes his remarks on "Outpost," "It is hard to imagine a better site for this confluence of outrage, experimental art, and politics than *Cosmopolis*" (23). Yet Conrad railed against the journal whose editors decided to break the story in half and offer it in two issues, June and July 1897. Writing in November 1896 to

Ted Sanderson, Conrad stormed: "I told the unspeakable idiots that the thing halved would be as innefective [sic] as a dead scorpion. There will be a part without the sting – and the part with the sting – and being separated they will be both harmless and disgusting" (CL 1: 320). Yet the bipartite structure was allowed to stand and even continued in the early editions of *Tales of Unrest*.

Among significant changes between manuscript and *Cosmopolis* is Conrad's description of Makola's communing with the Evil Spirit about the first white station manager who had died: "Perhaps he [Makola] promised him more white men to play with" (OP MS 2). Yet the sense changes dramatically in my view in *Cosmopolis* and in the Macmillan pamphlet which preceded it: "Perhaps he [Makola] had propitiated him [the Evil Spirit] by a promise of more white men to play with, by and by" (OP, Macmillan 61; OP, *Cosmopolis* 18: 610). "Promised" and "propitiated by" carry markedly different weights, so Conrad must have made the change himself in the typescript since the change first appears in the Macmillan pamphlet. If Makola only *promised* his Evil Spirit more white men to play with, the implication is quite muted compared to *propitiating* the Evil Spirit – this suggests appeasement or gaining favor through the promise of new white men as playthings, a particularly sinister implication of propitiation by human sacrifice – and a semantic change that comports with the mention of Father Gobila offering human sacrifice later in the story. The change provides early evidence of Conrad fine-tuning syntax to build the ironic structure which contains the tale and carries over into the first American and British editions of *Tales of Unrest* in 1898.

A lengthy omission from the *Cosmopolis* version (and the Macmillan pamphlet) which appears in the manuscript expands the narrator's reflections on the individual and the crowd:

> The individuals remain steady because of the equilibrium of the mass, and they feel and are safe just because of their individual insignificance which they understand instinctively cannot affect the

Chapter Four: "An Outpost of Progress": "The lightest part of the loot..." 193

general order of things and the present course of their own fate. The average individual can bear solitude easily enough, could live an hermit's life in a desert without losing his moral balance, for solitude by itself is only a negation; its whispers as such can be disbelieved; and in undisturbed memory there is always a refuge from the torments of the imagination. (OP MS 4-5)[59]

Had Conrad decided he'd written enough on the subject and would risk losing his audience if he delved too much into the psychology of the individual and the crowd?[60] Or had he concluded that there could be some misunderstanding or contradiction in construing the individual immersed in the mass while also capable of bearing solitude; a negation of the crowd, while at the same time seeking refuge in undisturbed memory? The passage is dense indeed, but Conrad will mitigate the confusion and develop the idea of negation/affirmation in contact with savagery as he continues to work through these ideas in the manuscript.

Another deletion which Conrad apparently made in the manuscript is: "for the mystery of the tropical life is too great to be solved at a glance" (OP MS 8). Hobson offers an explanation that Conrad may not have wanted to leave any possibility that the mystery could be solved at all ("Critical Edition" 57), but my view is that the clause is just too weak to convey Conrad's sense of the utter inexpressibility of the mystery of the tropics, so rather than leave in this limp description, he deleted it.

A further indication of Conrad's evolving irony, as Hobson points out, is found in the change from "They had really a strong affection for one another" (OP MS 8) to the much more cleverly nuanced "And *in time* they came to feel *something resembling* affection for one another" (OP, *Cosmopolis* 18: 614). The first straightforward expression of affection between the two characters in the manuscript is sharply modulated by "in time," "came to feel," "something," and "resembling," the swelling syntax ironically indicating the opposite, no real affection at all.

In a chilling foreshadowing of Kurtz's infamous declaration "Exterminate all the brutes!" the narrator conveys Carlier's rage at the natives in the manuscript: "He wanted to exterminate all the niggers" (OP MS 26). In *Cosmopolis* Conrad shifts this to: "but Carlier had a fit of rage over it, and talked about the necessity of exterminating all the niggers before the country could be habitable" (OP, *Cosmopolis* 19: 8). By adding "necessity," Conrad inscribes a sense of fate determining what must happen to make *white* habitation of the African continent possible while also pointing to what may have been the truest and most insidious of European colonialism's aims: eliminating the native population to remove any barriers to the rape of Africa's riches.

Several changes between the manuscript and Part I in *Cosmopolis* that Hobson doesn't note include: the description of the blacks who visit the station, "They were riddles, glossy black..." (OP MS 8), while in *Cosmopolis,* the natives are "naked, glossy black" (OP, *Cosmopolis* 18: 614). Conrad seems to shift the emphasis from the mystery (implied by "riddles") of the natives to their appearance, perhaps feeling that "naked" comports more closely with the rest of the sentence detailing physical description: "ornamented with snowy shells and glistening brass wire, perfect of limb" (614). In the manuscript, Conrad continues the description with "uncouth in speech, moving in a stately manner and sending quick wild glances out of their startled, ever moving eyes" (OP MS 8). But this changes in *Cosmopolis* to: "They made an uncouth babbling noise when they spoke, moved in a stately manner, and sent quick, wild glances out of their startled, never-resting eyes" (OP, *Cosmopolis* 18: 614). While the description of the natives' "stately manner" remains, it becomes fraught with the contradiction of their speech as "uncouth babbling noise," accentuating savagery by removing "speech" and replacing it with unintelligible noise.

A Tale of Three Henrys

A very significant substitution in the story in the first editions of *Tales of Unrest* (1898) occurs in the name change: "James" Price becomes "Henry" Price. Hobson reflects on the puzzling nature of the change, suggesting that Conrad

Chapter Four: "An Outpost of Progress": "The lightest part of the loot... 195

may have felt he'd already used the name "Jim" too much ("A Critical Edition" 68). But Hobson doesn't acknowledge the addition of an epigraph to the collection from Shakespeare's *Henry IV, Part 2*: "Be it thy course to busy giddy minds/With foreign quarrels" (*2H4* 4.3.342-43). This epigraph appears for the first time in the 1898 editions of *Tales of Unrest*. Set during a period of political rebellion, *Henry IV, Part 2* contrasts the nobility with low-life commoners who serve to frame the emergence of a king. Despite the appearance of the unforgettable Falstaff, the play is dark, a meditation on the troubled relationship between fathers and sons and the challenge of ruling during civil strife. Conrad's quotation is chosen from the scene where a dying Henry IV counsels his son unwisely, instructing him to distract his subjects with foreign wars to prevent their engaging in domestic strife. Conrad cautions his audience thereby about ignoring the troubles at home while focusing on imperialism in a foreign land. But we should remember that the epigraph pertains to all five stories and so reflects some aspect of each.[61]

In referencing the scene between the two Henrys as cautionary for his tale, Conrad implants a shift in identity for the dominant native character, the sole survivor of the three main inhabitants and the true "ruler" of the station. Henry Price/Makola has adopted an identity in the language of the colonizer but has been given another in the language of the colonized, so the imposition of a name chosen and a name imposed from without destabilizes the very notion of identity, just as language and meaning are destabilized throughout the tale. The Europeanized African "savage" looks back at empire and seems to say: "Go home and mind your own business!" – a nose-thumbing to Empire and an ironic reversal of Henry IV's advice to focus kingship on fomenting rebellion in far-flung colonies.

The irony of the surname Price should cause no surprise within the context of Conrad's indictment of "progress" and "civilization" understood rather as European greed. But there may be another irony lurking in the choice of the name Henry:

a nod toward the irrepressible Henry Morton Stanley, always, in my view, a specter in the background of Conrad's Africa, whose heroic reputation as the consummate African explorer, as we have seen, had been severely tarnished once more information emerged about the debacle of the Emin Pasha expedition 1887-1889. Of course there were certainly glimmerings of trouble with Stanley's reputation as early as 1872.

In 1897, Stanley's friend E. J. Glave published extracts from his diaries in several issues of *The Century Magazine* detailing the horrors of Leopold's Congo, including the chilling information that "twenty-one heads were brought to the falls, and have been used by Captain Rom as a decoration round a flower bed in front of his house!" ("Cruelty in the Congo" 76). To his credit, Stanley was incensed by this news and went to Belgium to suggest that the king investigate the atrocities. Yet despite his revulsion at the news coming out of the Congo, Stanley traveled to the Congo Exhibition in Tervuren in the same month that Glave published "Cruelty in the Congo," September 1897. It was for this exhibition that Leopold had commissioned the transport of 267 African men and women to be brought as living exhibits – like animals in a zoo – the organizers of the exhibition even posted a sign: "Do not feed the blacks" (Stanard 38). And Stanley saw it all as he toured incognito (Jeal 449).

Tim Jeal claims but does not provide evidence that Conrad read Glave's articles in *The Century*, especially the anecdote about Captain Rom, and used the image in "Heart of Darkness" (452). It would have been difficult, however, for Conrad to avoid reading about Congolese atrocities as there was so much of it reported in the British press, especially *The Times*, and it is likely that he did read Sidney Hinde's *The Fall of the Congo Arabs* (1897).[62] Stanley, therefore, may well have been in his thoughts as he created the wily, ivory-dealing and slave-trading Henry Price/Makola and the two Belgian bungling idiots Kayerts and Carlier who serve as his incompetent foils.[63] What an ironic tour de force if Conrad meant Henry Price to be Stanley's dark double!

Chapter Four: "An Outpost of Progress": "The lightest part of the loot... 197

Place Mappings: 8 Degrees North and 8.8 Degrees South of the Equator

From the first page of the tale, we the readers know that we are in Africa. Reinforcing that fact is the narrator's identification of the "third man on the staff" as "a Sierra Leone nigger" (OP MS 1; OP 77), and his wife as "a negress from Loanda." As Robert Hampson points out, the origins of this odd couple lie on the African coast, Sierra Leone to the north of the Congo River and Loanda (Luanda) in Angola in the south ("'An Outpost'" 219). These two locations are pivotal for centering between them the story's outpost deep in the interior where traders from the coast (Loanda), who can communicate with Mrs. Price in their common language, unmask the real nature of the slave trade hidden away in the African heart. Slave trade in the Portuguese colony Angola impacted nearly "all societies across the breadth of central Africa" (Ball 6). The primary destination for slaves exported from Angola was Brazil, where the volume of exportation grew until 1836 when Portugal prohibited the export of slaves across the Atlantic; but in reality, an illegal and clandestine slave trade clearly continued late into the nineteenth century, a trade which kept slaves in Africa working on African rather than Brazilian plantations.

When Stanley arrived in Loanda in 1877 at the end of the grueling trek of the Anglo-American expedition, he found the Portuguese exceedingly hospitable.

Stanley met with Portuguese explorers, Serpa Pinto, Brito Capello, and Roberto Ivens, pictured in the studio photograph below and wrote gratefully of the kindness of the Angolan government *(Through the Dark Continent* 2: 472). In fact, in the illustration, Stanley is showing the Portuguese explorers a map of the course of the Congo River to its mouth which he had just finished tracing. Perhaps to their chagrin, he had already accomplished what they initially set out to do; but Stanley only mentions the new explorations on which Pinto, Ivens, and Capello had determined to embark.

Henry M. Stanley describing his travels to the Portuguese Expedition (Ivens, Capello, Serpa Pinto) at Loanda. Stanley Archives, Coll. King Baudouin Foundation, entrusted to the AfricaMuseum, Brussels, Belgium

Stanley makes no mention of slavery in the Portuguese colony in *Through the Dark Continent*, but in 1878 he wrote a letter to the Secretary of the American Anti-Slavery Society on behalf of the Portuguese provinces to declare that while slavery "was not quite extinguished on the West Coast of Africa it has been suppressed so far that nothing but the embers of it remains" (*Stanley's First Opinions* 4). Such an opinion was naïve and premature; Stanley even argued that it is the "Portuguese African […] not the Portuguese European" involved in what remains of the slave trade (6). Yet later in his expedition to found the Congo Free State, Stanley's views had somewhat changed, and he not only expressed loathing for Portuguese traders, he also recognized that the Portuguese colony continued to engage in covert slave trading (Jeal 240, 271).

Chapter Four: "An Outpost of Progress": "The lightest part of the loot... 199

Despite the abolition of slavery in the Portuguese empire in 1875, labor in Portuguese Angola was, in form if not name, slavery (Clarence-Smith 216). Under the term "contract" labor, slavery persisted, and Stanley had been right early on about one fact – Africans were "the major slave-traders in the interior of the [Portuguese] colony" (Clarence-Smith 218). Clarence-Smith writes that the Ovimbundu tribe ranged far into "British, Belgian and German territory in their search for 'black gold'" in concert with Cokwe and Ovambo trading partners to the turn of the century (218). Mariana Candido insists that in Luanda (Loanda), among other African urban centers, slavery expanded during the nineteenth century (70). With the abolition of slave exports in the African Portuguese empire in 1836, "the use of local enslaved people expanded" (71).

In its approach to slavery, Sierra Leone provides a contrast to Loanda but masks an underlying ideology of white racial superiority. Although Conrad wrote Karol Zagórski from Freetown, Sierra Leone on May 22, 1890, he made no mention of whether he disembarked, and if he did, what he saw there, commenting instead on the dangers of fever and dysentery (*CL* 1: 51-53). While considered unhealthy for whites, Sierra Leone was established as a colony to combat slavery and offer former slaves a community where they could be free (Hampson, "'An Outpost'" 222). British warships even patrolled the coast off Sierra Leone to intercept ships illegally exporting slaves (223). On the west coast of Africa, some natives became proficient in Portuguese, English, and French, which made them useful to whites, and Hampson adds that with a culture of trade and enterprise, a "black bourgeoisie" emerged: children were sent to Britain to be educated, resulting in the development of a professional class (222). In the second half of the nineteenth century, Hampson, citing Christopher Fyfe, points to a "'far-ranging diaspora'" throughout Africa from Sierra Leone (223), revealing a trend in which Henry Price participated.

Writing in 1890 from the Underhill Station, Reverend J. Lawson Forfeitt acknowledged that "a great number of

English-speaking coloured Christians, many of whom belong to the Sierra Leone mission churches" are employed by the Congo Railway (7). "[O]ur Sierra Leone friends," Forfeitt continues, "are not afraid to let their light shine in the midst of much darkness and saddening superstition and sin" (7).

Fyfe expands on the history of Sierra Leone, populated by escaped American plantation slaves among others, and its emergence as an important trading center and a "province of Freedom" (174). White rule, however, persisted, as Fyfe points out, so policy decisions for the colony were made in London and executed by white officials in Sierra Leone (177). The social assumption that whites rule and blacks obey, widespread in Europe, prevailed in the late eighteenth century as black settlers recruited from Nova Scotia were duped and forced to pay for land that they had been promised would be free of rent (177).

White officers, however, suffered high mortality rates, giving Sierra Leone the label of the "White Man's Grave" (176). Stanley may have been first to give this name to Sierra Leone, writing in *The Congo and the Founding of Its Free State*: "Banana Point (six degrees below the Equator) only five feet above the brackish water of its creek, is proved to be much healthier than Sierra Leone, over eight degrees north, which has been called the 'white man's grave'" (2: 320). The echoes with the white man's grave in Conrad's tale are unmistakable, as is the coincidence that while writing Karol Zagórski from Freetown, Conrad describes his uneasiness about the dangers to health in the Congo: "What makes me rather uneasy is the information that 60 per cent of our Company's employees return to Europe before they have completed even six months' service. Fever and dysentery!" (CL 1: 52). Perhaps by choosing Sierra Leone as Henry Price's place of origin Conrad meant to parallel the "outpost" as another white man's grave.

Once in Sierra Leone, Africans known as "recaptives," liberated from slave ships, learned English to communicate and adapted to Christianity through the efforts of missionaries already there, often adopting European names taken from missionaries, officers, or prominent settlers (Fyfe 181-82). Fyfe

Chapter Four: "An Outpost of Progress": "The lightest part of the loot..." 201

points, however, to the ugly underbelly of the abolition of the slave trade in the area which caused, in the early history of freed slave colonies, the rise of the new imperialism (199). Instead of helping, Fyfe concludes, freed slave colonies "provided a model for the future extension of European sovereignty and softened West Africa for the coming European partition" (199).

Place Mappings: The Kassai

One day after he noted completion of the manuscript "An Outpost of Progress," July 21, 1896, Conrad wrote Fisher Unwin that he would send the story to Edward Garnett to place in *Cosmopolis* (*CL* 1: 293-94). The letter is both compact and incredibly dense; Conrad announced to Unwin "It is a story of Congo [...]. The exact locality is not mentioned" (294). But Conrad is careful to let Unwin know the exact location – "the life in a lonely station on the Kassai" (294). Perhaps Conrad chose this exact location as the result of lingering bitterness over having been denied the opportunity to participate in an expedition to the Kassai in September 1890 (58). Conrad had been led to believe that he was to command the steamboat for Alexandre Delcommune's expedition to Katanga on the Kassai, but that hope was blocked by Camille Delcommune, Alexandre's brother (Karl 299). What utter irony that the real-life Carlier would be chosen instead of Conrad to command the *Florida* on the expedition – so, I imagine, Conrad chose a lonely outpost on the Kassai for the fictional Carlier to die.

While he didn't travel up the Kassai, Conrad did pass its mouth, noted in his "Up-river Book," possibly on the third day, August 5th. He lists passing the entrance to the Kassai, bearing N 1/2 E about noon as he passed Pt XX, commenting "Entrance to Kassai rather broad. On Sth side a bright beach with a spreading dead tree above it mark the mouth" (UB MS). From there, Conrad records that the steamer docked at the Catholic mission, perhaps for a wooding stop – they were there for about an hour and a half.

In May 1882, Stanley did travel upriver against the current on the Kassai, entering what he named the Kwa at its mouth, and offering a lengthy description of the appearance of the river tributary as it enters the Congo. The Kwa, Stanley remarked, is "much more crooked than the Great River," requiring a series of traverses and some delay, but on the next day, he reached an old village of Gobila's (*The Congo* 1: 413). Stanley, though, instead of traveling along the Kassai after it joins the Kwa to debouch in the Congo, followed an upper tributary, the Mfini River, to discover Lake Leopold II.

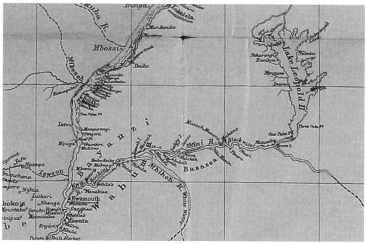
Detail from Stanley's *A Map of the Congo Basin*

Stanley's map attached to the first volume of *The Congo and the Founding of Its Free State* does not include the name of the River Kassai (he titles it first the Kwa, then the Bochini, followed by the Mbiheh River and then the White Water) because he didn't travel down that tributary but rather to the north; but by the time he draws the outlines of the map of his route on the Emin Pasha Expedition, Stanley has more information and detail, especially from the German explorer Wissmann, to include in his map about the length and trajectory of the Kassai River.

Chapter Four: "An Outpost of Progress": "The lightest part of the loot... 203

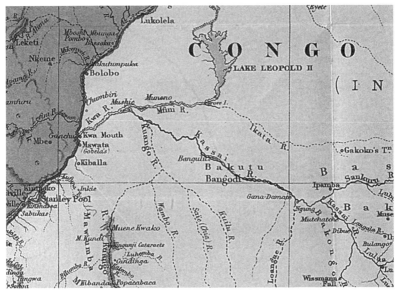

Detail from *A Map of the Route of the Emin Pasha Relief Expedition through Africa*

More details about the Kassai appear in other travel accounts; Henry Wack, for example, notes that the Kassai is the largest of the southern affluents of the Congo River, its exact course only recently (Wack was writing in 1905) discovered (50). The Kassai rises from Portuguese territory to the southwest of the Congo Free State and travels north and finally northwest to join the Congo. The largest rivers, including the Kassai, Wack reports, "are all patrolled by government steamers (55). By 1883, Wack continues, the Upper Kassai, so important for prosperity of the Congo region, was "brought under the influence of Belgian regeneration" (74). Wack trumpets the achievements of the Belgians before the Berlin Conference in 1885, writing that in

> five years discoveries of great value had been made in Darkest Africa, hundreds of tribes had been peacefully visited, over five hundred treaties of suzerainty had been made with the ruling chiefs, forty

stations had been erected [...] and five steamers on the Upper Congo were regularly communicating the affairs of a Government which now effectively controlled all the territory between the East Coast and Stanley Falls, between Bangala and Luluabourg. (74)

But the cultural insensitivity gets worse. Wack waxes eloquent about the progress in the Congo Free State:

> Thirty years ago what is now the Congo Free State was a wild tangle of luxuriant tropical growth through which hordes of black savages roamed, fought, and practised their unspeakable barbarities, living almost entirely on the spontaneous products of Nature. The *white magician* has waved his wand and the scene is transformed. (268, emphasis added)

Between Stanley's reports on the "Kwa" in 1883 and his more detailed map of the affluents of the Congo, including the Kassai, George Grenfell made exploring trips on the Congo River and the Kassai, from 1884-1886. At this time, the interior of the Congo basin east of the Congo River had not yet been extensively explored, so map knowledge as well as firsthand on-the-ground knowledge remained fluid through the middle of the 1880s. The names of rivers and tributaries indicate successive shifts as explorers penetrated more deeply into the interior, tracing the courses of rivers, trying to identify them through native names, but often naming themselves. George Grenfell, on his intrepid steamer *Peace* traveled numerous tributaries, writing a lengthy description of these travels to the Royal Geographical Society in 1886, "Exploration of the Tributaries of the Congo." Grenfell made part of this journey with the German explorer Hermann von Wissmann, whose *My Second Journey through Equatorial Africa* (in 1886-1887) offers detailed information of the Kassai (he names it Cassai) and the Luebo Station founded several hundred miles upstream from where the Kassai joins the Congo River. In a prime example of how knowledge about this major tributary evolved, Wissmann wrote: "I take this opportunity to mention that several cartographers [...] have given this

Chapter Four: "An Outpost of Progress": "The lightest part of the loot... 205

river the name of 'Sankurru,' whilst I, who have explored it in its full length, have called it 'Cassai'" (4-5). The reason for settling on this instead of the many other names the river had been called, Wissmann claimed, was to solidify the name the river was called through its longest stretch, to acknowledge it as the "part of the river system that had the greatest mass of water" (5), and to avoid confusion by not naming it "Nsaire," a native name also given to the Congo.

Wissmann would explore the "Cassai" on Grenfell's *Peace*, writing: "We could almost fancy we were transplanted into an antediluvian period. Fearless, as if man, the most dangerous beast of prey, were unknown in these regions, the huge pachydermata were moving about [...] marching along the river-side singly and in herds" (14).

Grenfell, on his earlier journey up the "Kasai" (another variant spelling of the name) in 1885, noted that he "journeyed upon the waters of that important tributary without knowing it" ("Exploration of the Tributaries" 627), another indication of how little was known of this interior at the time. In 1886, though, Grenfell, together with Wissmann, could identify where he was, describing the narrow, deep cut channel where the Kasai cuts into the Congo, 100 miles northeast of Leopoldville. The first 20 miles, he adds, are treacherous, filled with rocks that create reefs which the force of the river has not completely cut through. The Kassai enters the Congo River in a strong current, running 7-8 miles per hour, but after that, the river widens out to allow for smoother steaming. This river, Grenfell insists, is

> destined to play a most important part in the future commercial welfare of the Congo State. In fact, from what I have seen, I judge that this great affluent will be the first to show any "returns," as it furnishes a highway to countries where an extensive trade already exists. ("Exploration of the Tributaries" 629)

At the end of 1885, a new trading station, Luebo, was established at the confluence of the Luebo and Lulua Rivers, which once joined, feed into the Kassai to the north. The station, founded by Ludwig Wolf and Lieutenant Bateman, an

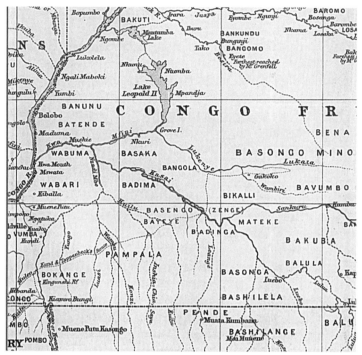

Detail from *Preliminary Map and Plans of the Congo and Its Tributaries*

Englishman employed by the Congo State, lies several hundred miles inland from the mouth of the Congo and may have served as one model for Conrad's outpost. Bateman, Jan Vansina writes, "promptly declared that he was taking possession of the whole region for the new Congo State, although no one ever informed the Kuba (the local tribe) of this" (20). What's interesting is that the location of this station formed a junction between various ethnic groups who provided assistance in the station's construction (Martens 70). Wissmann adds details about the appearance of the station in 1886:

> Four structures built of palisades, neatly lined with clay, and with far-over-hanging grass-covered roofs, filled up the end of the open space. Towards the land they were protected from any attack by a wall of

Chapter Four: "An Outpost of Progress": "The lightest part of the loot... 207

palisades leading from the Luebo to the Lulua. About 100 metres of ground was bare, with a dark wall of primæval forest towering behind. (59-60)

LUEBO STATION

Hermann von Wissmann. *My Second Journey through Equatorial Africa*

In 1886, the Congo State outsourced the post to the American Sanford Exploring Expedition, demoting it from a government station to a mere trading station. Luebo was then ceded to the *Société Anonyme Belge* with one lone agent year after year trading in rubber and ivory (Vansina 21). "Every single one of these traders," Vansina writes, "sought to establish profitable trade relations with the masters of most of the ivory, the successive Kuba kings, but to no avail" (21). A new state of affairs arose from 1891 onward. A permanent mission station was established by the Presbyterians, a proliferation of trading posts ensued, and as Luebo remained an area of free trade, it became the source of some of the best rubber in Africa (23).

In 1898, Alice Seeley Harris arrived along with her Baptist missionary husband to take residence in the Congo Balolo mission upriver from the Kassai on the Lulanga tributary. Harris' documentary photographs would gain world renown as evidence of Leopold's Congo atrocities after the turn of the century – especially the maiming of natives who failed to gather their quota of rubber in the rubber-rich region near Luebo. Harris' photographs are additionally interesting for charting the development of the stations and the missions nearby as they became more entwined in trade on the river. Her photograph below demonstrates the early stages in building a trading factory on the Kassai.

Clearing the Forest to Erect a Trading Factory on the Kasai. With kind permission of the family of Alice Seeley Harris

Additional information about the layout of trading stations appears in Frank Vincent's *Actual Africa* (1895). Vincent offers a textual map of the layout of the Luebo post:

> A large space of ground has been cleared for the station at Luebo, and has been neatly laid out with paths and rows of palm trees. In one part is an attempt at a flower-garden. There are several large buildings made of wattles and mud and roofed with grass – some of these are used for residence, and some for the storage of rubber and

Chapter Four: "An Outpost of Progress": "The lightest part of the loot... 209

various goods used in barter. The native huts are apart at one side, and separated from the European houses by a high fence, covered with the vines and fruit of the passion-flower [...]. A considerable amount of work has been done at this station. (450)

Space Mapping and Transculturation: The Imaginary Outpost and Its Fetish

Conrad, of course, never saw the Luebo station or any other station on the Kassai, for that matter, but his textual mapping of his outpost bears some resemblance to the layout of the buildings and space described by other explorers like Wissmann and Vincent. In "An Outpost of Progress," Conrad describes a clay storehouse with the grass roof containing trading goods, Makola's "low shed-like dwelling" to the side, and the large building for the white agents' residence; and most reminiscent of Wissmann's "dark wall of primeval forest," this outpost is flanked by "the impenetrable bush that seemed to cut off the station from the rest of the world" (OP 77-78). But the most symbolic residence is the one situated away from the residences of the living – the grave of the first chief of the station.[64] His dwelling suggests and symbolizes the "burial" of Kayerts and Carlier in an outpost approximately three hundred miles away from the nearest station. The grave also suggests and symbolizes stasis as opposed to "progress," further underscoring the irony of Conrad's title. The Director's comment as he steams away reinforces the static "planting" of the "imbeciles": "I bet nothing will be done" (78). The stasis of inactivity accelerates in the months that follow: "Together they did nothing – absolutely nothing – and enjoyed the sense of idleness for which they were paid" (81). While all around them there is motion they are "unable to see," the jungle, "throbbing with life," the river which "seemed to come from nowhere and flow nowhither," and "canoes, and men with spears in their hands would suddenly crowd the yard of the station" (81).

The warriors have come to trade, and the center of this outpost, which marks it as a trading post is the "fetish." "Take that herd over to the fetish (the storehouse was in every station called the fetish perhaps because of the spirit of civilization it contained)," Carlier instructed Makola, "and give them up some of the rubbish you keep there. I'd rather see it full of bone than full of rags" (82). Conrad, through his narrator as mouthpiece, acknowledges a collapse in the distance between a Europeanized conception of African *nkisi* and its identification with the European commodity.[65] Thus Conrad's later dismissal of displays of "variegated rubbish" like those in the Great Exhibition of 1851 in "Autocracy and War" resonates with his image of the Congolese storehouse as the container for the commodity transcendent in "An Outpost of Progress."

Makola is the middleman, the "linguist," the term Kajsa Friedman uses to denote middlemen in the Congo who knew multiple languages and "handled the contacts with the African population, or more correctly, the suppliers of African export products" (*Catastrophe and Creation* 51). Friedman's discussion of European "factories" – the commercial trading stations located along the Congo River and its tributaries – is invaluable for expanding a reading of Conrad's specific use of this term. Friedman writes, "The storehouse where the European exchange goods were kept, was sometimes called *nkisi* [fetish] [...] by the Africans, to the derisive joy of the Whites" (55). As a container for these exchange goods, the storehouse became viewed as a container for the life-force, just as the *nkisi* operated as a container for a materialized life-force and source of power. In this space of transculturation, Friedman notes the origin of "fetish" as the Portuguese word "feitiço," the "manufactured object" (133).

Friedman's observations about the storehouse as a "fetish" are borne out in a source published in 1911 by Reverend John Weeks entitled *Congo Life and Folklore*. Beginning in 1882, Weeks spent thirty years in the Congo, and in the notes to Part I, "Life on the Congo as Described by a Brass Rod," Weeks remarks:

> The early traders on the Congo placed in their large stores a fetish to deter the natives from robbing them. It was generally a large, gaudily-

Chapter Four: "An Outpost of Progress": "The lightest part of the loot... 211

coloured, hideous image put on the top shelf opposite the door, from which position it was supposed to dominate and guard the contents of the whole building. Many traders called their store "the fetish" because of the presence of this ugly figure in it. (343-44)

This description clearly marks transculturation as the main feature of the European storehouse, and Conrad's narrator's depiction of European trade goods as the "spirit of civilization" underscores both the unmistakable irony and the significance of such cultural mingling – especially if Conrad was aware of the practice of installing an *nkisi* in storehouses to protect European "rubbish." To underscore this notion is the fact that, as William Pietz contends, "the fetish, as an idea and a problem, and as a novel object not proper to any prior discrete society, originated in the cross-cultural spaces of the coast of West Africa during the sixteenth and seventeenth centuries" ("The Problem of the Fetish, I" 5).

Culture in Crisis: The Conflicted Nature of the Fetish

The history of the *fetish/nkisi* in the Congo reveals the ugly reality of a culture in crisis and a slippage in meaning as fetishism becomes "an increasingly indeterminate catch-all term" (Böhme 5). For example, Hartmut Böhme questions if Christian "cult images" brought with Portuguese explorers as early at the fifteenth century could be one source for African sculpture fetishes (138). The word *fetish*, Böhme continues, does not exist before the beginning of Portuguese colonial history (140), and fetishism as a concept comes into play when Charles de Brosses coined the term in 1757 (Pietz, "Fetishism and Materialism" 131). Zdenka Volavkova cites Olfred Dapper, who, writing in 1676, remarked that "the people in the Kongo, had 'two arrows in their bows,' Catholic and Pagan ones, mixing the objects of both rituals" (55). Europeans debated about the nature of the fetish as "worship of terrestrial, material objects" (Pietz, "Fetishism and Materialism" 131), and therefore the lowest form of religion; however, this notion ignores the fact that for the African the fetish was not an "idol" to worship but rather a source of power to be controlled. While the fetish is always a material object, it is also more than that; it incorporates "something 'other' than itself into itself: meaning, symbols, forces, energies, power, spirits, ghosts, gods, etc." (Böhme 18). Samuel Taylor Coleridge, although misconstruing the nature of the fetish as an idol, makes an insightful observation about the very materialism of the fetish object, further suggesting its connection to trade and capitalism: "From the fetisch of the imbruted African to the soul-debasing errors of the proud fact-hunting materialist we may trace the various ceremonials of the same idolatry" (qtd. in Pietz, "Fetishism and Materialism" 131).

At the turn of the nineteenth century, Friedman argues, the changing nature of fetishism in African culture represented a society in "dissolution and crisis" (*Catastrophe and Creation* 140). "The magically inclined fetishism of the lower Congo," Friedman continues, "is not a primitive phenomenon in a primitive society, but, on the contrary, a crisis phenomenon in *a society that had been crushed and that lived under the acute threat of extinction*" (140, emphasis added). Thus the *fetish/nkisi* may have represented the only means by which Africans felt they could control their fate – Friedman cites Buana's definition of *nkisi* as:

> Nkisi is usually translated with *fetish*. But this is not quite correct. The word nkisi includes in fact the idea of medicine, the therapeutic method which the nganga [Kikongo for spiritual healer] uses, magic and religion. Nkisi is the abode for a protecting ancestor. It is also the place where the supernatural power is concentrated. Nkisi is the object through which one enters into contact with this power. (qtd. in Friedman 133)

While Conrad's tale does not include a fetish object, identifying instead the European rubbish in the storehouse with the concept, I want to return briefly to the discussion of *minkisi* I initiated in the first chapter – the reference to a nail fetish from Boma displayed in *The Stanley and African Exhibition*. Nail fetishes or *minkisi* were particularly powerful

Chapter Four: "An Outpost of Progress": "The lightest part of the loot... 213

objects in African culture due to their terrifying and threatening aspect – missionaries and explorers sought to eliminate them as a result. In *The Congo and the Founding of Its Free State*, Stanley acknowledges the power of the African *nkisi*, describing the "great gods of Banza Uvana" and includes an illustration which suggests the worship of nail fetishes. Stanley describes his encounter with a nail fetish:

> In this village there is a double-headed wooden bust, with its crown adorned (?) with old iron scraps and bits of mirror glass, and two wooden idols, about 4 feet high, ferocious in appearance, placed under a small shed, as a chapel, I suppose. These are the great gods of Banza Uvana. (*The Congo* 1: 199)

Stanley's image displays the transculturation that nail fetishes represent; as I noted in the discussion of the *nkisi* from Boma in Chapter One, these objects incorporated iron nails, mirrors, knives, even bits of cloth, some of which could not have existed before the arrival of Europeans who brought trade items to Africa's shores. Stanley brought back *minkisi*, exhibiting one in *The Stanley and African Exhibition,* nor was he alone in doing so.

Fetish Idols

As a foreign phenomenon, the factory/storehouse represented an "enclave" of civilization for white traders in a "strange and exotic Africa," while for Africans, the factory established a hierarchy which aligned whites and their trade goods with the supernatural, above Africans, and therefore closer to the highest powers (Friedman, *Catastrophe and Culture* 54, 55). European trade goods, Friedman argues, "constituted or represented the life-force and were placed in a house that came to act as a container for this force. Like an ordinary 'fetish'" (55). William Pietz reinforces his claim about the transcultural nature of the fetish first argued in his initial essay on "The Problem of the Fetish" while adding in his second essay that a commercial space was needed to establish contact between radically different cultures: "The idea of the fetish originated in a mercantile intercultural space created by the ongoing trade relations between cultures so radically different as to be mutually incomprehensible" ("The Problem of the Fetish, II" 24).

The African Perspective: Culture Clash and Makola

Conrad's omniscient narrator's perspective on the clash of cultures in "An Outpost of Progress" suggests an African backlash at the European effort to force its version of civilization in the remote interior of the continent, exhibited by the attempt to overcome the dominant invading culture through the power of the fetish. Makola/Henry Price embodies the cross of two cultures, performing a continual slippage between the two. His chosen name, or shall I say, the name he "maintained" was his, "Henry Price," points to his own identification with a Europeanized version of civilization consonant with the coastal culture of Sierra Leone from which he came.[66] However, the "natives down the river" (OP 77) had given him the name of Makola with no reason assigned to that choice, but it stuck to him. Despite Makola's wish to be known as Henry Price, neither the narrator nor Carlier and Kayerts call him anything but Makola throughout the narrative. This may be meant to underscore a tenuous African identity while that identity is continuously challenged. And Makola speaks both English and French, but he does so with a "warbling accent" (77), suggestive of the melody of bird song as Makola adapts the sound of those European languages to his own African linguistic rhythms. While apparently proficient in two European languages, Makola seems unable to communicate with the armed ivory traders in their Loandan dialect later in the tale, or perhaps he understands too well their meaning.

We never "see" Makola, that is to say, the narrator never offers a physical description, but has much to say about his character, abilities, opinions, and beliefs. On the one hand, he writes "a beautiful hand" and understands "book-keeping," but these seemingly civilized qualities are immediately undercut by the narrator's addition "and cherished in his innermost heart the worship of evil spirits" (77). In fact, Makola's knowledge of accounting is further undercut by the narrator's observation that he "*pretended* to keep a correct account of beads, cotton cloths, red kerchiefs, brass wire, and other trade goods" (77, emphasis added) – the holy trinity of European trade goods in the Congo is specifically referred to here by name. Are we being told that Makola's "civilization" is nothing but a veneer or that these trade goods as examples of civilization are not worth keeping an accurate account of? Makola, in the narrator's view, appears "taciturn and impenetrable" (OP 77) yet the fact he despises the two white men is not impenetrable to the reader.

Makola's indifference extends to an "I told you so" attitude toward the death of the first station chief, and what would he have told the white artist – that white men in Africa were only meant for a "White Man's grave"? For with the passing of the artist/station chief, Makola can continue to keep his account books while dwelling alone with "the Evil Spirit that rules the lands under the equator," perhaps even "propitiat[ing]" his "god" with more white men to play with in the future (78). Again, his veneer of civilization wears thin.

His civilized veneer also thins as his linguistic competence shifts. Makola is capable of correct syntax in quoted English speech yet occasionally slips into a staccato "pidgin" English. Months pass before the narrator records Makola's first quoted speech at the appearance of the African ivory traders from the coast. When asked what "lingo" the men speak, Makola begins with the grammatically correct, "'I don't know'" and ends with "'They are perhaps bad men'" (85). And even though he denies it, Makola does seem to understand the leader while at the same time seeming to forget "French – seemed to have forgotten how to speak altogether" (86). So presumably Makola speaks to Kayerts and Carlier in French yet his quoted speech in the text is English. Once the capture of the station workers is complete, Makola slips into the terse "'Some villages burn'" (87). Then even more pointedly in pidgin: "'Do you like get a little more ivory?'" (87). This is followed by several far more grammatically correct sentences. Makola's articulation continues to shift from competence to pidgin, for example – "'Better get a fine lot of ivory – then he say nothing'" – an example of simple present tense for what would be better spoken future tense with a helping verb *will* (88). Once Kayerts has shot Carlier, Makola's articulation clearly indicates linguistic competence as his manner demonstrates control: "'Yes, I saw,' said Makola. 'There is only one revolver. Where's his?'.... 'I will go and look for it,' said the other [Makola] gently" (96). Makola's decision, once he knows that Carlier had no weapon, is to cover up the incident as he covered up the slave trading: "'I think he died of fever. Bury him tomorrow'" (97). In his final quoted speech in the text, Makola reverts more closely to a rapid-fire pidgin, again resorting to simple present tense rather than present progressive and future with the helping verb: "'Steamer! Steamer! They can't see. They whistle for the station. I go ring the bell. Go down to the landing, sir. I ring'" (98). Overall, Makola's staccato, terse speech seems to undercut the narrator's claim about his "warbling" accent, further destabilizing his language and the fixity of identity.

Previous scholars have written on the issue of Makola's conflicted identity, considering him as an example of the "mimic

Chapter Four: "An Outpost of Progress": "The lightest part of the loot... 217

man" who seemingly has assumed the manners and behaviors of another, dominant culture.[67] The very nature of mimicry, Homi Bhabha argues, is "an *ironic* compromise" (*Location of Culture* 122), the result of the tension between the need for the stasis of identity and the counterpressure of changing history. Thus, mimicry continually produces "its slippage, its excess, its difference" (122). Yet, Bhabha continues, mimicry is also "the sign of a double articulation […] which 'appropriates' the Other as it visualizes power" (122). Fundamentally the civilizing mission is threatened by the "displacing gaze of its disciplinary double" (123). In constructing the figure of Makola, Conrad is not only, as Harry Sewlall observes, "engaging in the delectable exercise of deconstructing stereotypes" (7), but also seems to have anticipated what Bhabha would write about the character of the "mimic man" almost a century later. Perhaps the ultimate irony is that Makola as the "mimic man," whose identity and language are fluid, is the one left standing at the end. Without doubt, he does not escape culpability for his actions nor does he escape the narrator's ironic twists in the development of his characterization, but he is the one who *belongs* there while the Belgians do not.

Indeed, Makola's mimicry extends to the slave trading of the colonizers as well as that engaged in by numerous African tribes. Makola initiates the pivotal moment in the action when he trades the ten African station workers for six magnificent tusks of ivory. Kayerts is slow to realize "'Why!' he shouted, 'I believe you have sold our men for these tusks!'" (OP 89). Hesitating to admit that he's "sold" the workers into slavery, Makola continually attempts to shift the emphasis to the fine quality of the ivory he's received in exchange. "'I did the best for you and the Company,' said Makola imperturbably – 'Why you shout so much? Look at this tusk'" (89). This is hardly a regular trade, as Makola points out, with no entry in his books as no trade goods were taken from the "fetish," and Makola, and later, Kayerts and Carlier can quietly cover up their complicity in slavery.

An Unadulterated African: Gobila

If Makola is a complex and transcultural "pivotal figure in the narrative," able to "negotiate" and "manipulate" two cultures in contact and conflict, as Robert Hampson argues ("'Outpost'" 218), he is counterbalanced by the more "unadulterated" African, Gobila. Whether or not Conrad ever met the historical Gobila is unknown, but he clearly appears in the narratives of Stanley and others. Comber mentions meeting "the jolly old chief Ngobela" (a variant phonetic spelling of Gobila) on his expedition on the tributaries of the Congo River (Grenfell and Comber 354).

Stanley is more voluble about his encounter with Gobila: "an exceedingly stout man, of about forty-five, very unkinglike in dress" (*The Congo* 1: 405). Stanley's Gobila announces to him that he is "only an ivory trader" (406) and not in charge of offering land to Stanley for a station. In May 1882, Stanley comes to an agreement in a palaver with several chiefs controlling the land and chooses the spot where he will build the station at Mswata, located above Stanley Pool and just below the mouth of the Kwa into which the Kassai River feeds as it joins the Congo. Stanley's Lieutenant Janssen distinguished himself so well in beginning construction of the station that "Papa Gobila [...] regarded him with paternal pride" and "with rare humour, christened his white son 'Susu Mpembe,' or the 'White Chicken'" (409). One year later, Janssen had completed the station, building for himself "a genteel farmhouse in appearance, with a cool and shady porch, where he holds his palavers and chats twice a day with Papa Gobila" (507).

The illustration of Stanley's "genial, aldermanic Gobila – Papa Gobila" (510) offers a visual representation for Kayerts' friendly greeting to Gobila, "'How goes it, you old image?'" (OP 84).[68]

Conrad's Gobila, however, provides quite a different image from Stanley's; the narrator describes a "grey-headed savage, thin and black, with a white cloth round his loins and a mangy panther skin hanging over his back" (83). Hardly a match for Stanley's image – but the staff is there "as tall as himself" (83).

Chapter Four: "An Outpost of Progress": "The lightest part of the loot... 219

Papa Gobila of Mswata

And Gobila's village in Conrad's text lies on the tributary, the Kassai, near the distant outpost, not on the Congo River itself. We know from his "Up-River Book" that Conrad passed Ganchu Point, across the river from Mswata, at approximately 9:15 a.m. on August 6, 1890. (The date is not certain as Conrad kept good records of times but not dates, but it appears he reached this location two days after the last date he marks in his notebook, August 4th, UB MS). While he may well have seen Gobila's village ("Gobela's" clearly marked on Stanley's map below), he doesn't note that, focusing his attention instead, as I noted in the last chapter, on navigating sandbanks, dead trees, rocks, and other hazards to steaming upriver on the Congo.

Stanley's Gobila is somewhat of a buffoon, if a likeable one – with quite an affection for "Kiyanzi beer," becoming rather intoxicated and "rude" until he was persuaded to be "happy and good," as if he were a child to be placated (*The Congo* 1: 407-408). Conrad's Gobila comes to visit, squatting in the common room of the station, "making a speech" to Kayerts

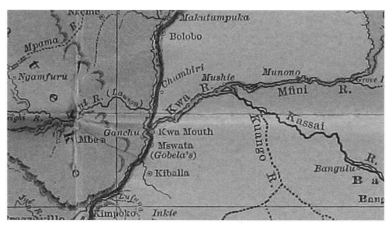

Gobela's, detail from *A Map of the Route of the Emin Pasha Relief Expedition through Africa*

"which the other did not understand" (OP 84). This Gobila is "incomprehensible," but "paternal, and he seemed really to love all white men" (84), whom he viewed as immortal, believing even that the dead artist/station chief "pretended to die and got himself buried for some mysterious purpose of his own into which it was useless to inquire" (84). The narrator's record of Gobila's thoughts is tinged with irony throughout, his eloquent expression undercutting Gobila's apparently naïve world view. Misguidedly, Gobila transfers his "absurd affection" to the new white men, providing them with provisions, while Carlier and Kayerts treat him mockingly, striking off matches to amuse him[69] and letting him sniff the ammonia bottle (84). Gobila's affection swiftly shifts to fear once the slave trading crew have abducted the station workers and killed one of his people, and in "his fear the mild, old Gobila offered extra human sacrifices to all the evil spirits that had taken possession of his white friends" (92). The narrator ironically challenges Gobila's mildness by crossing it with the reference to human sacrifice. Feeling this betrayal by his white men, Gobila utterly shuts down communication with Kayerts and Carlier from this point on, "His people must keep away from them and hope for the best" (92).

Chapter Four: "An Outpost of Progress": "The lightest part of the loot... 221

African Ivory: Slave Traders and Their Victims

Conrad's Africans include more than those singled out for special attention, Makola and Gobila, for Conrad populates the outpost with ivory and slave traders passing by as well as the indentured station men who reside at the outpost. A few months into their installation in the outpost, Kayerts and Carlier are occasionally visited by "men with spears in their hands" who came out of the "void" of the river bringing ivory (81). The narrator's description highlights both their beauty and their savagery: "They were naked, glossy black, ornamented with snowy shells and glistening brass wire, perfect of limb" (81). Unlike Makola, who speaks European languages with a "warbling" accent, these natives "made an uncouth babbling noise when they spoke" their own dialect, yet "they moved in a stately manner and sent quick wild glances out of their startled never-resting eyes" (81). The uncouth nature of their speech is counterbalanced by their stately movements which is then further offset by the "wild glances" and "startled" eyes. The narrator's carefully nuanced description gives way to the attitudes of Kayerts and Carlier toward the natives as "[f]ine animals" who "stink"; "'You Makola! Take that herd over to the fetish'" (82). Kayerts adds, "'This is the tribe that lives down the river – they are rather aromatic'" (82).

But these traders' visits are rare, and after a few months, a more threatening group of armed men come out of the forest. Not from the area, their appearance is quite different from the earlier visitors; "They were tall, slight, draped classically from neck to heel in blue fringed cloths and carried percussion muskets over their bare right shoulders" (85). Having come from the coast, closer to European penetration, these natives bear signs of European goods – the dyed blue fringed cloths from England, the US, or even India, and muskets.

The leader of the slavers makes a long speech which "sounded like one of those impossible languages which sometimes we hear in our dreams" (85). Makola immediately senses the threat, "'Bad fellows' […]. 'They fight with people and catch women and children. They are bad men and have got guns'" (OP 87-88). Perhaps realizing that he has little choice, Makola seems able to recover sufficiently to make his infamous trade, for the bad men have brought a '"fine lot'" of ivory (89). The ten station men captured by the slave traders had been earlier locked into indentured servitude to the Company, taken far from their homes where they miss, among other things, the "festive incantations, the sorceries, the human sacrifices of their own land" (87), their filed teeth a possible gesture toward cannibalism.[70] They've sickened and weakened on a bad diet and "no power on earth" could induce them to perform their tasks efficiently (87). While Kayerts and Carlier reflect on the horror of slavery, they fail to realize that their own station men are already enslaved and dying as a result, and now, because of the utter ignorance Kayerts and Carlier exhibit, headed toward an even worse fate at the hands of the "bad men."

The "pioneers of progress": Kayerts and Carlier

In writing about Europeans in Africa and the African climate in *The Congo and the Founding of Its Free State,* Stanley remarked on the ineptitude of many Europeans who came to Africa as pioneers. His descriptions seem well fitted to the fictionalized Kayerts and Carlier:

> As they appeared on the Congo, one after another, singly or in threes, or in larger groups, supremely ardent, grandly proud that at last the mettle of which they boasted was about to be proved in distant Africa, it was an interesting study to note how the sudden or slow descents to far below zero – often from the topmost altitude of assurance – were effected; to observe how the exaggerated anticipations, by which they had duped themselves, took quick flight before the revelations of reality. (*The Congo* 2: 239)

In further remarks about the African climate and the necessity for Europeans to pay attention to the vicissitudes of this climate when situating river stations, Stanley writes of dangers to health that could be encountered in Africa, when

Chapter Four: "An Outpost of Progress": "The lightest part of the loot... 223

> you add months of poor diet, bad cooking, and other indescribable discomforts, you wonder that the African continent has an evil character, and that so many unfortunate *pioneers of trade and exploration* have left their bones in its earth. (297, emphasis added)[71]

Kayerts and Carlier, of course, in a Conradian phrase that seems to echo Stanley, are "two pioneers of trade and progress" (OP 82) who will soon leave their bones in the earth at the outpost of progress; and while Stanley laments the ignorance of so many Europeans coming to Africa to promote trade (read: find their own fortunes), Conrad highlights with unmistakable irony, hammering home that word *progress,* the entire futility of the European colonial project.

It would be a delicious irony to imagine that Conrad deliberately based the names of his two characters on the historical figures he met or knew about while in the Congo: Keyaerts, who traveled on the upriver voyage of the *Roi des Belges* with Conrad, and Carlier, who got command of the *Florida* for its Kassai expedition in place of Conrad (Mahood 16). Indeed, that biographical connection is enhanced by the depiction of the fictional Kayerts and Carlier as Belgian since the "home" paper they read is so suggestive of sentiments expressed by Leopold II and carried by Belgian and British newspapers as well as the hint from the narrator that Kayerts and Carlier speak French. Carlier remarks about the speech of one of the Loandan traders: "'In the first moment I fancied the fellow was going to speak French'" (OP 85) and Makola seems to have forgotten his when questioned about the appearance of the strangers (86).

Regardless of whether Conrad meant to skewer the two historical figures in the ironic depiction of his fictional ones, their apparent namesakes, the focus on these comic doubles as the butt of a cosmic joke is clear. In writing about Makola, I reflected on his dual identity in the context of his transculturation. His station bosses, Kayerts and Carlier, externalize that duality, embodying mirror images which reflect both sameness and difference. The narrator opens with what appears to be an indistinguishable duo, "There were two white men in charge of the trading station" (77). There is irony ensconced in the very first sentence claiming that the two *white* men are "in charge" of the station – of course, they are not, even though the very fact of their being "white" would deem them superior to the natives in the context of nineteenth century racial views. That irony will be carried throughout and further nuanced by the collapsing of racial stereotypes and undermining of colonial power as it is increasingly clear that it is Makola/Henry Price who is in charge.

In appearance, the men would certainly suggest cartoon characters Mutt and Jeff if indeed those cartoons had been available to Conrad in 1896. What was available was the depiction of two comic figures – one tall and one small – in Flaubert's unfinished satire *Bouvard et Pécuchet*, "characters whose lives and attitudes would embody and exemplify the principal features of bourgeois stupidity"[72] (Simmons and Stape, Introduction 8). Kayerts is short and fat; Carlier is tall "with a large head and a very broad trunk perched upon a long pair of thin legs" (OP 77) – neither reflects a particularly appealing description. The Director caps the characterization, lumping both men together: "'Look at those two imbeciles. They must be mad at home to send me such specimens [...]. I always thought the station on this river useless – and they just fit the station!'" (78). "'They will form themselves there,' said the old stager with a quiet smile" (79). The "old stager," i.e., old-timer, knows what is inevitable – the narrator inserts an ironic, knowing character for just a moment to strike the note of foreshadowing.

And they do form themselves, to the degree that they have any agency to do so but are perhaps more formed by the space which they are powerless to shape. The space of the outpost is suggestive of Foucault's concept of "heterotopia"— the space of the other – cultural spaces, for example, which are different, disturbing, even contradictory and transforming (Johnson 790).[73] Peter Johnson, following Foucault, argues that heterotopias are "emplacements" within cultures which seem to "celebrate the discontinuity and changeability of existence" (794). Furthermore, these "counter-sites" indicate a complex relation between time and space; recent research, Johnson continues, "focuses on a social or cultural space that is both in place and out of place" (797). Johnson's contention that in these spaces "'normality is suspended'" is especially compelling; heterotopia, he adds, "disturbs and unsettles wherever it sheds its *light*: cultural spaces, disciplinary borders and notions of subjectivity" (800, emphasis added).

As an example of the unsettling, disturbing effect of the spotlighted, heterotopic space of the outpost, sunlight is almost continuously shed, adding an estranging and even deadly effect. The narrator mentions the sun six times and sunshine five; several of those references connect the sun to illness, particularly fever. As they pass the first agent's grave site, Kayerts and Carlier remark that he died of fever after exposing "'himself recklessly to the sun'" (OP 80).[74] As a heterotopia within a heterotopia, the "cemetery" space of the agent's grave is an absolute space of otherness, of the utterly unknowable, but also predicts the space that awaits the two agents who will, by the end, form themselves as corpses driven to madness by fever and the sun. Sunshine is ever present except at the end; it seems benign when Makola's children roll about in its light, but its appearances become more ominous, as the outpost becomes increasingly defamiliarizing. For Kayerts and Carlier, utterly blind to their larger surroundings, the "brilliant sunshine disclosed nothing intelligible" (81). In an even more powerful description of the African sun, the narrator reports there are days when the "vibrating brilliance of vertical sunshine" poured down on the outpost's empty courtyard – leaving "the pioneers of trade and progress" with no profit from ivory (82). Later, the ill-gotten ivory tusks "looked very large and valuable in the sunshine" (90), and after Gobila abandons them to their fates, what is familiar for Kayerts and Carlier – home and people like them – recedes "into distances made indistinct by the glare of unclouded sunshine" (92). Blinded by the sun's glare, both men sink deeper into heterotopic space: "And out of the great silence of the surrounding wilderness its very hopelessness and savagery seemed to approach them nearer, to draw them gently, to look upon them, to envelop them with a solicitude irresistible, familiar and disgusting" (92).

As they are enveloped and fixed by the wilderness, Kayerts and Carlier are also formed in stasis – Conrad's narrator glosses motion with the freezing of time in an outpost that has, in reality, become an *inpost*. Carlier, for example, reflects "trailing a sulky glance over the river, the forests, the impenetrable bush that seemed to cut off the station from the rest of the world" (78). Despite their apparent activity early on, both men will quickly descend into inactivity: "Together they did nothing – absolutely nothing" (81). Time and motion flow around them, but they are "unable to see the general aspect of things. The river, the forest, all the great land throbbing with life were like a great emptiness" (81) which not even the "brilliant sunshine" could illuminate (81). Mired in stasis, Kayerts and Carlier experience "[t]hings [which] appeared and disappeared before their eyes in an unconnected and aimless kind of way" (81). But the motion of the river is unceasing, marking the inevitable changeability of space/time despite the inability of Kayerts and Carlier to comprehend their own pivotal position in inertia: "[t]he river seemed to come from nowhere and flow nowhither. It flowed through a void" (81).

Two months earlier, just at the point of being left to their own devices at the outpost, Kayerts and Carlier ascend the slope toward the station "arm in arm," and continue walking arm in arm "drawing close to one another as children do in the dark and they had the same not altogether unpleasant sense of danger which one half suspects to be imaginary" (79). This collapse of individuality as the physical boundaries between the two men blur also wraps the narrator's philosophical aside on the nature of "civilized crowds" (79). The reflections of Conrad's narrator suggest a link to Gustave Le Bon's theory of crowds, for in Conrad's tale the two "imbeciles," having been left alone in the wilderness, have lost the security protection of the higher organization of the crowd. It is the crowd not the individual, the narrator contends, to which "every great and every insignificant thought belongs" (79). Le Bon's *Psychologie des Foules* appeared in French in 1895 and in English translation in 1896 – Le Bon was the most popular writer on the theory of crowds in his day and the work continues to be reprinted and cited in our own. Le Bon's conception, however, bears important distinctions from the philosophical reflections by Conrad's narrator. Le Bon's task, for example, was inflected by his study of the rise of mass culture at the *fin de siècle* and entrenched in the history of western Europe; and his opinion of the crowd is far from kind, in fact, the "crowd" differed little, in his view, from the level of imbecility enjoyed by Kayerts and Carlier. Modern scientific and industrial change, Le Bon argued, had created the moment of transformation at the "present epoch" of his writing (xiv). In further elaboration, Le Bon wrote in bold "The age we are about to enter will in truth be the ERA OF CROWDS" (xv). Le Bon insists that the individual forming part of a crowd is an automaton no longer guided by his will, and that in such an organized crowd, "a man descends several rungs in the ladder of civilization. Isolated, he may be a cultivated individual; in a crowd, he is a barbarian – that is, a creature acting by instinct" (13). In his examination of institutions, such as parliamentary assemblies, Le Bon suggests that the functions of government increase

> in proportion as the indifference and helplessness of the citizens grow. They it is who must necessarily exhibit the initiative, enterprising, and guiding spirit in which private persons are lacking. It falls on them to undertake everything, direct everything, and take everything under their protection. The State becomes an all-powerful god. Still experience shows that the power of such gods was never either very durable or very strong. (226)

This sort of crowd-driven government seems to be what Conrad's narrator has in mind when "he" comments that the crowd "believes blindly in the irresistible force of its institutions and of its morals, in the power of its police and of its opinion" (OP 79). The supposed "high organization of the civilized crowds" (79) forms a protective barrier for Kayerts and Carlier who could not exist otherwise. Yet in commenting that the crowd believes blindly in the force of its institutions and both great and "insignificant" thoughts belong to the crowd, the narrator hints at what Le Bon makes explicit when he states that in the organized crowd, the individual descends the ladder of civilization. The protection of the "civilized" crowd gone, Kayerts and Carlier are left alone to face "contact with pure unmitigated savagery, with primitive nature and primitive man, [which] brings sudden and profound trouble into the heart" (79). However, within or outside of their "crowd" protection, the two men hardly rise far above the level of savagery with which they have been brought face to face. With the usual negated, the "unusual" is affirmed, raising the prospect of danger, and creating fear when as individuals, Kayerts and Carlier are confronted with the unknown and unknowable, and as "children [...] in the dark" they fleetingly glimpse danger (79).

Reestablishing some contact with the "civilized" world, Kayerts and Carlier delve into the "torn books," the "wrecks of novels" (82) left behind by their predecessor – historical fiction which Conrad seems to have chosen carefully to reflect periods of social upheaval and the rise of the masses. Beginning in the order in which they are named, the reference to Dumas' *The Three Musketeers* through the reference to its characters D'Artagnan and Cardinal Richelieu points to a time set in the seventeenth century during the reign of Louis XIII but written in 1844 during the July Monarchy in France. This novel would surely appeal to Kayerts and Carlier for its swashbuckling adventures, but the deeper meaning for its appearance in the text is the reflection between the setting of the novel and the time of its writing more than two centuries later – both display periods of social unrest. The power of the *Ancien Regime*, under Louis XIII and his successors is destined to break under the violent upheaval of the French Revolution, and the July Monarchy will fall in the revolution of 1848, leading to the end of the House of Bourbon. Hawkeye (Hawk's eye in Conrad's text), James Fenimore Cooper's hero in *The Last of the Mohicans* (1826) is

Chapter Four: "An Outpost of Progress": "The lightest part of the loot... 229

the second character named. We know that Conrad admired Cooper's sea tales, writing in 1898:

> In his sea tales, the sea inter-penetrates with life; it is in a subtle way a factor in the problem of existence, and, for all its greatness, it is always in touch with the men, who, bound on errands of war or gain, traverse its immense solitudes. ("Tales of the Sea," Stape 48)

Yet it is not Cooper's tales of the sea like "The Pilot" that Conrad chooses for his imbecilic characters to read; rather, it is that novel on which Cooper's fame mainly rests, set in 1757 during the French and Indian War as France and Great Britain battled for control of North America. Clearly, Cooper's novel suggested a theme, prevalent in the day, that the indigenous people were disappearing, allowing for full-scale white settler expansion across the continent. At the conclusion of the novel, as the Delawares bury their dead and Chingachgook and Hawkeye solidify their bond of friendship, Tamenund disperses the crowd, saying "The pale faces are masters of the earth, and the time of the red-men is not yet come again [...]. In the morning I saw the sons of Unâmis happy and strong; and yet, before the night has come, have I lived to see the last warrior of the wise race of the Mohicans!" (Cooper 295). Sublimated beneath Kayerts and Carlier's facile, superficial reading of the novel lies the cautionary tale for the African subjected to implacable colonial rule, mingled with the ability to overturn colonial power, if ever so briefly, in the survival and even dominance of Makola and Gobila. The last of the novels, *Père Goriot* (1835) begins in 1819 during the turbulence of the Bourbon Restoration when profound changes occurred in a French society filled with the tension between the aristocracy and a growing bourgeoisie as the lowest classes struggled with unbearable poverty. Balzac was deeply influenced by Fenimore Cooper, but instead of the "noble savage," Balzac saw a human barbarism that resisted attempts at civilization. Even more notable, Balzac wrote in the Preface to the 1835 edition that Goriot, who had become rich selling vermicelli during widespread famine, was "an Illinois of the flour trade" and "a Huron of the grain market" (qtd. in Kanes 4-5). Balzac further elaborated this theme when the character Vautrin remarks that Paris is a "forest of the New World where twenty varieties of savage tribes clash" (qtd. in Hunt 92). Completely misunderstanding what he had read and unwittingly enhancing the irony of the deeper implications, Kayerts could have been referring to any of these characters, "'I had no idea there were such clever fellows in the world'" (OP 83).

But Kayerts and Carlier also found old copies of a home paper, presumably Belgian, where the benefits of "'our colonial expansion'" were extolled, with the usual blather about "the rights and duties of civilization," "the sacredness of the civilizing work," the merits of "bringing light and faith and *commerce* to the dark places of the earth" (83, emphasis added). Such language could have been found in newsprint all over Europe at the time, but an important referent for the language that encapsulates the major claims is found in King Leopold II's speech at the international geographical conference he convened in September 1876. In it, Leopold reminded those gathered for the conference that the goal was

> To open up to civilisation the only part of our globe which it has not yet penetrated, to pierce the *darkness* in which entire populations are enveloped, is, I venture to say, a crusade worthy of this age of *progress*, and I am happy to perceive how much the public feeling is in favour of its accomplishment; the tide is with us. (qtd. in Banning 152, emphasis added)

The King was to lay before the members attending the conference a plan which Henry Morton Stanley would later follow: establishing bases of operation at the mouth of the Congo, opening up the interior by establishing trade routes, and creating committees to oversee the work, all goals whose explicit purpose was the abolishment of slavery but whose real purpose, the rape of the Congo's resources, was cloaked, in Conrad's tale, in "high flown language" (OP 83).

Kayerts and Carlier, reading in those old newspapers about the importance of the work they were engaged in, began to imagine the future of their station. Carlier even thinks of himself and Kayerts as "'the first civilized men to live at this very spot'" (83), and offers a pretty vision: "'In a hundred years there will be perhaps a town here. Quays and warehouses and barracks ... and ... and ... billiard rooms. Civilization my boy, and virtue ...... and all'" (83). Of course, they are not the first, they've forgotten their predecessor and fail to acknowledge any of the explorers who had entered the interior of the continent decades before them. Stanley, for example, saw visions of the future as he prepared the ground for founding the government station at Vivi in 1879:

> The mind works rapidly and eagerly when its interest is excited. As fast as the eye searched for all these details the mind leaped into the future. I already viewed the completed station, the broad, well-travelled turnpike-road, the marching columns of tradespeople, the stream of traffic, and the incessant moving to and fro of multitudes. (*The Congo* 1: 127)

Stanley sees trade writ large traveling the highways of commerce he will carve through the interior of the continent. And trade means the movement of commodities in which Kayerts and Carlier deal, while delegating negotiations for those trades to Makola.

What Carlier has pictured relates as closely to the reality of trade in the future as Stanley's vision – quays, warehouses, and billiard rooms especially suggest the link, with a lurking irony in the reference to billiard-rooms, linked contiguously to billiard balls, which in the 1890s were made of ivory. Early on, Kayerts and Carlier are largely unsuccessful in obtaining ivory – their primary reason for being deposited as agents at their outpost station. The narrator relates that "profitable visits were rare" (OP 82). What they have for trade lies in the "fetish," the "rubbish" and "rags" which comprise the "spirit of civilization" (82) – the "beads, cotton cloths, red kerchiefs, brass wire" that are the mainstay, the holy trinity of commerce in the Congo.

But months later with the arrival of the strangers from the coast, that changes with the acquisition of six magnificent tusks, which come at quite a high price. Conrad makes quite clear the connections between ivory trading and slavery as Kayerts and Carlier slowly become complicit in the sale of their ten station men. "'Slavery is an awful thing,' stammered out Kayerts in an unsteady voice. 'Frightful … the sufferings …'" (90). Their demise as a result of this complicity, which can't be hidden in the brilliant vertical sunshine, is even chillingly foreshadowed when shortly after congratulating themselves on the importance of their work, Carlier plants the cross over the prior station manager's grave, the cross that will serve as Kayerts' gallows – "'It used to make me squint whenever I went that way […]. So I just planted it upright. And solid, I promise you. I suspended myself with both hands to the cross-piece. Not a move. Oh, I did that properly'" (83). Kayerts' and Carlier's frustration increases as the weeks become months, the station deteriorates, no steamer arrives, and supplies dwindle. As madness ensues for both men raging over sugar, Kayerts shoots Carlier; on the next day, the penetrating sunshine that has illuminated the station for months, disappears in the fog. The mist, the narrator describes, "the mist penetrating, enveloping and silent; the morning mist of tropical lands, the mist that clings and kills, the mist white and deadly, immaculate and poisonous" envelops Kayerts in "the white shroud of that land of sorrow" (98). This is *progress,* the narrator insists.

> Progress was calling to Kayerts from the river. Progress, and civilization and all the virtues. Society was calling to its accomplished child, to come, to be taken care of, to be instructed, to be judged, to be condemned; it called to him to return to that rubbish-heap from which he had wandered away – so that justice could be done. (98)

Kayerts' response to that call is a refusal to return, condemning instead progress, civilization, and the very society calling to him as he hung "by a leather strap from the cross": "And, irreverently, he was putting out a swollen tongue at his Managing Director" (99).[75] As Laurence Davies presciently

Chapter Four: "An Outpost of Progress": "The lightest part of the loot... 233

observes: "Something remarkable is happening here. Even before 'Heart of Darkness,' a nineteenth-century voice is yielding to a twentieth-century one," and the balance of both voices, evidenced in Conrad's unwillingness to split the text in two allows for the emergence of mingled "outrage, experimental art, and politics" ("Don't You think" 23).

Chapter Five: "Heart of Darkness": Conrad's Centerpiece in the Congo[76]

Mapping the Evolution of the Tale

> "It is a story as much as my Outpost of Progress was"
> (*CL* 2: 139-40)

According to a letter to Edward Garnett on December 18, 1898, Conrad's first impulse for writing "Heart of Darkness" was propelled by the need for money, "Now I am at a short story for B'wood which I must get out for the sake of the shekels" (132). Serendipitously, Blackwood wrote to Conrad just two weeks later to solicit a contribution to appear in the February edition of *Blackwood's Edinburgh Magazine*. Delighted by this request, Conrad responded with a brief summary of the tale under construction.

> I am (and have been for the last 10 days) working for Maga. The thing is far advanced [...]. It is a narrative after the manner of youth told by the same man dealing with his experiences on a river in Central Africa. The idea in it is not so obvious as in youth – or at least not so obviously presented [...] tho' I have no doubts as to the workmanship I do not know whether the subject will commend itself to you for that particular number. (139)

While the writing was derailed briefly as Conrad worried about his son's illness, Conrad had completed enough of the text by January 9, 1899, to send fifty-eight typed pages followed by thirty-two pages of manuscript to David Meldrum, Blackwood's literary advisor. Conrad asked Meldrum to have the manuscript pages typed since, due to illness, his wife Jessie could not continue typing. This represented approximately half the story – but it continued to evolve, and on January 16, Conrad wrote to Meldrum, "The thing has grown on me. I don't think it will be bad" (153). By February 7, still not finished, Conrad instructed Blackwood where to end the first installment; at this point he thought it would be about half of the finished tale and promised to hurry to finish the rest. In that February installment of *Blackwood's* "The Heart of Darkness" – Conrad had not yet eliminated "The" from the title – ended on page 220 with Marlow's anticipation of a meeting with Kurtz: "Still, I was curious to see whether this man, who had come out equipped with moral ideas of some sort, would climb to the top after all, and how he would set about his work when there" (HD Blackwood's 220).

Tracking backward to the inception of the tale, we find that what remains of both the manuscript and typescript of "Heart of Darkness" is fragmented. There are only thirty-five pages of typescript extant, housed in the Henry W. and Albert A. Berg Collection at the New York Public Library, and 113 leaves of a first batch of manuscript copy inscribed on recto and verso, beginning on page 11 as numbered by Conrad, followed by a second batch of 25 recto leaves, housed in the Beinecke Library, Yale University. Yet as Owen Knowles describes it, the typescript together with the manuscript present the best copy texts for coming closest to Conrad's intentions, thus they serve as the base for the Cambridge edition. Knowles contends, and a close examination bears out, the manuscript of "Heart of Darkness" is atypical among Conrad's manuscripts, for, writing under pressure against a deadline, Conrad needed to produce a fairly clean text devoid of extensive revision ("Copy-texts" 306).

From manuscript and typescript to initial publication, Conrad demonstrates, as Knowles points out, the process of "authorial self-withdrawal" (Introduction xlii). Clearly, Conrad meant to withdraw increasingly from topicality to stamp the tale with the timelessness it now displays. There is, however, one passage that was excised in the published version of the text to which I'd like to give attention here.

Chapter Five: "Heart of Darkness": Conrad's Centerpiece in the Congo 237

The passage describes the government station (at Boma) and constitutes a textual mapping of the space, an architectonic structure which does not appear in Conrad's manuscript "Congo Diary" (CD MS) since its text begins in Matadi, further upriver from Boma. In the manuscript "The Heart of Darkness," Conrad writes:

> We went up some twenty miles and anchored off the seat of the government. I had heard enough in Europe about its advanced state of civilization; the papers, nay, paper-vendors in the sepulchral city were boasting about the steam tramway and the hotel – especially the hotel. I beheld that wonder. It was like a symbol at the gate. It stood alone, a grey high cube of iron with two tiers of galleries outside, towering above one of those ruinous-looking foreshores you come upon at home in out-of-the-way places where refuse is thrown out. To make the resemblance complete it wanted only a drooping post with the legend: rubbish shot here, and the symbol would have had the clearness of the naked truth. (HD MS 40-41)

The typescript includes part of this passage with a few changes, e.g., thirty instead of twenty miles, but ends with "To make the resemblance complete it only wanted a" (fragment above page section numbered 25 in HD TS). More on the Boma station follows in the manuscript but the reference is collapsed in the first published version to simply "We anchored off the seat of government. But my work would not begin for some two hundred miles farther on. So as soon as I could I made a start for a place thirty miles higher up" (HD Blackwood's 204).

The section of the manuscript passage quoted above, however, makes the point I wish to pursue about an evolving withdrawal from factual placement which Conrad achieves with more concision in the published text, but I'm also interested in what the deletion might have added had it been left intact. First, notice the link drawn between the sepulchral city and the "seat of government" – a link that stretches across the ocean, to establish the boast that the colony is a reflection its Empire can be proud of – but this observation becomes unnecessary as evidence overturning it abounds throughout the published version. Then, there follows Conrad's well-known disgust with newsprint – the hotel and tramway have been touted in the newspapers, while what Marlow sees is hardly a "wonder," a comment clearly made tongue in cheek; and the case about newsprint has already been pounded home in Marlow's parting scene with his aunt. Yet there is a small something lost in the elimination of the wondrous hotel that stands at the gate to the interior and symbolizes the horror that lies beyond. In Marlow's view, the hotel is hardly an attractive sight, standing guard over a "foreshore" where "refuse is thrown out."

Boma: Post Office, with Rail Tracks

The image above appears on an official Belgian postcard, dated approximately 1912, and while it identifies the post office, the building on the left, it does not identify the hotel which is the taller structure on the right. It is clear that this image is the hotel from another illustration of the same building displayed in the December 13, 1890 issue of *The Graphic*. This is what Conrad saw but not what Marlow describes, and while this image doesn't appear as revolting as Marlow portrays it, the description clearly reveals Marlow's and Conrad's revulsion against the Belgian government's pride in its progress in the Congo. And Conrad hardly wished to invoke a real image, which most if not all of his readers would never see anyway, choosing an imaginary and symbolic one instead. What the disappearance of the lengthy manuscript passage signifies may be that Conrad had decided it was extraneous and failed to add necessary details to what Marlow would describe as the Outer Station. Or it stands as an example of his withdrawal. But what it adds to an extra-textual study of the novella is a revelation of the hotel as a Dantesque structure, the "symbol at the gate," towering over a scene of waste. Textually, indeed, the nod to Dante will not be entirely lost, for Marlow will tell his listeners shortly, "but it seemed to me I had stepped into the gloomy circle of some Inferno" (HD 58).

Material History as Dreamscape

"Inferno" strikes the keynote for where we, as readers, are about to embark – a symbolic descent into the darkness of an unknown combined with a literal journey through a material landscape scarred irrevocably by imperial greed. The evolution of the text negotiates a delicate balance between dialogue with its moment in material history, pitting textual reality against the unknowable *Real*,[77] and a "political unconscious" which emerges within a dreamscape. As we have seen, Conrad arrived in the Congo in the wake of Henry Morton Stanley's efforts to force the region into modern history on European terms once the Congo had been pried open to the European gaze through mapping, exploration, and trade by Stanley and a whole tribe of explorers both before and after him. As Conrad wrote in his Author's Note to *Youth, Heart of Darkness, The End of the Tether*, "Heart of Darkness" is "experience pushed a little (and only a very little) beyond the actual *facts* of the case" (HD 6, emphasis added). Sensing something just beyond the reach of language, a looming presence that defied symbolization, Conrad wrestled with the symbolic to give the Real textual form. Conrad's novella is far more than a tale of the history of transatlantic trade in the Congo, but that tale, once exposed, produces an indictment of colonialism/imperialism writ large. However, as Fredric Jameson's observation below suggests, the objects of trade populated in Conrad's text, though only a liminal presence, point to a political unconscious, a *reality* which demands to be acknowledged.

> [H]istory is *not* a text, not a narrative, master or otherwise, but that, as an absent cause, it is inaccessible to us except in textual form, and that our approach to it and to the Real itself necessarily passes through its prior textualization, its narrativization in the political unconscious. (35)[78]

We glimpse a Congolese reality in 1890-1899 – the years covering Conrad's actual presence in the Congo and Marlow's fictional reminiscence/the scene of Conrad's writing – in the codes embedded in the political unconscious, waiting to be deciphered.

All narratives create desire for an ending, and in Conrad's text, desire pulls us deeper into the political unconscious, toward cracking those embedded codes, structuring narrative motion for the reader, the narrator, the protagonist, and the characters. Desire functions, for example, as a palpable lust for the riches an object of trade like ivory can bring; that lust, felt by both the fictional characters and the real ones they represent, becomes embodied in the echoing of the word *ivory* which reverberates throughout the narrative. Unlike his cast of characters, though, Marlow experiences desire in his thrust to reach the "Other" figured as the remains of Kurtz, reduced to little more than an ivory-like skeleton and a voice by the time Marlow reaches him. Finally, the reader (and the anonymous narrator, her double) is driven by desire to penetrate the continuously hinted-at unknowable and to face it as the narrative dies.

Spatial historian Paul Carter writes that the explorer's experience reveals an interesting "parallel with psychoanalysis" (84), a point I mean to explore further. As the explorer trusts the inner logic of the track, plotted by latitude and longitude, which it is her/his responsibility to find and follow, the analyst relies on tracking the dream narrative of wish fulfillment. As we have seen throughout the preceding chapters, Conrad asserts that his passion for maps and the stories of polar exploration "'sent me off on romantic explorations of my inner self'" (GSE 10). So, the journey, as the interpretation of a dream, should lead to the true path of self-knowledge. But space, even in successful explorers' narratives, according to Carter, was a place of "'distortion' or 'transposition,'" and the "association between travelling and dreaming (both awake and asleep) was, in fact, a commonplace of the explorer literature" (84). Conrad's narrative of Marlow's (and his) Congo journey is no exception. Marlow, Conrad's alter-ego and fictional explorer shaped in his own mold, exposes a spatial history of the place by marking the objects of trade which litter the dreamscape of his river journey. But Marlow continuously maps a dreamscape whose features distort and threaten as the track leads farther and farther toward the center – in Freudian terms, the "dream's navel," where, at the root of every dream, Lacan, following Freud, locates the Real in its momentary contact with the Symbolic (23). Freud wrote:

> There is often a passage in even the most thoroughly interpreted dream which has to be left obscure; this is because we become aware during the work of interpretation that at that point there is a tangle of dream-thoughts which cannot be unravelled and which moreover adds nothing to our knowledge of the content of the dream. This is the dream's navel, the spot where it reaches down into the unknown. (528)

Note that despite the fact that we as readers and analyzers will travel to the narrative navel, what we find there may well correspond to the anonymous narrator's conception of Marlow's meanings as "misty halos that, sometimes, are made visible by the spectral illumination of moonshine" (HD 45). It is into the center of this textual whirlpool, the dreamscape's navel, that "Heart of Darkness" leads us.[79]

The Preamble: on board the *Nellie*

Raising the specters of ill-fated explorers with the image of Sir John Franklin and his ships the *Erebus* and *Terror*, the anonymous narrator first invokes the metaphor of dreaming through the "dreams of men" fed by a greatness which "floated on the ebb of that river [Thames] into the mystery of an unknown earth!" (45), as he builds a textual dreamscape with light, dark, and gloom – the Chapman lighthouse illuminates the Thames – it "shone strongly," while a "brooding gloom" casts its shadow at sunset over the "monstrous town" in the west (45). As a framing device this nameless narrator shapes our anticipation and reception of the inner tale, Marlow's narrative – Marlow's tale nests within that of the anonymous voice which also listens.[80] Marlow's imaginary voyage begins on the Thames where he offers his listening and reading audience several resonating analogies with Roman occupation of Britain and Gaul – the darkness at the "very end of the world," as well as "[s]and banks, marshes, forests, savages," which could as easily describe the Congo as the Thames; as they "must have been dying like flies" could describe the fate of whites in the Congo (46).

Marlow, as Conrad's quintessential narrator, makes his first appearance in the story "Youth" which precedes "Heart of Darkness" in the volume *Youth, Heart of Darkness, The End of the Tether*. As Conrad's *doppelgänger*, Marlow displays an off-center relationship to Englishness; John Galsworthy even remarked that "'though English in name,'" Marlow is "'not so in nature'" (qtd. in Knowles, Introduction xxxiii), clearly suggestive of Conrad's own dual nature as both Englishman and Pole. Owen Knowles contends that this results in a strained relationship between Marlow and his projected audience (xxxii), indicating that Marlow's politics are increasingly disaffected from *Blackwood's* party line. Marlow's support of British colonialism, for example, is ambiguous.[81]

Conrad's support for this ambiguity and his sense of identification with Marlow seems unwavering. Of Marlow, Conrad writes affectionately in his Author's Note to the *Youth* volume:

> He haunts my hours of solitude, when, in silence, we lay our heads together in great comfort and harmony; but as we part at the end of

Chapter Five: "Heart of Darkness": Conrad's Centerpiece in the Congo

> a tale I am never sure that it may not be for the last time. Yet I don't think that either of us would care much to survive the other [...]. Of all my people he's the one that has never been a vexation to my spirit. A most discreet, understanding man.... (HD 5-6)

It is Marlow who is best equipped to voice the tale of the Congo that Conrad might not have been able to tell without him.

Beginning with his oracular and unforgettable pronouncement, "And this also [...] has been one of the dark places of the earth" (HD 45), Marlow extends the imagery of light and dark. The meaning he takes away at the "furthest point of navigation and the culminating point of [his] experience" (47-48) of the Congo seems now, onboard the *Nellie,* "to throw a kind of light" (48) on the place where Marlow, as an "emissary of light" (53) would bring civilization to the heart of darkness. Africa as the "white patch" (48) for a boy to "dream gloriously" over has become a "place of darkness" (48). Light and dark, one signifying visibility and illumination, while the other signifies impenetrability and negation, are visually analogous to ivory and ebony and allude to a buried pattern of signification whose gradual exposure reveals the overdetermination of meaning at its core. That signification will increasingly point to and expose the exploitation of the black African in the European plunder of white ivory.

In fact, a tiny detail linked to ivory and ebony emerges in the mention of the dice on board the *Nellie,* dice which are, in fact, not cast.[82] While not cast literally, the dice are certainly cast figuratively, for as the company aboard the *Nellie* plan to play a game of dominoes which never gets played, the stage is set for the inevitability of Marlow's tale. And those dominoes, traditionally carved from ivory or bone, bring the first tangible intimation of Africa to the *Nellie.* Thus, the image of the Congo looms over the Thames before Marlow's tale follows him to Africa's shores, and the imaginary throw of the dice compels the company onboard to listen.

As the narrative unfolds, ivory often appears in close connection to a waterway – its vehicle of transportation to trading centers – and as the anonymous narrator notes, the Thames is "a waterway leading to the uttermost ends of the earth" (44). Those uttermost ends have returned ivory in huge quantities to the Thames, the gateway to England, the largest importer of ivory in Europe in the nineteenth century (Beachey 290). The dominoes, the visible sign of British consumption of this commodity, are brought out by the accountant, who toys with them "architecturally" (HD 43), as though building the monetary structures of empire on the banks of the Thames. Perhaps that gloom over London in the west includes, along with its pessimistic view of terrestrial extinction, a veiled indictment of British imperialism contradicting Marlow's later observation that in Africa's red, British colonies, "some real work is done in there" (50). England has produced the "seed of commonwealths, the germs of empires" (45). Conrad, through the anonymous narrator, strikes the notes of money, commerce, and trade with these preliminary, half-buried references, and soon Marlow will link these realities to the dream-like state in which he travels, marginally witnessing the phantasmagoria of European commodities along the Congo River.

Conrad knows, furthermore, that ivory serves not only as an exchangeable and usable commodity figuring prominently in empire-building, it also serves as a fetish around which the "faithless pilgrims" surge: "The word ivory rang in the air, was whispered, was sighed. You would think they were praying to it. A taint of imbecile rapacity blew through it all like a whiff from some corpse" (65). Just like the anonymous narrator's conception of the redeeming idea behind colonialism, ivory is "something you can set up, and bow down before, and offer a sacrifice to" (47). Indeed, the very comment about *sacrificing* to the redeeming idea undercuts its claim to redemption, for idolatry to false idols hardly exemplifies Christianity's claim to redeem the "savages." Marlow sits onboard the *Nellie* like an idol, "yellow" and "ascetic" (43), invoking the image of a Buddha carved in ivory – again, not a Christian icon. Conrad, to this point, has developed a matrix of associations in whose web he will embed meaning – ivory is both valuable commodity and fetish supreme, desirable and deadly.

Mapping the Scramble at the Center of Colonial Empire

Alternating textual associations among ivory, yellow, bones, and idols continue when Marlow arrives in the city like a "whited sepulchre" (50), a city which whitewashes the truth of its colonizing evil in the Congo. The image of Conrad's fictional Brussels, so closely associated with its Company and the ivory trade, reveals this commercial center as a charnel house. The Company was "going to run an overseas empire" and planned to "make no end of coin by trade" (50).

In a primal reminiscence of his passion for maps, Marlow points to that initiatory impulse to go to the great white heart of Africa: "When I grow up I will go there," echoing Conrad's own passion for exploring African space repeated in "Geography and Some Explorers" (GSE 14) and *A Personal Record* (PR 26). Marlow remembers the course of the river "resembling an immense snake uncoiled, with its head in the sea, its body at rest curving afar over a vast country and its tail lost in the depths of the land" (HD 48). But in the office of the "whited sepulchre" he is most struck by the "large shining map marked with all the colours of a rainbow" (50). Marlow's penchant for irony bursts out as he adds signification to each color: British, the "vast amount of red – good to see at any time because one knows that some real work is done in there," French "a deuce of a lot of blue," Italian green, Portuguese orange, and a jab at the Germans' purple "where the jolly *pioneers of progress* drink the jolly lager-beer" (50, emphasis added).[83] But the yellow, designating the Congo Free State, "[d]ead in the centre" is his destination, "[a]nd the river was there – fascinating – deadly – like a snake" (51).[84]

And since Conrad himself arrived in the wake of Stanley's exuberant popularity in the historical Brussels, perhaps Marlow, in his imaginary world, does too. Marlow notices that his aunt's comment about "'weaning those ignorant millions from their horrid ways'" is but one example of "a lot of such rot let loose in print and talk just about that time," and his aunt, "the excellent woman," got "carried off her feet" (53). Marlow's affectionate dismissiveness of his aunt's naivete surfaces in his remark about women in general, "They live in a world of their own and there had never been anything like it and never can be. It is too beautiful altogether; and if they were to set it up it would go to pieces before the first sunset" (53).[85]

But Conrad works the aunt in for more than a pessimistic view of a world constructed by women matched with the justification for masculine domination; he intends as well to let Marlow point to a European justification of colonization in the interests of the 3 capital C's: Christianity, Civilization, and Commerce. Marlow's comments also underscore Conrad's own distaste for the newspaper spreading such "rot" like Stanley's dispatches to British and American newspapers trumpeting his achievements in Africa. In just the jingoistic vein that Marlow (and Conrad) deplored, Lord Northcliffe's *Daily Mail*, begun just a few months before Conrad started work on "An Outpost of Progress" in 1896, announced that it would be "the articulate voice of British progress and *domination*. We believe in England. We know that the advance of the

Mr. H. M. Stanley's Return to England

Chapter Five: "Heart of Darkness": Conrad's Centerpiece in the Congo   247

Union Jack means protection for weaker races, justice for the oppressed, liberty for the downtrodden" (qtd. in Hay 119, emphasis added). Later in his narrative, in a rare and possibly veiled ironic jab at Stanley, Marlow notes that Kurtz "desired to have kings meet him at railway stations on his return from some ghastly Nowhere where he intended to accomplish great things" and "had been writing for the papers and meant to do so again 'for the furthering of my ideas. It's a duty'" (HD 116). The illustration above is a suggestive example of Stanley's triumphant arrival at Victoria railway station and the news media sensation he had become.

Coasting

From the relative safety of the *Nellie*'s deck, Marlow begins charting his return to Africa, constructing a plot dominated by desire for union with an unknown and unknowable at its navel as it skirts the banks of two rivers and the coasts of two continents. Feeling as though he's "set off for the centre of the earth" (53), Marlow collapses the distance between Europe and Africa, declining to narrate the ocean voyage and leaving the only vestige of his sailing from Europe in the words "I left in a French steamer" (54). It's as though, in Marlow's narrative, the two continents present a continuous front as they almost do, and, in fact, Marlow, sailing south in the North Atlantic, would have sighted the northwestern coast of Africa before completely losing sight of the Strait of Gibraltar, Portugal, and Spain. Thus, Marlow reaches Africa, where, as the "formless coast" presents itself to view, he thinks of the "merry dance of death and trade" (55) and feels oppressed by "a still and earthy atmosphere as of overheated catacombs" (55), metaphorically linking the African coast with the city like a whited sepulchre. Marlow brings the African coast into view as his ship calls at "every blamed port they have out there" (54). Coasting south and then east, Marlow muses on the enigmatic nature of a formless coast whose depths seem impenetrable, both inviting and threatening; and in a series of accumulating, combatting adjectives, Marlow begins textually mapping what he sees: "Watching a coast as it slips by the ship is like thinking about an enigma. There it is before you – smiling, frowning, inviting, grand, mean, insipid or savage, and always mute with an air of whispering – Come and find out" (54). Yet what Marlow sees seems impenetrable as he looks southeast down the coastline, steaming along the Bight of Benin: "The edge of a colossal jungle, so dark-green as to be almost black, fringed with white surf, ran straight, like a ruled line, far, far away along a blue sea whose glitter was blurred by a creeping mist" (54). The interior reveals nothing other than "specks [...] with a flag flying above them perhaps," as the ship lands both soldiers and custom-house clerks whose work would be conducted in "a God-forsaken wilderness, with a tin shed and a flag-pole lost in it" (54). "Every day," Marlow continues, "the coast looked the same, as though we had not moved; but we passed various places, trading places, with names like Gran' Bassam, Little Popo; names that seemed to belong to some sordid farce acted in front of a sinister back-cloth" (54). Significantly, as Marlow passes Gran' Bassam, he is literally passing by a "sinister back-cloth," sailing east on the southern coast of the most infamous region for slave trading in the seventeenth through the nineteenth centuries, the Ivory Coast and the Slave Coast, in the Bight of Benin. It's small wonder Marlow feels disconnected, experiencing only a "momentary contact with reality" when he sees boats paddled by "black fellows" who "wanted no excuse for being there," their "intense energy of movement" was "as natural and true as the surf along their coast" (54); but Marlow feels kept "away from the truth of things within the toils of a mournful and senseless delusion" (54) – perhaps removed from the irony that these "free" black fellows paddle in the surf of slave-trading country. In the map illustration below, "Lit. Popo" appears on the coastline just below Togo, however, Gran' Bassam does not appear on this section of the map as it is located further west on the Ivory Coast near the western coast of Ghana.

Chapter Five: "Heart of Darkness": Conrad's Centerpiece in the Congo 249

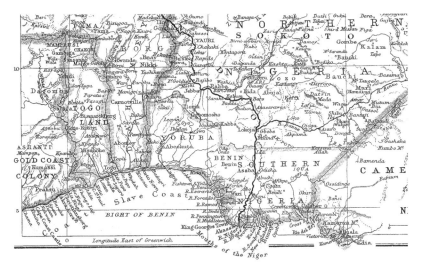

The Slave Coast

Marlow skirts the coast for a month before reaching the mouth of the river where he will map the signposts left by enforced European trade along its banks, creating continual metaphoric and metonymic links to the center of colonial empire, the "whited sepulchre" of Brussels and, just as importantly, to the river Thames leading to the "uttermost ends of the earth." "Nowhere," Marlow tells the listeners onboard the *Nellie*, "did we stop long enough to get a particularized impression but the general sense of vague and oppressive wonder grew upon me. It was like a weary pilgrimage amongst hints for *nightmares*" (55, emphasis added). From the mouth of the river at Banana, Marlow travels to Boma first, but spends no time there nor does he describe it other than to say he left as soon as he could. In fact, reminiscing later about Boma, Conrad remarked, "I arrived at that delectable capital Boma, where before the departure of the steamer that was to take me home I had the time to wish myself dead over and over again with perfect sincerity" (*PR* 27).

The First of the "Holy Trinity" of Commodities: Cloth

Marlow's first mention of disembarkation occurs thirty miles upriver, where the "blinding sunlight drowned all this at times in a sudden recrudescence of glare" (HD 56). While not named, Marlow's outer station is Matadi, 25.19 nautical miles from Boma. At the outer station, Marlow witnesses large scale waste and destruction, rusty remnants of the effort to build a railroad. His comments must express Conrad's sentiments at the Belgian state railroad under construction when he arrived in the Congo – for Leopold II, of course, the railway was vitally necessary, given the difficult topography of the lower river's cataracts, to transport ivory and trade goods. Here Marlow will witness his first "chain gang," black men whose necks are bound by iron collars, linked together with chain – enslaved, forced laborers on the railroad. In addition to the rusting railroad components and slave gang, Marlow finds, in a grove of dying Africans, another unmistakable link to Europe in the "bit of white worsted round" (58) a dying African's neck. The African's thread necklace resonates with the iron collars Marlow has just witnessed, linking it metonymically and metaphorically with slavery. "It looked startling," Marlow says, "round his black neck, this bit of white thread from beyond the seas" (59). "Worsted," named for Worstead, a manufacturing center for this cloth dating back to the twelfth century, unmistakably links this undyed worsted yarn to England, suggesting a veiled connection between British imperialism and the dying African (Kerridge 27). Conrad has chosen a specific word for this "thread," it is not cotton or generic wool, it is high quality yarn with a long fiber consisting of straight parallel strands, subject to separating into strands, one of which the African wears round his neck.

Marlow has more to say about the reasons for the African's thread necklace: "Why? Where did he get it? Was it a badge – an ornament – a charm – a propitiatory act?" (HD 58). These comments cement a link to the notion of the fetish, an effort on the African's part to yoke European power through its cloth in releasing him from this deadly servitude, but the white

Chapter Five: "Heart of Darkness": Conrad's Centerpiece in the Congo

thread from beyond the seas can't save him – it serves instead as a sign of his enslavement.

There is more to read in this scene as Marlow draws attention to the sharp contrast of black and white; the reader familiar with the connections between ivory and the slave trade is reminded of David Livingstone's observation that " 'black ivory carried white ivory'" on its back (qtd. in Beachey 276n7). Here, of course, the dying African youth has been subjected to enforced labor in building a faster, more efficient means of transporting the ivory to Europe than on his back. The sharp contrast of white yarn on black skin refers the reader back to an earlier association to black and white, and to wool, fate, and death in the image of the mysterious women ushering Marlow into the Company offices in that city "like a whited sepulchre" while "knitting black wool as for a warm pall" (HD 51). Just as important, though, the appearance of white worsted is the first note struck in the text of the actual presence of an object of trade. Ivory as an African export has so far been present in the text only tangentially, manufactured into an object of use on the *Nellie* or metaphorically connected to yellow idols and bones; it will, of course, soon be seen in its raw tusk form.

But the white worsted thread from beyond the seas is textually present first, and in his reference to it, Marlow points to the power in nineteenth-century European trade of a constellation of commodities in Conrad's Congo – as I have noted in previous chapters – the "holy trinity" of trading commodities in central Africa: cloth, beads, and brass wire. Inasmuch as Marlow seems determined to dismiss and even disparage the holy trinity, the liminal textual presence of these objects opens a window on the trading reality that Conrad himself witnessed. The history glimpsed in this first reference to a trade item points to England, a wool merchanting center in the nineteenth century, importing raw wool from colonies like Australia, New Zealand, and South Africa, and distributing it to manufacturing centers both at home and abroad, where it was processed and then exported back out to the colonies (Barnard 4). Wool, cotton, and worsted from beyond the seas traveled around the world, in fact on several of

Conrad's own ships like the *Duke of Sutherland* and the *Loch Etive*, to reach the interior of Africa and be reborn in Conrad's fictional reality as the worsted necklace metaphorically strangles a dying African. Clearly linked to England, the African's thread "necklace" introduces textiles more broadly as a premier trade item which had established itself in coastal African culture and daily life as early as the seventeenth century. Imported European cloth was traded for ivory, copper, and slaves, even linked through its use in trade for slaves in Africa to its harvesting in the New World by slaves transported from Africa. Gradually, European cloth replaced indigenous cloth woven of raphia palm as well as cotton cloth woven in India, and by the 1880s, cheaply manufactured cotton from Manchester was driving local cloth off the market in the major trading center at Stanley Pool, along the Congo tributaries, and the Congo plateau (Martin, "Contesting Clothes" 404).

That catastrophic change in a native African economy was foreordained with the onset of the Industrial Revolution, when England, continental Europe and the US began to dominate global trading, creating a "great divergence," the period when the world separated into industrialized and non-industrialized states, between colonizer and colonized (Beckert xiv). Inventions in the eighteenth century like the flying shuttle and the spinning jenny as well as the emergence of Liverpool as a major port for overseas trading fostered an industrial revolution in cotton textile production (Inikori 76). An "empire of cotton"[86] tied America, Europe, Africa, Australia, and Asia into a complex commercial web where ships carrying slaves from Africa to the US provided the slave labor necessary to grow and harvest cotton, ships from the US to Europe carried the raw cotton to be manufactured in (predominantly) Lancashire mills, and ships from England, other countries in Europe, and India both shipped wool from Australia to Manchester and carried manufactured cotton cloth to Africa to be traded for slaves and ivory (Beckert 36).

By 1868, commodities to and from Britain, France, and the US constituted 83% of African trade; and in the decade

Chapter Five: "Heart of Darkness": Conrad's Centerpiece in the Congo 253

1861-1870, "about 57 million yards of imported textiles of all kinds were traded annually" to Africa (Eltis and Jennings 938, 953). By the time Conrad and his fictional counterpart Marlow arrived in central Africa, the African market was flooded with European textiles. Yet with such an immense volume in commodity trade with Africa, it is wrong to assume, as Marlow seems to do, that the African consumer was easy to please with poor quality, trashy cloth. In fact, foreign cloth represented a luxury item for Africans, as it was exotic and higher in quality than native-produced cloth; so Africa was not just "a dumping ground for cheap cloth" (950). But Marlow sees no value in trade cloth, for he never notes African consumption of that cloth, only observing it warehoused at the central station and describing it as "rubbishy" (HD 65).

Marlow doesn't know, given his limited interaction with Africans in his fictional Congo, that for the African consumer, cloth was an important cultural indicator – if he did, he might not have applauded the consuming blaze. During the eighteenth and early nineteenth centuries, Indian prints and calicoes were quite popular with African traders and consumers, but increasingly in the nineteenth century, Manchester traders traveled to West Africa to obtain samples of favored indigenous cloth in order to make copies, and European cloth was woven expressly for the African trade (Nielsen 469). "Guinea" cloth, originally woven in India and shipped to Europe to be re-exported to slave traders on the Guinea coast, was replaced by European weaves in imitation of Indian cloth. Blue baft, or guinea blue cotton cloth, for example, was consistently popular with the African consumer. Two of Conrad's natives, the cannibal headman and the helmsman, both appear in blue cotton. "Their headman, a young, broad-chested black, severely draped in dark-blue fringed cloths […] stood near me" (HD 84), and the helmsman "wore a blue cloth wrapper from the waist to the ankles, and thought all the world of himself" (89). While Conrad provides only a peek at clothed Africans – the cannibal headman, the helmsman, and the African woman who appears later in the text "draped in striped and fringed cloths" (107) on the bank of the Congo – an alternative material history does emerge through the glimpses of what Marlow sees.

The importance of cloth in nineteenth century African material history for the African consumer was that cloth and clothing represented in microcosm the aesthetic, moral, cultural, and communal ideals of the wearer. For the interpreter of African life at this period, cloth becomes "a document which records, when considered in its proper social setting or cultural context, the historical, ethnographic, and aesthetic qualities of an individual, group of individuals, or nation as a whole" (Steiner 103). At some level Marlow might guess at this reality, detailing as he does the pride with which his helmsman sports his "blue cloth wrapper." However, African use of cloth

Togoland Beauties

Chapter Five: "Heart of Darkness": Conrad's Centerpiece in the Congo 255

revealed even more: according to Steiner, cloth manufactured by one society expressly for use by another, becomes a "visible symbol representing a delicate stylistic and functional balance struck at a particular historical moment between two cultures in contact" (104): *transculturation*.

The image above, an unacknowledged photograph in Lethbridge's *West Africa the Elusive*, offers powerful visual proof of the balance between two cultures in contact. Writing about the image, Steiner suggests that the women in the photograph wear three versions of cloth – a continuum from native enhanced to European manufactured: the wrapper pictured on the left is an African design "painted or dyed on a lightweight commercial cloth," i.e., an indigenous cloth (105). The one in the middle appears to be a European manufactured cloth printed with an African motif. And the one on the right is clearly wearing European-made cloth with a European motif – Steiner suggests Dutch, British, German, or French. The prime indicator for Steiner is the "regularity and precision" in the African and European patterns printed on European cloth as opposed to hand-stamped or painted patterns on the indigenous cloth (105).

In the effort to reconstruct African ethnohistory, Steiner insists, "textile arts […] ought to be more thoroughly integrated into what has recently been labeled 'a continuous interdisciplinary dialogue'" (104, qtd. from Obenga 85).[87] Steiner concludes with a profound statement of the importance of recognizing the transformational nature of the commodity in Africa: "the example of the Euro-African textile trade epitomizes the shattering of Europe's distorting glass of preconceptions, thus bringing to a head the potential sensitivity and refinement in Europe's image of Africa in the 19th and 20th centuries" (106).

As a further example of transculturation produced by the African trade in cloth, the African woman pictured on the postcard below also displays two cultures in contact: she wears cloth wrappers produced both in Europe and in Africa; her large wrapper appears to be a European manufacture in a beautifully

Congo. Femme Acra

detailed print suited specifically to African taste – notice the regularity in the design which would indicate manufactured cloth. The bodice wrap is more difficult to identify, but the fringe on the waist wrap may be European as well.[88] In addition to the significance of transculturation in cloth, African access to imported goods in general and cotton cloth in particular was viewed as the essence of power (Martin, "Power, Cloth" 4-6). Imported cloth took hold in political and social contexts as well as serving as a primary form of currency and as a visible marker of one's place in society (2, 7), but Marlow largely misses the implications, seeing only that European manufactured cloth is simply "rubbishy" – his apparent lack of insight, though, points to his larger purpose, to indict an inequity in trade which he believes disadvantages the African.

Chapter Five: "Heart of Darkness": Conrad's Centerpiece in the Congo   257

From the Outer Station to the Central Station: the Overland Journey

Marlow soon turns his attention to caravans moving through the Outer Station, strings of dusty Africans carry "a stream of manufactured goods – rubbishy cottons, beads and brass wire – set off into the depths of darkness and in return came a precious trickle of ivory" (HD 60). On the track toward that ivory and Kurtz, Marlow must first trace the steps on the overland journey that Conrad traveled a decade before. Having retrieved his Congo journal several years earlier as he began "An Outpost of Progress," he may have revisited it for details of Marlow's overland, "two hundred mile tramp" (61).[89] His pages of description and brilliant sketches in the "Congo Diary" are collapsed here to a few sentences:

> Paths, paths everywhere; a stamped in network of paths spreading over an empty land, through long grass, through burnt grass, through thickets, down and up chilly ravines, up and down stony hills ablaze with heat; and a solitude, a solitude, nobody, not a hut. The population had cleared out a long time ago. (HD 61)

The depopulation described here seems a bit exaggerated for artistic effect, but not entirely off the mark from the accounts I've included in preceding chapters; the riverine tribes had without doubt been decimated by slaving and many had fled the dreaded Force Publique press gangs.

Conrad's experience, re-molded to the shape of this new narrative, allows many sights from the "real" of the past to resurface. There is added description of dead Africans on the trail; Marlow notes "a carrier dead in harness, at rest in the long grass near the path, with an empty water-gourd and his long staff lying by his side" (61), as well as government agents patrolling the roads: "a white man in an unbuttoned uniform […] with an armed escort of lank Zanzibaris, very hospitable and festive, not to say drunk" (61-62). In his "Congo Diary" dated July 3, 1890, Conrad noted passing apparently efficient government Zanzibaris traveling by canoe with a register for some unstated purpose. Marlow, however, sees nothing to respect in either the disheveled white officer or the Zanzibaris – surely jabs at both the Congo Free State administration and perhaps at Stanley's privileging of Zanzibari escorts in his narratives. As I've noted earlier, Stanley depended on Zanzibari warriors for help in building all his stations, but by the time Conrad arrived in the Congo, Zanzibaris in service to the Congo Free State were abusing their power by assaulting the natives and causing depopulation of the trade routes.[90]

More reminiscences from Conrad's own overland journey surface in the description of the "middle-aged negro with a bullet-hole in the forehead" (62) – ignored by the officer and Zanzibaris Marlow has just passed. And Harou, mentioned anonymously, makes an appearance here – "a white companion too, not a bad chap but rather too fleshy" (62), Harou's spill at the hands of his carriers is recorded, causing "no end of rows with the carriers" (62). Conrad's uncomprehended speech to the bearers mentioned in his "Congo Diary" surfaces as well, "I made a speech in English, with gestures, not one of which was lost to the sixty pairs of eyes before me" (62), but regardless of their attention, the bearers drop the white companion, Harou's double, the next day. Marlow feels he's becoming "scientifically interesting" (62).[91]

Marlow is far from done denigrating trade objects, commenting once he's arrived at the Central Station (presumably Kinshasa / Leopoldville[92] at Stanley, now Malebo, Pool), "One evening a grass shed full of calico, cotton prints, beads, and I don't know what else, burst into a blaze so suddenly that you would have thought the earth had opened to let an avenging fire consume all that trash" (65).

The grass shed invites comparison to the "fetish" storehouse encountered in "An Outpost of Progress," its fetish power here ironically burned to the ground. Marlow's disgust with trade goods erupts again a few days later: "And several times a week a coast caravan came in with trade goods – ghastly glazed calico that made you shudder only to look at it, glass beads value about a penny a quart, confounded spotted cotton handkerchiefs" (71).

The Second of the "Holy Trinity" of Commodities: Beads

The irony of the context in which Marlow's comments are set is that these objects arrive but not the rivets needed to repair the steamer, nonetheless, Marlow has allowed a glimpse into the reality of African trade. Glass trade beads, "cheap" in Marlow's view, were second in importance to cloth in the trinity of commodities and bear nearly as much significance in African trading networks as cloth. Portuguese trading ships arrived during the fifteenth century to trade glass beads as their major currency for gold, slaves, ivory, and palm oil. In the Kingdom of Kongo, glass trade beads served as a major form of currency dating from about 1858 (Verhaeghe et al. 25). Along with textiles, beads were "among the foremost items of long-distance trade" (Sciama 7). "Trade," writes Lois Sherr Dubin, "became a focal point for organizing human affairs: empires grew out of markets" (129). Dubin dates bead trading in Africa as far back as the fourth century CE, but the majority of this trade occurred from the fifteenth-nineteenth centuries, when the Dutch, English, Belgians, and Germans brought *millions* of Venetian, Dutch, and Bohemian beads to Africa. Glass beads, largely undervalued in Europe, became a "primary export good and in the period of European expansion they were transformed into a powerful currency" (Trivellato, "Out of Women's Hands" 48). Earlier, Portuguese merchants left records of the high trade value placed on glass beads; one such merchant wrote in 1554 that Africans would receive "beads in exchange, which they consider as great a treasure as are gold and jewellery with us" (qtd. in Klehm). Travelling in Murano in 1728, Montesquieu found that the manufacture of cheap glass and beads was predominantly for the African slave trade. Later, he added in his travel accounts that glass pearls made in Murano and fashioned in Venice were sent from Italy "*pour les Sauvages & Nègres*" (1: 46, qtd. in Trivellato, "Murano Glass" 165n90). In fact, glass beads are often the only imported commodity to survive in African archeological sites.

In the 1850s, Richard Burton remarked that "African specie" consisted of cotton cloth, brass wire, and beads, all used to barter for ivory (1: 20). Burton observed at least 400 varieties of beads in trade, also noting that what the trader might feel was a large amount didn't really go far. In Burton's Eurocentric view, like Marlow's, beads were "rubbish" and "toy[s]" to the "savage" (136). Yet their disbursement was widespread; Burton noted that there was such a vast demand for beads that they were traded "throughout the vast terra incognita of the central African basin" (136). In 1867, David Livingstone noted the use of beads as currency in his journals, writing as an aside

> We may here add a few particulars concerning beads, which form such an important item of currency all through Africa. With a few exceptions they are all manufactured in Venice. The greatest care must be exercised, or the traveler – ignorant of the prevailing fashion in the country he is about to explore – finds himself with an accumulation of beads of no more value than tokens would be if tendered in this country for coin of the realm. (*The Last Journals* 150)

Both Burton and Livingstone acknowledged that beads had a critical function in the entire African monetary system; beads served as the "link between long-distance trade and African inter-regional trade" (Pallaver 20). Comprising the largest portion of African caravans, beads, along with cloth and metal wire, were used to buy food and pay taxes. Trading in beads was tricky, however, as Burton, Livingstone, and Stanley all learned, for there was a constant fluctuation of demand; in Stanley's view "[t]he various kind of beads [to be carried into the interior] required great time to learn, for the women of Africa are as fastidious in their tastes for beads as the women of New York are for jewelry" (qtd. in Pallaver 25). Indeed, Stanley's remarks suggest not only his own Eurocentric view of the reason for the fluctuation in taste for beads, but also his lack of understanding of their function in African society and of the agency of Africans in making choices as consumers. But he was a sufficiently wily trader to recognize how necessary it was to carry the

Chapter Five: "Heart of Darkness": Conrad's Centerpiece in the Congo

most desirable collection of beads, as indicated by the sample box from his collection illustrated below containing eighteen separate compartments of beads on threads, each named with a small tag. Outfitting a caravan in Zanzibar in 1876, Stanley insists, requires careful attention to the kinds of cloth, beads, and wire in demand by different tribes. The "intending explorer," Stanley writes, spends all his daylight hours "in the selection and purchase of [...] bales of unbleached cottons, striped and coloured fabrics, *handkerchiefs*" (emphasis mine – compare Marlow's "confounded spotted cotton handkerchiefs") and red caps, bags of blue, green, red, white and amber-coloured beads, small and large, round and oval, and coils upon coils of thick brass wire" (*Through the Dark Continent* 1: 24).

In general, the more unusual a bead, the more attractive it was to the African consumer. Burton pays tribute to the immense variety of beads in circulation in Africa in an appendix

Box of Bead Samplings. Stanley Archives, Coll. King Baudouin Foundation, entrusted to the AfricaMuseum, Brussels, Belgium

to his *The Lake Regions of Central Africa*, naming several varieties like the *samesame* – a small coral bead made of scarlet enameled on a white ground – pink porcelain beads, and blue porcelain beads, among others (2: 330). The coarse porcelain bead was a staple of commerce, and, as I've noted, beads frequently changed in and out of favor to create temporary standards of value. Catalogs of bead cards such as the Moses Levin's catalog of bead samples[93] and *The Venetian Bead Book* from the mid to late nineteenth century provide valuable information about the types of beads in circulation. Biconical disks, bicones, and tubes in opaque golden yellow or ocher decorated with stripes or eye-like designs, beads decorated with "squiggles," beads with black bases and white eyes with pink or blue pupils, and beads with plant-like decorations or spiral lines were popular (Peter Francis 27, 39), as well as, according to Richard Burton, "blue bohemian glass beads cut into facets" (2: 333, qtd. in Francis 39). This is by no means an exhaustive list of varieties of beads imported in Africa, but only a few favorites. The sample display from the Levin catalog below provides a variety of shapes, sizes, colors, and designs found in African trade beads.

Beads Employed in the African Trade for Ivory. © The Trustees of the British Museum

Chapter Five: "Heart of Darkness": Conrad's Centerpiece in the Congo 263

If, as Burton and Marlow thought, beads were only rubbish, there would be no need to explore their significance further; but the opposite is the case when we examine the uses to which beads were put in African culture. Beads were not only objects for adornment or used as currency in trade, they were also important in rituals, a fact that is clarified by archeological discoveries at burial sites. Dubin argues that they played a major role in African culture and in rituals ensuring the continuity of the community (151). The graves of slaves at burial sites on southern plantations in the US indicate that for these descendants of central Africans – approximately 40% of the ten million Africans brought to the US through the middle of the nineteenth century originated in Kongo and Angola (Stine et al. 49)[94] – beads were an important part of African American material culture whose underlying meaning was closely associated with its African roots – "a pan-cultural phenomenon" (53). These graves yielded blue beads in much larger numbers than any other color (50), suggesting the power of blue in these communities for producing spiritually protective charms that operated in a similar manner to the *nkisi* or "fetish." According to Stanley, for example, sacrifices of white *merikani* beads were made to the god of Lake Tanganyika; Stanley's guide insisted that "those who throw the beads generally get past without trouble, but those who do not throw the beads into the lake get lost and are drowned" (*How I Found Livingstone* 1: 400, qtd. in Pallaver 25).

Used as ornaments, beads, according to Sciama, "in their different colours, arrangements and styles, are important symbols of collective, as well as individual identity for many social groups" (18). In nineteenth-century Tanzania, Pallaver argues further, beads were used to decorate hair and beards, to "embroider cloths, masks and dolls, and to make jewellery, like necklaces, bracelets, and so on" (25). Most importantly, though, glass trade beads help us, more than a century later, to infer different cultural narratives revealed by these objects of material culture that go beyond the limits of ancient texts (Klehm), and, in the case of "Heart of Darkness," to continue to insert the history of a material culture back into the discussion of a mythic narrative.

Upriver from the Central Station

Having witnessed the trade in European goods (rubbish?) for ivory firsthand, Marlow spends two months on the upriver journey from the Central Station, facing similar struggles to navigate a dangerously powerful river that Conrad himself faced assisting Captain Koch in 1890. Through Marlow, though, the emotions suppressed in Conrad's diary can emerge as a metaphoric return to the origins of the earth, the navel of the narrative: "Going up that river was like travelling back to the earliest beginnings of the world, when vegetation rioted on the earth and the big trees were kings" (HD 77). Marlow as navigator has to "keep guessing the channel; I had to discern, mostly by inspiration, the signs of hidden banks; I watched for sunken stones" (77). Additionally, Marlow has to identify wooding spots to keep the steamer, "like a sluggish beetle crawling on the floor of a lofty portico" (78) afloat. Notice the bird's eye view here in Marlow's metaphoric description of the slow progress of the steamer; perhaps, as he writes, Conrad is visualizing once more the bird's eye views of the track of the steamer *Roi des Belges* as he drew his directional maps in the "Up-river Book." So much more emerges here than Conrad, nine years earlier, could have expressed in his journal at the time, because now, instead of maintaining a steady focus only on the perils in the river, Marlow recreates the space, "The earth seemed unearthly," "travelling in the night of the first ages, of these ages that are gone, leaving hardly a sign – and no memories" (79).

In a fog like "heap of cotton-wool" (87), Marlow thinks of the dangers in his approach to "Kurtz grubbing for ivory in the wretched bush" (87) while providing a touch of comic relief in the characterization of the cannibal crew. Their payment – "three pieces of brass wire, each about nine inches long" (85) – seems senseless to Marlow as he reckons that there is no opportunity for the cannibals to buy provisions along the banks of the river for there are either no villages or the natives are hostile.

The Third of the "Holy Trinity" of Commodities: Brass Wire

Conrad also acknowledges, through his narrator, a widespread practice of using brass wire as money in the Congo. Brass wire in Conrad's text is sent out into the wilderness along with the other manufactured commodities, cottons and beads, in a caravan from the Outer Station – and in return Marlow sees only that "precious trickle of ivory" (60). By the mid nineteenth century, the introduction of brass wire in the Congo had produced significant change, a change which dramatically impacted market forces in the Congo – dragging the Congo even more into contact with Europe and definitively changing the nature of its reality.

In his history of metals, Leslie Aitchison remarks that metals have attained "an almost unquestioned supremacy among the materials used by man" (1: vii), and in exploring that history from the earliest periods, Aitchison unveils the importance of metal trading back to the Neolithic period in Asia Minor (50). Copper was one of the earliest commodities traded in Africa, bangles of fine-drawn copper wire date back to the twelfth century when copper was prized by Africans more highly than gold. But as early as 1713, the brass and copper industry in Bristol was thriving from its trade with west Africa (Inikori 468). With the dawn of the nineteenth century, metal, turned out in Birmingham brass factories, "flooded African markets," bringing European metal ware into direct competition with "indigenously produced metal [...] trade brass drove out African copper in almost all the arenas where the two met head on" (Herbert 154).

Both Burton in the 1850s and Livingstone in the 1870s witnessed the lively trade of native copper, and Stanley saw copper bars traded for ivory in the mid 1880s. But European trading companies pushed increasingly into the interior to find new markets for brass and copper kettles among natives eager to trade for ivory. Imports replacing indigenously produced copper wire invaded the Congo basin, aided by Stanley himself, who introduced brass rods as a form of payment into the upper Congo (171). Brass rods or *mitakos* were unknown on the Upper Congo before Stanley's arrival in the 1870s, but post Stanley, according to Herbert, the brass *mitako* superseded copper currency – "a tangible symbol of the 'opening up' of the continent to waves of explorers, missionaries and traders" (171). Stanley himself observed in 1877 that as tribes in the interior were increasingly exposed to the novelty of exotic foreign items for exchange: "copper was despised, but brass wire was gold – anything became purchasable with it except canoes" (*Through the Dark Continent* 2: 286). Johnston points out that "there is no race in Africa which combines zinc and copper to make brass," yet brass is found "in use among African tribes that have never seen a white man, possibly never even heard of a white race" (*British Central Africa* 463).

In the 1860s, W. C. Aitken published a history of brass manufacture, remarking that large quantities of brass wire made in Birmingham were being exported to the Gold Coast in the form of "guinea rods" used for trade (95). But brass wasn't just in use as money for trade, it was also an item of embellishment, converted into ornaments. Richard Burton, for example, wrote about brass "bangles," massive brass rings, worn by the Wanyamwesi – their weight demonstrating wealth and respectability (qtd. in Aitken 96). Livingstone commented as well on a "Makololo woman" attired in "Dame Nature" (a euphemism for nudity) aided by "a Birmingham brass wire manufacturer" (qtd. in Aitken 96). Livingstone's facetious description is worth quoting at some length for its resonance with the adornment of Conrad's magnificent African woman:

> Sebituane's sister [...] wore eighteen solid brass rings, as thick as one's finger, on each leg, and three of copper under each knee; nineteen

Chapter Five: "Heart of Darkness": Conrad's Centerpiece in the Congo 267

> brass rings on her left arm, and eight of brass and copper on her right, also a large ivory ring above each elbow. She had a pretty bead necklace, and a bead sash encircled her waist. The weight of the bright brass rings round her legs impeded her walking, and chafed her ankles; but as it was the fashion, she did not mind the inconvenience. (*Narrative of an Expedition to the Zambesi* 283-84, qtd. in Aitken 96)

Sebituane's sister, left unnamed in Livingstone's text, is adorned transculturally: indigenous ivory and copper, European brass and beads.

Traveling up the Mfini River, the upper tributary of what would later be named the Kassai River, Stanley was on a voyage of exploration which would ultimately result in the discovery of Lake Leopold II in 1882. On that voyage, Stanley found that brass ornaments had penetrated deeply into the interior of the Congo, remarking:

> [The] women, like the Wy-yanzi, affect heavy brass collars, from ten to sixty pounds weight of brass around their necks, while leglets and armlets were also massive. The hair was in towering top-knots. They carried spears like Zulu assegais; the shafts being slender and long, and beautifully grooved. (*The Congo* 1: 428-29)

Just a few years earlier in 1875, during his expedition to trace the length of the entire Congo River, Stanley visited the court of Mtesa, Emperor of Uganda, where he witnessed "Mtesa drilling his Amazons and playing at soldiers with his pets. They are all comely and brown, with fine virginal bosoms. But what strikes us most is the effect of discipline" (*Through the Dark Continent* 1: 314). In Stanley's photograph reproduced below, the women, like those later in the village on the Mfini River, carry spears and sport anklets and necklaces, possibly made of brass; but what is even more striking is the recognition that such "warrior" women existed.[95] The similarities to Marlow's African woman are remarkable.

By 1890, the brass rod or wire was the "money of by far the larger number of the people on the Lower and Upper Congo"; variable lengths of brass rods,[96] were the medium of exchange and the unit of value (Weeks, *Congo Life* vii), and indigenous

Mtesa's Amazons

copper mining and production of metal goods did not survive once the "flood" of Birmingham metals had begun – the native economy had been forever changed.

Ivory: The Commodity Transcendent

European objects of exchange, viewed as inferior by Marlow, appear marginally in various places in the text; the value of those "rubbishy cottons" in Marlow's opinion, for example, falls far below that of the ivory which they buy. And Marlow, to this point, sees only a tiny bit of ivory – a "trickle," but its symbolic presence pervades. At a crucial juncture for the journey of ivory from Africa to Europe, Marlow sees only a trickle because ivory supplies will, in fact, soon begin to dwindle. From its height in 1890-1891, the ivory trade exported 950,000 pounds of ivory worth more than £300,000 to Europe, in fact, to the Thames, the gateway to England, the largest importer of ivory in Europe in the nineteenth century (Beachey 290). Translated to tons, Britain imported 500 tons of ivory each year from 1850-1910,

Chapter Five: "Heart of Darkness": Conrad's Centerpiece in the Congo

with world consumption of ivory amounting to 1,000 tons in the late nineteenth century (Meredith 111-12). Ivory could be manufactured into so many products in the West – from buttons, beads, bracelets and knitting needles to piano keys, billiard balls, and *dice*. However, this monstrous consumption required the killing of approximately 65,000 elephants annually to meet the demand (112). German explorer Georg Schweinfurth warned:

> Since not only the males with their large and valuable tusks, but the females also with the young, are included in this wholesale and indiscriminate slaughter, it may easily be imagined how year by the year the noble animal is being fast exterminated. (qtd. in Meredith 112)

Martin Meredith suggests that the flow of ivory from Africa reached around the globe in the nineteenth century, prized because it was "finer-grained, richer in tone and larger than Indian ivory" (107). In fact, ivory was the "plastic of the era," responding to cutting and polishing so well that it could be sliced into transparent, thin sheets like the one displayed at the Crystal Palace – "fourteen inches wide and fifty-two feet long" (107).

But by the end of the decade, as Conrad wrote "Heart of Darkness," the imposition of game regulations to preserve the African elephant shrank the size of ivory exports to just 100,000 pounds per year – almost ten times less than just ten years before (Beachey 287). Marlow, like his author, lives in two moments, time past and time present – then, in the Congo, and now, on the *Nellie;* as Conrad inhabits the 1890-1891 Congo in memory and resurrects it in 1899. By the time he wrote, Conrad knew what had become of the ivory trade.

Kurtz, Marlow notes, is in the "true ivory-country" (HD 60), but that's still more than 1,000 miles away, and as desire drives him to follow the track of ivory and reach Kurtz, it is only the word *ivory* which, once Marlow arrives at the Central Station, within sight of the "big river," "rang in the air, was whispered, was sighed" (65). Both ivory and Kurtz are ephemera, beckoning from the wilderness, their interlocking associations as word and icon becoming ever stronger and reaching an epitome once we reach the physical presence of the man himself. And both beckon, as the wilderness itself beckons: "Come and find out" (54).

Men, who appear to Marlow like a lot of "faithless pilgrims," mill about, their rapacity giving off an odor like "a whiff from some corpse" (65). With no appearance of ivory, only the word, Marlow remarks presciently about the power of ivory over the "pilgrims," "[y]ou would think they were praying to it" (65). Marlow raises the specter of ivory as an object of worship, a deadly fetish, which cloaks its object-hood in mystery. Ivory's power lies in its exchange value for money – not in Africa, where it is sufficiently undervalued by Africans to be exchanged for "rubbish," but indeed in Europe where it represents great wealth.[97] However, Conrad's narrative construction continuously underscores a metonymic linkage between European capitalism in the Congo, desire, and death – the pilgrims' greed stinks like a corpse.

As Marlow waits interminably for the means to mend his steamboat in a dreamscape of waste and senselessness, Marlow senses that the "silent wilderness [...] struck [him] as something great and invincible, like evil or truth" that simply waits "patiently for the passing away of this fantastic invasion" (65). Even the brick maker, the Manager's spy whom Marlow describes as a "papier-mâché Mephistopheles"(68) whose body, if poked, would yield "only a little loose dirt may be" (68), invites metaphoric linking with the city like a whited sepulchre. The brick maker, along with the others in that station are all waiting for something – "to get appointed to a trading post where ivory was to be had" (66). Yet they are all at present enveloped by a "wall of matted vegetation standing higher than the wall of a temple," through whose gap Marlow could see "the great river [...] glittering, glittering, as it flowed broadly by without a murmur" (69). From that "immensity," Marlow "could see a little ivory coming out" (69) and he has known for some time that the tantalizing Kurtz is in there as well. As he reflects upon the presence of Kurtz in that "dumb thing," "the immensity" of darkness, Marlow hints at how far, in the future, he will go to lie for Kurtz and insists upon his hatred of the lie, which has "a taint of death, a flavour of mortality" (69). The metaphors knitting Kurtz, ivory, lies, and death tip into an ever-expanding web of associations, strengthening Marlow's desire and his determination to penetrate space to reach the center of those associations.

In knitting this web of associations, Marlow senses the "unreal" nature of his experiences: "Do you see him?" he cries out to his listeners on the *Nellie*.

> "It seems to me I am trying to tell you a dream – making a vain attempt – because no relation of a dream can convey the dream-sensation, that commingling of absurdity, surprise and bewilderment in a tremor of struggling revolt, that notion of being captured by the incredible which is of the very essence of dreams...." (HD 70)

Marlow wrestles with the disparity between the experience of the dream and its narration, forced into repetition in his efforts to make knowable the unknowable. Anticipating the notion advanced by Paul Carter much later that the relationship between exploring and dreaming is a commonplace of the literature of exploration, Marlow (and Conrad) senses the peculiar unreality of his experience. The dream-sensation, "that notion of being captured by the incredible which is of the very essence of dreams" carries Marlow on a dream-journey through a dreamscape, ever heading toward the navel of the dream where, he will realize, "We live, as we dream – alone..." (70). Communication fails.

Commodity Fetishism, the Biscuit Tin, and the Tin-Pot Steamer

The ghost of Stanley, as the premier representative of trade in the Belgian Congo, rises from Marlow's narrative and points the way to the means of transportation by which trading commodities lead to ivory – the wretched old steamboat is the fictional representation of Conrad's actual steamboat, the *Roi des Belges*, used by Stanley on his expeditions a few years before.[98] It is here that Marlow makes that intriguing observation, one overlooked by many commentaries on this novella. The "battered, twisted, ruined tin-pot steamer" rings under Marlow's feet like a Huntley & Palmer biscuit-tin "kicked along a gutter, she was nothing so solid in make and rather less pretty in shape" (71).[99] Both pieces of tin serve as mounting evidence of trash and waste – one "ruined" wreck and the other so omnipresent as to be found in the street and "kicked along a gutter" (71). Admittedly, Marlow uses the trademark ubiquitous biscuit tin of the 1890s as an analogy only, not as a trade commodity, but the connection of such a strong and lovely object to Marlow's (as well as Conrad's) steamboat is striking for the detail it offers about Conrad's knowledge of European, specifically English, commodities and artifacts in the Congo. Huntley and Palmers tins could keep biscuits exported from Reading, England, fresh for years as they traveled around the world, and the tin itself became as much a symbol of the British Empire as Coca Cola (or maybe now McDonalds) symbolizes the United States. By 1867, Joseph Leete, Huntley and Palmers' sales representative, had secured a warrant of appointment from Leopold II, so that biscuit tins were widely circulating in Africa, with evidence found in Uganda, Sierra Leone, and the Sudan (Corley 84).

Counterpointing Africa's raw resource, ivory, the standard of value, fetish supreme, and object of desire that pervades Marlow's narrative, the biscuit tin marks one point on a "fetish" continuum where the commodity seems wholly secular and immersed in the world while ivory marks the opposing point, verging on the religious, sacred, iconic. The biscuit tin by itself, in contrast to ivory, would appear to have very little intrinsic or exchange value despite the many ways in which it might be used; thus, the tin is both commodity and *not* commodity – at one time it had use and exchange value but now in the gutter, it has none. Unhinged from its original purpose, the tin – in

Chapter Five: "Heart of Darkness": Conrad's Centerpiece in the Congo

Conrad's metaphor – is free to signify otherwise. Certainly, Conrad means for the tin to represent the worst of modern capitalism and advertising as the commodity transcendent, but kicked by the mule, the tin breaks free of what it may have been meant to do.

It can, however, be shaped into something of artistic value – and linked to work, which was always for Conrad linked to art. The passage that begins with a reference to the tin closes with a meditation on work, and the hard work expended on the tin-pot steamer that made Marlow love it. His work on the steamer, the biscuit tin's reflection, offers Marlow a kind of redemption, a "chance to come out a bit" (HD 72), a chance to find himself. "[Y]our own reality," Marlow continues, " – for yourself – not for others – what no other man can ever know. They can only see the mere show – and can never tell what it really means" (72). As Conrad would observe later in *The Mirror of the Sea:*

> Efficiency of a practically flawless kind may be reached naturally in the struggle for bread. But there is something beyond – a higher point, a subtle and unmistakable touch of love and pride beyond mere skill; almost an inspiration which gives to all work that finish which is almost art – which *is* art. (*MS* 37)

Self-making, or self-fashioning in Stephen Greenblatt's term, requires that Marlow, as part of that process, must remake the tin-pot steamer and set it afloat, becoming the artist through the work of making.

Both the tin-pot steamer and the biscuit tin, its absent metaphor, merge in the Congo, with clear photographic evidence that, by Conrad's and Marlow's time, the biscuit tin had arrived in the Congo.[100] Note the caption of the photo: "Huntley and Palmers Biscuits foremost again," as the photograph below offers a view of one of the Belgian trading steamers on the Congo around 1890. Little is known of the provenance of this photograph housed in the Huntley and Palmers Gallery of the Reading Museum, but the photographer identified in the caption at the bottom of the photograph is Baptist missionary R. D. Darby, who helped found the Lukolela mission in 1887 (Hawker 239). The tin, with its recognizable garter and buckle is faintly visible on the steamer's roof just to the right of the steam funnel in the middle of the picture. In fact, the central figure in white with white safari helmet bears a strong facial resemblance to Stanley, thus the photograph may have been taken earlier than 1890, possibly dated almost a decade earlier, for the steamer shown in the illustration appears to be the *En Avant,* skippered by Stanley during the founding of the Congo Free State stations from 1879-1884. At Banana Point in 1879, Stanley wrote of the *En Avant:*

> The *En Avant* was guilty of extraordinary freaks, and as stubborn as the donkey is generally supposed to be. At one moment she had over ten atmospheres of steam, and rushed madly on, while we, expectantly watching the first signs of an explosion, were ready to jump overboard, but suddenly the gauge indicated descent, and the paddle-wheels could scarcely revolve, while the rudder never had the slightest control of her movements. (*Congo* 1: 68-69)

But due to its improving performance – the first boat to steam up to Stanley Falls under the guidance of a new engineer –

Belgian Trading Steamer. Upper Congo River.
Huntley and Palmers foremost again.[101] With kind permission
of the Reading Museum (Reading Borough Council)

Chapter Five: "Heart of Darkness": Conrad's Centerpiece in the Congo   275

The *En Avant*, *A.I.A.*, and *Roi des Belges*

Stanley grew to love the steamer, writing in his usual ebullient manner: "Oh, an epic poem might now be written of the brave little boat!" (70).

Thus in addition to its other achievements, the *En Avant* must have carried those "foremost" biscuits as it plied the river for a decade. However, what makes Conrad's reference to the biscuit tin an even more striking coincidence is that if Conrad was so familiar with the biscuit and its tin, then he may have seen the Huntley and Palmers picture trading card showing Stanley at the head of his expedition to rescue Emin Pasha, facing African bearers carrying the clearly recognizable garter and buckle of Huntley and Palmers tins. The postcard unmistakably adds to the accruing evidence not only of the ubiquitous presence of the biscuit tin worldwide but also of Stanley's success in turning all of Africa into a European consumer culture.

Ivoried Kurtz

Ivory is the focus for Stanley and for Marlow, though, not rubbishy cotton, beads, brass wire, or even biscuit tins – as

Stanley's Expedition to Relieve Emin Pasha. With kind permission of the Reading Museum (Reading Borough Council)

it clearly is for the Eldorado Exploring Expedition whose *"tin boxes, white cases, brown bales"* (emphasis added) add to the "muddle of the station" and suggest "the loot of innumerable outfit shops and provision stores, that, one would think, they were lugging [...] into the wilderness for equitable division" (HD 73). The tension in Marlow's irony is palpable. As the Central Station Manager notes to his uncle in the conversation Marlow overhears, a great deal of ivory has been coming out of the interior in the year or more since word has been heard from Kurtz, "'Ivory [...]. Lots of it – prime sort – lots – most annoying from him'" (74). And with the ivory comes Kurtz's bill – the invoice for his commission on the volume of ivory he has boated down the river. The ivory has been floated downriver by an English half-caste who reports that Kurtz had turned back rather than come into the Central Station with the ivory, a fact which adds to Kurtz's ephemeral, mysterious presence in the text as well as to Marlow's and the reader's desire to reach him. Word has come as well of one other, a "'wandering trader – a pestilential fellow snapping ivory from the natives'" (75);

this is the Russian harlequin – associated both with ivory and the dying Kurtz – whom Marlow will shortly meet.

Marlow, however, has still seen only a trickle of ivory. Yet symbolically, he's surrounded by it. Once on the river steaming toward Kurtz, Marlow passes small stations along the banks where the "word ivory would ring in the air for a while – and on we went again into the silence" (78). Ivory is still largely a word. It is just now that Marlow takes the helm, commanding the tin-pot steamboat upriver, exploring anew the shoals, currents, and soundings as he goes. He, not Stanley, is the explorer now, "You lost your way on that river as you would in a desert and butted all day long against shoals trying to find the channel till you thought yourself bewitched and cut off for ever from everything you had known once – somewhere – far away – in another existence perhaps" (77). Marlow is "bewitched," his past flooding back in the shape of an "unrestful and noisy dream remembered with wonder amongst the overwhelming realities of this strange world" (77). He is one of the "wanderers on a prehistoric earth, on an earth that wore the aspect of an unknown planet" (79), while the steamboat moves on through the silence of a dreamscape of high tree walls lining the banks of the river. He is at the mercy of an "implacable force brooding over an inscrutable intention" (77). So much of this upriver journey draws Marlow into contemplation that he figures himself as taking his place among the ranks of explorers; he feels that he is one of the first white men to penetrate this territory or the first in so long that memory of its exploration has been lost. The trace of Stanley has been, for the moment, erased, and, alone and unsupported, Marlow balances at the threshold of an experience of the Real, knowing it only as "[t]he inner truth [that] is hidden – luckily, luckily" (77). And it is only through "looking awry," through a distorted lens, to cite Slavoj Žižek, that Marlow can glimpse the Real; for Marlow, traveling on an unearthly earth, must question where reality lies – is reality an illusion and does the veil only slip momentarily when the dreamer is near the presence of the Real? It is "only in dreams that we encounter the *real* of our desire," Žižek argues, and "our common reality [...] turns out to be an illusion that rests on a certain 'repression,' on overlooking the real of our desire. This social reality is then nothing but a fragile, symbolic cobweb that can at any moment be torn aside by an intrusion of the real" (17). Marlow is at the threshold of such an intrusion.

But first Marlow finds that there is a sign of white presence when he lands just below the Inner Station and enters the hut left by the man known only to us as a Russian dressed like a harlequin. In that hut, Marlow finds a familiar book, *An Inquiry into some Points of Seamanship* by Towzer or Towson, an English master in His Majesty's Navy. Marlow the mariner, traveling through this "unearthly" earth, finds a comfortable, familiar presence, which, though replete with dull "repulsive tables of figures" represents "the right way of going to work" (HD 81).[102] However, the book is defamiliarized by being coded; Marlow thinks that notes written in cipher have been placed in the margins surrounding the text – in "this Nowhere [...] an extravagant mystery" (82). Homi Bhabha remarks that the English book's appearance as a sign of authority "reveals that they [these appearances] represent important moments in the historical transformation and discursive transfiguration of the colonial text and context" ("Signs Taken for Wonders" 147). In his critique, Bhabha shifts emphasis in reading Marlow's comment, "He must be English," from *who* must be English to an examination of the English book – and by extension, the book's presumably English author, Towson (148). In constructing this argument, Bhabha concludes that "both Marlow and Conrad owe" a particular debt "to the ideals of English 'liberty' and its liberal-conservative culture," and that "Towson's manual provides Marlow with a singleness of intention" (148). "[I]t is in between the edict of Englishness and the assault of the dark unruly spaces of the earth," Bhabha writes, "through an act of repetition, that the colonial text emerges uncertainly" (149). Bhabha identifies the uncertainty of Conrad's text and its ambivalence regarding colonial authority over those dark unruly spaces, but I believe

Chapter Five: "Heart of Darkness": Conrad's Centerpiece in the Congo

the implications of Marlow's find are even more far-reaching when we revisit Marlow's observation in its textual space. Bhabha has quoted the text but not reflected on the fact that the Manager complains about the "white man" (the harlequin) who has left wood for them at the wooding stop, "'It must be this miserable trader – this intruder,' exclaimed the Manager looking back malevolently at the place we had left. 'He must be English' I said. 'It will not save him from getting into trouble if he is not careful,' muttered the Manager darkly" (HD 82). Countering the manager's malevolence, Marlow seems to approve that the owner of the English book must be the white man he has not yet met. The unmistakable irony is, of course, that the "miserable trader" is Russian, and as Christopher GoGwilt suggests, "[t]he full force of Bhabha's reading lies in the recognition that the cultural ground, or text of *Heart of Darkness* is fundamentally unstable and mistaken" (125). While this passage does shift the ground beneath the reader's feet, Marlow counters the ambiguity with his acknowledgment of "having come upon something unmistakably *real*" (HD 82, emphasis added). Just how real, though, is Marlow's find when he confuses the notes written in Towson's book for ciphers?

Increasing the irony associated with this seaman's text is, of course, that the harlequin, the owner of the book, is not English at all but Russian, and the code or cipher Marlow finds in the margins of the book is written in Russian (100). Indeed, Marlow may well claim the "trader's" Englishness specifically to needle the Manager, whom he despises. Reading the scene in which the English book is marginally inscribed with Cyrillic print – a fact that Bhabha does not directly address but which offers an intriguing instance of East/West transculturation – suggests an important extension of Bhabha's argument. No doubt Conrad has increased the perplexity of the book's appearance by de-stabilizing "English" authority through the introduction of a "hybrid" text. Later Marlow will learn that both he and the harlequin have followed the sea; such knowledge could mitigate the harlequin's "Russianness," repugnant to Conrad, born a Pole, his family devastated by Russian imperialism.

Yet Conrad never affords the "harlequin" a name, the only reference is to a long "unreadable" signature left on the message at the woodpile. Thus the anonymous harlequin may represent Conrad's erasure of Russian identity, but the clear hybridity of Russian/English identification reveals, at the same time, the link between two imperialisms experienced by Conrad himself, Russian control of his native land and English colonialism in Africa. Englishness rises again in the harlequin's question to Marlow: "'You English?'" (98) – an echo of Marlow's comment about the harlequin "'He must be English.'"

Marlow can't bear to tear himself away from the book, "the shelter of an old and solid friendship" (82), a harbor which seems to invite safety in the imminent presence of the Real, so he takes away the mariner's manual as his guide. But the text itself, so familiar and yet so foreign to Marlow, serves as a metaphor of a bifurcated and bi-directional narrative flow which trembles between reality and the Real. The fictional work within a work is, indeed, a fiction, never published by John Towson, whose calculations in his actual *Tables to Facilitate the Practice of Great Circle Sailing* (1848) advanced global navigation at the dawn of the Age of Steam by providing the latitudes, courses, and distances for the shortest global shipping lanes necessary to support the massive proliferation of trade during the last decades of the nineteenth century (Cotter 220). Conrad's Marlow recognizes this fictional book by naming a real author of navigational manuals; in fact, like Conrad, we might imagine that Marlow studied Towson – as so many British mariners did – for his mates' exams. And in its "physical" appearance in the text, the white cotton thread which has stitched and bound the fictional book together forges an additional textual link to a growing indictment of colonialism by resonating with the eeriness of the bit of white worsted round the dying African's neck and, as I have observed, the omnipresence of English textiles in the Congo.

Towson's fictional book can't shelter Marlow now, though, for he is in the presence of real danger – not only from the river which could sink his steamboat but also from the banks, where

Chapter Five: "Heart of Darkness": Conrad's Centerpiece in the Congo

something immobile lurks, as though waiting for Marlow and all on board. Hoping that he is less attractive to danger than the pilgrims, Marlow recognizes a silly "touch of fantastic vanity which fitted well with the dream-sensation that pervaded all my days at that time" (HD 85-86). In the midst of a heavy fog, a fog like "a heap of cotton-wool," Marlow thinks of the dangers in his approach to this "Kurtz grubbing for ivory in the wretched bush" (87).

Having sustained an attack by the natives, navigated the snags and sandbanks in the river, and lost his helmsman, Marlow approaches the river bank where he will finally meet the "miserable trader," the harlequin who beckons him to the shore; Marlow notices his patchwork clothing – patches of blue, red, and yellow covering cheap, disintegrating brown holland cloth – offering an association with the clownish harlequin figure in European comedies for centuries.[103] The brightly colored patches themselves call out for association with the colors of African colonization – French blue, British red, brown (Dutch) holland cloth, and Belgian yellow – and the map in the office of the city like a whited sepulchre. The nameless harlequin figure is eager to establish national identity, "'You English?'" (98) he calls out to Marlow; admitting sadly that he is not. The harlequin, that "pestilential" wandering trader the Manager despises, has sent a little ivory back, has served on English ships, and is admittedly the author of the Russian notes to Towson (whose name is now confirmed in the text as Towson and not Towzer, 100). He tells Marlow of Kurtz's travels in the interior and his discoveries of "lots of villages, *a lake too* [...] but mostly his expeditions had been for ivory" (101-02, emphasis added). In what appears to be another of his rare, veiled references to Stanley, Conrad may refer here to Stanley's journey up the "Kwa" – the mouth of the Kassai on the Congo River and his discovery of Lake Leopold II at the furthest point of the Mfini River – perhaps this was on Conrad's mind in the aftermath of having published "An Outpost of Progress." This nexus of just three words "a lake too" binds together three strands of reference: to Stanley's voyage to and discovery of Lake Leopold on the *En Avant*, to Stanley's traveling on the Mfini, a tributary of the Kassai, to discover that lake, and of course to "An Outpost of Progress" set on the Kassai.[104]

As he listens to the harlequin, Marlow thinks in navigational images of the way in which Kurtz and his Russian acolyte had "come together unavoidably, like two ships becalmed near each other, and lay rubbing sides at last" (101). Without goods to trade, Marlow wonders how Kurtz has managed to secure ivory; there were cartridges left, the harlequin tells him, so Marlow confirms, "'To speak plainly he raided the country'" (102). Having made himself "adored" by the natives for his superior firepower, Kurtz even threatened to shoot the harlequin for the small bit of ivory he'd collected. And only recently had Kurtz emerged from the wilderness with his adoring tribe, to slake "the appetite for more ivory" (103). It is hardly an accident that at this point in the text Marlow realizes that the "round knobs" on stakes around Kurtz's compound are, in fact shrunken heads – "a head that seemed to sleep at the top of that pole, and, with the shrunken dry lips showing a narrow white line of the teeth, was smiling, too, smiling continuously at some endless and jocose *dream* of that eternal slumber" (HD 103-04, emphasis added). The black shrunken heads re-invoke the color imagery of light and dark as they surround and pay homage to Kurtz's own head, an "ivory ball" (93), while the head which faces Marlow seems to laugh at the prospect of an eternal slumber, itself a dream.

Marlow is about to see Kurtz, the man who has "stolen more ivory than all the other agents together" (92). Indeed, Kurtz himself, now little more than a voice, has amassed "[h]eaps of" ivory, "stacks of it [...] [t]he old mud shanty was bursting with it" (93), Kurtz, whose "lofty frontal bone" was "impressively bald. The wilderness had patted him on the head, and behold, it was like a ball – an ivory ball; it had caressed him and – lo! – he had withered" (93). Disintegrating to bone himself, Kurtz views his ivory filling the steamboat, piled on the deck; Marlow listens as Kurtz expounds, "'Everything belonged to him'" (94).

The worship of ivory has turned Kurtz into the commodity he most reveres – he is his own fetish.

In Marlow's first vision of Kurtz, whose body appears "pitiful and appalling as from a winding-sheet […] the cage of his ribs all astir, the bones of his arm waving," Kurtz is, as Marlow gazes, an "animated image of death carved out of old ivory" (106).

The "gorgeous apparition" of a Woman

Kurtz's physical presence will soon fade from the text, as Marlow's listeners and readers sail within sight of the dream-text's navel: the farthest reach of the navigable Congo, presumably below Stanley Falls with its "subdued thundering mutter" (GSE 14), and the furthest point of the interpretation of the text. In writing about H. Rider Haggard, Rebecca Stott argues compellingly about the white explorer in Africa: "Africa invites the white male explorer, it challenges him and it tempts him. The white man must explore and penetrate this foreign territory, but he must also resist it or be threatened with absorption into otherness: cultural otherness and sexual otherness" (77). An image of Africa, Marlow's "wild and gorgeous apparition of a woman," stands at the metaphoric navel and the innermost geographical point in the text. Adorned with ivory, she "must have had the value of several elephant tusks upon her" (HD 107), and her body glitters with brass, glass beads, and charms. She collects all the commodities of trade, both indigenous and imported, around her body as she "tread[s] the earth proudly, with a slight jingle and flash of barbarous ornaments" (107). The woman bears the evidence of commodity production on her own continent in the weight of the elephant tusks and charms from witch doctors with which she is adorned. But she also bears the mark of the West. Her brass leggings and "brass wire gauntlets to the elbow" may have come from Birmingham, her glass beads are from beyond the seas, likely from Venice, and her cloth draperies, striped and fringed, very likely African designs printed on Manchester cotton. She is the clash of cultures personified, but representational even in the transculturated blur of commodified East and West of an Africa unbowed, refusing to surrender, ready, as her helmet-shaped hair suggests, to fight back. Rather than appearing as a strange and unique anomaly in African culture, this woman is reminiscent of warrior women reported by both Livingstone and Stanley as well as the famous "Amazon" women warriors of Dahomey in the nineteenth century (Bay 200-09).[105]

She returns Marlow's gaze, refusing to reveal herself as transparent to his look, rejecting his power over her, resisting colonization.[106] Yet colonization is inevitable and her only recourse is to vanish rather than surrender, gleaming only for a moment as an emblem of raw power soon swamped by the flood of commodity trade. Even more, she is Woman with a capital W: the wilderness, the darkness, woman unknowable – the navel of the narrative, the mirror of the Real. "[T]he immense wilderness, the colossal body of the fecund and mysterious life seemed to look at her, pensive, as though it had been looking at the image of its own tenebrous and passionate soul" (HD 107). As the wilderness gazes at her, the warrior woman returns that gaze in its reflection, what the wilderness and the woman know of each other remains unknown and unknowable to us.[107] Stott writes:

> The horror at the centre of Africa, the horror that is persistently associated with woman, the horror at the centre of the text threatens to release itself. To lift the veil, to penetrate too deeply into the mysteries of woman or into the mysteries of Africa, is to risk releasing something dangerous and potentially deadly. (75)

Marlow the explorer has reached the final bend in the river of his dreamscape and, shaken to his core, has found the heart of darkness in the bronzed female body; but as she retreats into the bush, "her eyes gleamed back at us in the dusk of the thickets before she disappeared" (HD 108). Kurtz's, and Marlow's, glimpse of the void, the nothingness of the Real, "The horror!" is here.[108]

Desire for an ending increases as the narrative gathers speed to reach its inevitable conclusion: Kurtz, whose presence once so eagerly desired, and now one with his ivory, lies exposed as a fraud with only a voice. Once the "apparition" of the African woman recedes into the bosom of the wilderness, Kurtz is heard insisting to the Manager, "'Save me! – save the ivory you mean […]. You with your little peddling notions – you are interfering with me'" (108). He is hardly in doubt about where his value lies – and the Manager tells Marlow "'there is a remarkable quantity of ivory – mostly fossil. We must save it at all events'" (108). The effect on Marlow is that he feels "buried in a vast grave full of unspeakable secrets" (109), echoing the imagery of the charnel house and the whited sepulcher. After having foiled Kurtz's failed and feeble effort to escape back to the tribe, Marlow guides the steamboat downstream, and time moves swiftly as Marlow witnesses Kurtz's dying moments. His "ivory visage," with its "expression of sombre pride, of ruthless power, of craven terror – of intense and hopeless despair," as though rending "a veil" of illusion, yields to the moment when Kurtz whispers his dying words, "'The horror! The horror!'" (117). And with those words, Kurtz leaves Marlow alone to "dream out the nightmare to the end" (117). *The real is that which always comes back to the same place*" (Lacan 42).

The Return

Marlow returns to the sepulchral city to bring the Intended her letters and her picture; everything of Kurtz's, including his ivory, has passed out of Marlow's hands, and now all that remains is for him to finalize the matter with the Intended. Leaving Marlow's supervision in the Congo, Kurtz's ivory can only have arrived at Belgian ports under the control of the Company. Marlow feels that the vision of Kurtz joins him in entering the house whose street seems as "still and decorous as a well-kept alley in a cemetery." The irony of Kurtz's words, "'This lot of ivory now is really mine. The Company did not pay for it. I collected it myself at a very great personal risk,'" rings in Marlow's mind as he moves toward the drawing-room (HD 121). Inside, in the gathering dusk, the polished surfaces of the drawing room gleam. The contrast of light and dark, the glow of ivory and ebony, are invoked once more in the "monumental whiteness" of the marble fireplace and the "dark gleams on the flat surfaces" of the grand piano, that "sombre and polished sarcophagus" (122). The Intended's "pale head" surrounded in black, floats toward Marlow in the dusk. As he listens to the Intended plead for information about Kurtz, Marlow is forced to repeat his memories and once again hears Kurtz's dying words; he wants to cry out to her "'Don't you hear them?'" (125) as the whisper of the Real seems "to swell menacingly like the first whisper of a rising wind" (125). Death stalks the room, its gathering and enveloping darkness held at bay only by "that great and saving illusion that shone with an unearthly glow in the darkness" (124) of the Intended's faith. As he speaks the lie, Marlow leaves the Intended with a word linking her name forever with "The horror!" And as the Intended stretches her arms "after a retreating figure" (125), Marlow sees in her the image of another, the "tragic and familiar Shade" stretching her "bare brown" arms "bedecked with powerless charms" over "the glitter of the infernal stream, the stream of darkness" (125). Both women are now linked inextricably to the "horror" – one present raising her arms to the power of illusion and the other absent, in Marlow's vision raising her arms to the power of the Real, glimpsed at the edges of a now retreating dream.

Marlow's tale of the Congo has exposed a textual, political unconscious which re-enacts and repeats a dreamscape, haunted by the presence of the Real as a sublime threat. But at the same time, it has unveiled a historical reality littered with the relics of explorers like Stanley, the devastating effects of European colonization, and the destruction of native economies through British/European trade. By inserting the biscuit tin into his metaphoric Congo, we might imagine that Conrad meant to represent it as a negative icon, representative of the commodity transcendent, kicked in the gutter; but instead, it stands in sharp contrast to the rubbish constituting the commodities for

Chapter Five: "Heart of Darkness": Conrad's Centerpiece in the Congo

trade in the Congo. Mechanically reproduced, the tin aligns with Benjamin's argument that in mechanically reproduced art, authenticity ceases to be applicable to artistic production, and the function of art is reversed; instead of being based on ritual, art grounds itself in politics ("The Work of Art" 224) and becomes a "cipher" for "abstractness, that irritating indeterminateness of what it is" (Adorno, *Aesthetic Theory* 21-22).

> The work of art translates the aura of the commodity form into an enigma, even into a kind of frustration, a maddening puzzle that abjures easy consumption and so attempts to threaten the endless process of consumption as a whole, with its claim that that is all there is and that to live is to consume. (Wall 139)

"If," as Adorno theorizes, "everything must metamorphose into a thing in order to break the catastrophic spell of things," then it follows that art itself, both commodity and fetish, must metamorphose into a "thing." ("A Portrait of Walter Benjamin" 233). Conrad's lowly biscuit tin, beyond its function as fetish object in his text, in its "gratuitousness and specificity always intimate[s] more than [it] appears" (Wall 140).

Taking charge of his tin steamboat in his return from the heart of darkness, Marlow as seaman, and Conrad as artist steam back down the river, having summoned the image of Africa unbowed, the dying European ivory idol, and an iconography of the commodity transcendent in the heart of Africa to complete his tale. Refusing closure, however, Marlow rests in the pose of a meditating Buddha as the anonymous narrator pronounces the final word of the text, the very gloss on the enigma of the Real: "darkness."

Conclusion:
Conrad, Commodities, and the Work of Art

I view this conclusion as a rich opportunity to bind together the central themes that have dominated my discussion of Conrad's texts and to add new perspectives on what I have written. Throughout I have focused on the detail – that tidbit of information that Conrad dropped into a narrative, that, when expanded, opens new avenues of interpretation for each text. Most often, that tidbit was grounded in the material culture of the work: the hints/echoes of Stanley despite the effort to silence him, the traveling biscuit tin, the sketch of the overland journey drafted with a double vision, the much-maligned holy trinity of commodities for trade in the Congo, and the shifting nature of the fetish as opposing cultures collide; these are a few examples of the details I've pursued.

Here's a new tidbit: Stanley writes in the Preface to *The Congo and the Founding of Its Free State,* "There is a law pretty generally recognized among the advanced nations, that every honest labourer is worthy of his hire, but only the conspicuously meritorious deserve special commendation" (1: xiv). And here's an echo you'll recognize from Charley's aunt: "'You forget, dear Charles, that the labourer is worthy of his hire,' she said brightly" (HD 53). Then, as we know, Marlow goes on to reflect, "It's queer how out of touch with truth women are! They live in a world of their own and there had never been anything like it and never can be" (53). So, who is out of touch – women in general or Stanley in particular? I don't presume to write that Conrad read Stanley (or that Marlow's aunt did), but the reflection of Stanley's rhetoric so pervasive in the culture at the time is unmistakable, and I think what most scholars have viewed as an indictment of an impossible and "feminine" view of the world may be expanded to indict the *colonizer's* view of the world, *à la* Stanley.

Remember, Marlow is one of the "Workers, with a capital [...] a sort of lowly apostle" (53), and the language reflects the "rot let loose in print and talk" (53). Of course, the phrase didn't originate with Stanley; it first appears in the Bible, Luke 10:7 – with which Conrad's choice of "apostle" to describe Marlow truly resonates – and is repeated in Chaucer's *Summoner's Tale* with a satiric twist against greed and corruption in the Catholic church. Chaucer's reference that the worker should be adequately compensated for work performed is ironically mocked when the Friar – the labourer for salvation – asks to be compensated by a poor peasant for the Friar's prayers. For Stanley and for Charley's aunt, that aphorism applies to Colonization with a capital C. The context for Stanley's remark is his notice in the text for those of his companions in the expedition to found the Congo Free State who have proved to be extraordinary in the performance of their duties and whose names appear in his chapter on *Europeans (The Congo* 2: 255-79). The context for Marlow's aunt's remark is similar, promoting Marlow's efforts to wean "'those ignorant millions from their horrid ways'" (HD 53).

Colonization and the Commodity (with capital Cs) have been at the heart of my work, but an examination of Conrad's texts as works of art has been there too. Through my use of the intersection of text and image in this study, I have worked toward making visible the liminal detail to redefine the intersection between the commodity and the work of art. From 1899-1924 – the period during which Conrad wrote the works discussed in this study – the East and the West, Europe and Africa, experienced a time of great social upheaval, fueled largely by what Walter Benjamin described as the age of mechanical reproduction and a rising awareness of material culture. With the new age came the fetishizing of the commodity, initiated by the appearance of the Crystal Palace. Where is the place of art in such an age? I think this is at its core Conrad's dilemma.

Adorno musing on Baudelaire, would write, the "absolute artwork converges with the absolute commodity" (*Aesthetic Theory* 21). That pronouncement does seem especially

Conclusion: Conrad, Commodities, and the Work of Art

prescient in describing the Walters Museum tusk featured in my Introduction – the tusk as art and commodity is both in and of the world in the East and in the West. The artisan carving the tusk coded major themes about the social transformation of Africa in the nineteenth century, destined for a European collector, with its base the very commodity which would bring about the destruction of a uniquely African way of life. The tusk embodies art as politics, heralding the emancipation of the artform from myth and ritual in the modern age and its immersion in the world.

I have argued that the biscuit tin that appears liminally in the beginning and end of my study – both as a display at the Great Exhibition of 1851 and then as an absent presence in the Congo of "Heart of Darkness" – becomes a metaphor of strength and beauty while emblematizing the very steam power of the Congo steamboat that brings colonization to Africa. Marlow's tin is a commodity and *not* a commodity, once a container of a commodity, but now empty. As a mechanically reproduced object traveling in a London gutter, Marlow's tin advertises through its globally recognizable garter and buckle design that one form of the commodity transcendent is here and has metaphorically arrived in the African jungle.

The infusion of the social into the artwork and its reverse, the artwork into its culture, however, always results in an uneasy alliance. Working backwards through the texts examined in my study, we can acknowledge that Marlow's disgust with the commodities of trade in the Congo clearly suggests a disgust with the whole notion of colonization and the "selling" of the Congo, and rightly so. With the opening up of the great central basin of the Congo by Stanley, the flood of commodities is in full swing when Marlow arrives there, and the specter of Stanley peeps out from the veiled reference to Kurtz's desire to "have kings meet him at railway stations" and to write "for the papers [...] 'for the furthering of [his] ideas'" (HD 116). The commodity transcendent must be reviled, but it cannot be denied nor can the history it helped to create be erased. Even the art of going about work the right way, Marlow's retrofitting the tin-pot steamer to perform its service on the great river, results in the transportation of those commodities. And indeed, the premier commodity, the ivory tusk is much more than just an elephant tusk, it is the "fetish" around which the worshipping pilgrims surge.

Kayerts and Carlier find and read classic novels in "An Outpost of Progress" – models of literary art that are hardly free of political taint – each is set in a time of social turmoil reflective of the cultural turmoil in the African interior, and they are balanced, as well, against the old, mechanically reproduced newspapers which reiterate the blather about what colonization can do for the African. Makola may be the prime example of what colonization can do for the African – made in Africa, formed by Europe, Makola is the twisted result of that transformation.

Just as important to highlight cultural intrusion and transculturation is the narrator's deliberate recognition of the "fetish" as the warehouse for European commodities, a miracle of irony in its recognition of the commodity as an object of worship. Also remarkable is the manipulation of the notion of the fetish from its indigenous roots in an artifact like a nail fetish, acting as a receptacle empowered by the insertion of "medicine," to the storehouse as the receptacle empowered by the insertion of the holy trinity of commodities. The entire tale, indeed, becomes a perfect jewel of irony, for very limited trading takes place and when magnificent tusks of ivory are offered, the price is the enslavement of the African station workers. Laurence Davies' cogent observation about the tale bears repeating here, "An Outpost of Progress" represents mingled "outrage, experimental art, and politics" ("Don't You Think" 23).

Conrad's Congo journals, grounded in geographical and navigational awareness, give witness to an African interior that has been shaped beforehand by Henry Morton Stanley's will, wresting the Congo Free State from the African jungle. But Conrad continues to ignore Stanley's prior presence, while his sketches mark his own work as artist, draftsman, geographer,

Conclusion: Conrad, Commodities, and the Work of Art 293

explorer, mapping and describing the terrain through which he travels. He is both seeing and seen, subject and object, in his sketches which trace his walking along hills and ravines beside the Congo River. In his narrative of the journey, Conrad is a firsthand witness to the administration of the Belgian Congo, dropping tantalizing hints about what he saw, but was not yet ready to process into the artforms that his African tales would become.

Writing near the end of his life, Conrad looks back briefly at his time in the Congo, perhaps subliminally erasing Henry Morton Stanley altogether to install himself as navigator through the Torres Strait. The explorers that Conrad privileges are artists – Cook, Livingstone, Mungo Park – they know the right way of going about work, creating art in their maps, their photographs, and their illustrations, while unmistakably embedding the politics of the moment in the coding of the map to the centerpoint of the map's world – Greenwich.

Heralding a new age, a watershed moment in material culture, The Great Exhibition presented the transcendent commodity to the world and paved the way for a later exhibition promoting the scramble for the wealth of the African continent, *The Stanley and African Exhibition*. The brief reference to the Crystal Palace in the center of Conrad's "Autocracy and War" reveals in microcosm the commodity as the root cause of the troubled state of the world, allied to Conrad's vision of the specter of Russian autocracy and the rise of Prussian autocracy that threatens the future.

At its inception, the Great Exhibition was imagined as a global display of *manufacture* and *arts*, a grand testament to modernity. Emphasis was placed, though, and priority given, to machines and mechanical reproduction – photography, steam engines, the printing press dominated the spectacle contained within the huge glass and iron structure. Art seems to have appeared rather randomly in the displays; the life-size sculpture of the Greek slave, for example, while never mentioned by Conrad because he could not have seen it in 1851, displays the female body in classic marble form – in chains. The political message of the sculpture uniting gender, power, and slavery cannot be denied.

In an age of mechanical reproduction, according to Benjamin, art becomes political, rising from its material culture, and shaking the domain of art to its core. This is an observation with which, I am well aware, Conrad might never have agreed, and I wonder if, in fact, "Heart of Darkness" turns Benjamin's core observation about aesthetics in modernity on its head. While "Heart of Darkness" can never free itself from the political indictment of European colonization, isn't it so much more than that? "Heart of Darkness," endlessly reproducible and endlessly analyzed, reaffirms the primacy of art as modernity transformed into myth.

NOTES

[1] For a closer look at this magnificent tusk, visit the Walters Museum website where the image can be downloaded and enlarged for a magnified view of the scenes. Even though only one side of the tusk is displayed in the image, there is sufficient detail to interpret the carvings, and additional views of all sides of the tusk are provided in black and white photographs included in an "Additional Views" link. The museum website also offers more information about the scenes on the tusk, but there is some disparity between several of the museum's descriptions and those found in Strother's article, "Dancing on the Knife of Power." My interpretations, in my effort to close-read the tusk, align more closely with Strother's. The tusk is 42 and 1/2 inches high and weighs 23 pounds. <https://art.thewalters.org/detail/10458/elephant-tusk-with-scenes-of-african-life/>.

[2] I am indebted for this understanding of transculturation to Nicholas Mirzoeff's insights deeveloped from his reading of Cuban theorist Fernando Ortiz and Cuban novelist Antonio Benitez-Rojo (131).

[3] Richard Curle assigned titles to the first, untitled manuscript journal because Conrad did not give it a title. Conrad did, however, entitle his second manuscript journal "Up-river Book," and the Houghton Library has assigned that title to both manuscript journals. When Curle published only the first manuscript journal, he gave it two titles: *Conrad's Diary* in *The Yale Review* and *Joseph Conrad's Diary of His Journey up the Valley of the Congo in 1890* in Strangeways and *The Blue Peter*. Therefore, to clarify, when I refer to the manuscript in my text, I use quotation marks, "The Congo Diary" and italics, *Congo Diary* (using the shorter of his titles), when referring to Curle's editions. In parenthetical citation for this first manuscript journal, I use the abbreviation CD MS, while the abbreviation *CD* refers to Curle's published editions and includes the publisher to identify which of the three editions I'm quoting.

[4] The Cambridge edition of *Notes on Life and Letters* is a valuable edition for the wealth of information about the evolution of the text, its variants, and notes. The textual variants of the five published editions I've looked at reveal a story in themselves regarding editorship whether by Conrad or by an anonymous editor; in fact, a comment by the editor of the Cambridge edition makes an important point: "this essay is with 'The Censor of Plays' and 'Certain Aspects of the Admirable Inquiry' among the most vivid examples in *Notes on Life and Letters* of how thoroughly Conrad's writing was edited and, from the viewpoint of standard phrasing and usage, seemed at times almost to cry out for it" (Stape, "The Texts" 269).

[5] There is a significant variant between the two published editions of *Notes on Life and Letters*, the Cambridge edition and the *Uniform Edition* (1924), as well as the typescript, *The Fortnightly Review,* and *North American Review*. "Produce" in the *Uniform Edition* (106) *suggests* the fate of humans to labor in the production of commodities for consumption, while "purchase"

in the Cambridge edition indicates its necessary reverse, in casting the fate of humans to consume those commodities. Thus the Marxist notion of the worker's alienation from his/her labor glimmers in the choice of "produce," but equally important is the concept of a consumer society created by capital and directly invoked in the word "purchase." It is unknown or unclear whether Conrad or an anonymous editor made this change; "produce" appears in the Syracuse typescript and the *North American Review* versions, while "purchase" appears in *The Fortnightly Review* version and the Thomas Wise privately printed pamphlet of the essay (Stape, "Apparatus 327, 88.10).

[6] Conrad's essay actually appears in Volume 84 of *The Fortnightly Review* dated July 1, 1905.

[7] Keith Carabine argues that inscribing the unlikely motto "*sine ira et studio*" may be Conrad's way of masking the "Polishness" and deep personal involvement of his polemic (*The Life and Art* 84-85).

[8] This is the frontispiece illustration in Henry Mayhew's *1851: The Adventures of Mr. and Mrs. Sandboys*.

[9] Armstrong offers a vivid decription of the Victorian experience of the Exhibition, quoting from Tallis' *History and Description of the Crystal Palace and the Exhibition of the World's Industry in 1851*, "The soul was approached through its highest senses, flooded with excitement; all its faculties were appealed to at once, and it sank for a while, exhausted, overwhelmed" (79n13, Tallis 3: 1).

[10] The company, however, in an advertisement memorializing the centennial of the Great Exhibition, claimed that "[a]t the Great Exhibition of 1851 Huntley and Palmers received the highest awards for biscuits" (Auerbach, *The Great Exhibition* 255).

[11] For a contemporary description of the erection of the Albert Memorial, see *Bow Bells: A Weekly Magazine of General Literature and Arts* 180.

[12] A very similar illustration of a "Fetish from the Congo State" appears in Figure 7.1, "Sketches at the Stanley and African Exhibition" (*Illustrated London News*, 29 March 1890) in Felix Driver's *Geography Militant* 154.

[13] Instead of the word *fetish*, I call attention to the African words: singular *nkisi* and plural *minkisi* to identify African artifacts mislabeled by Europeans.

[14] Crush cites Biebuyck's 2-volume work *The Arts of Zaire* and Louise Tythacott 168, as sources for his conclusions about the multiple functions of *minkisi* in African society.

[15] Sakhalin is now the largest of Russia's islands, but was contested space between Russia and Japan throughout the nineteenth and twentieth centuries until Russia seized the island at the end of World War II.

[16] As an interesting though tragic irony, Stead died in the *Titanic* disaster, which also resulted in the loss of Conrad's manuscript of "Karain" being sent to John Quinn, the American collector.

[17] Bismarck died the same year that he made this prophetic statement – the "damned foolish thing" is, of course, the assassination of Archduke Franz Ferdinand of Austria by a Bosnian student on June 28, 1914. This act led to

a declaration of war by Austria-Hungary against Serbia in July, followed by declarations of war by Germany against Russia and France in August. Britain declared war on Germany and Austria-Hungary in August after Germany invaded Belgium.

[18] Andrew Griffiths, referring to prior discussions of Stanley in Brantlinger, GoGwilt, and Rubery, attempts to establish that Conrad was influenced by Stanley's *In Darkest Africa* when he wrote "Heart of Darkness" (*The New Journalism* 122-54). In the absence of solid proof that Conrad read Stanley's work, my argument about the "spectral presence" of Stanley follows a different path in this chapter.

[19] The first reference is to the page number in Conrad's manuscript housed at the Beinecke; the second is to the transcription of the manuscript in Stevens and Stape.

[20] I am indebted to Laurence Davies ("More railways and Saddle Island") for pointing to the name Saddle Island as an explanation for Conrad's "doodle" in the manuscript.

[21] Conrad refers to the location as Torres Straits (GSE 15), but the contemporary name is singular, Torres Strait.

[22] The legend added by another hand down the left side of the map reads "*verkleinen* of 15 ½ cm." In Dutch, *verkleinen* means reduction. In communication with me, Beinecke librarian Natalia Sciarini reports that an archivist would not have marked an original with anything other than a call number, so the marking may have been made by a prior owner before the Beinecke received the map.

[23] A memory board, constructed of beads, shells, and pegs to depict and perform the history of the Luba people in the Democratic Republic of Congo. The board is "read" by touching its surface with the right forefinger – the configuration of the objects dictates the information to be read by an expert "memory man."

[24] Denis Cosgrove quotes this stunning passage from Pynchon's novel *Mason & Dixon* as the headnote for the introduction to his edited collection *Mappings*. The passage refers to Mason and Dixon witnessing the transit of Venus at Cape Town.

[25] The description of the vast central part of Africa as unknown appears in bold on Henry Schenk Tanner's 1823 map entitled "Africa." The map could be viewed at <https://www.davidrumsey.com/luna/servlet/detail/RUMSEY~8~1~1354~100122: Africa--Engraved-&-Published-by-H-S>.

[26] Tanner's map can be viewed at <https://exhibits.stanford.edu/maps-of-africa/catalog/ms639jm9954>.

[27] Herman Moll's map is found at the website: "Evolution of the Map of Africa." <https://library.princeton.edu/visual_materials/maps/websites/africa/maps-continent/continent.html>.

[28] See "1851 Map," *Evolution of the Map of Africa*. <https://lib-dbserver.princeton.edu/visual_materials/maps/websites/africa/maps-continent/1851%20tallis.jpg>.

[29] See *Livingstone's 1871 Field Diary: A Multispectral Critical Edition*. <http://livingstone.library.ucla.edu/1871diary/site_guide.htm>.

[30] The map section illustrated here is found on the Christie's website with valuable details about the status of the map, and fortunately still available to view despite the fact that it was sold almost twenty years ago. It is the map used and annotated by Stanley as he plotted the course of the Congo River with "pencil dots and holes representing the noon-day reckonings, points that were then linked in pencil" (Ian McKay 58+). The map was sold by Christie's to a private collector in 2003.

[31] There are two halves to the map, each included in one of the two volumes of *Through the Dark Continent*; "Map Showing the Eastern Half" is located in the back pocket of volume 1 and "Map Showing the Western Half" is located in the back pocket of volume 2. The entire map may be viewed at the website: <https://maps/princeton.edu/catalog/princeton-44558g13k>.

[32] The Beinecke at the Yale University Library has these two navigational charts in its Conrad Digital Collection, <https://collections.library.yale.edu/catalog/16637392>.

[33] The editor of Stanley's newspaper reports, Norman Bennett, has used the spelling "*Despatches*" in the title of his collection; so when I refer to the title, I use his spelling; otherwise, though, I use the more common American spelling "*dispatch*."

[34] This method measures distance following a particular compass bearing for a particular number of hours at an estimated average speed; based on the number of hours walking, distance can be determined.

[35] Dr. Thomas Parke in Stanley's expedition actually saw the Ruwenzoris first but declined to contradict Stanley's assertion that he was the first European to see the mountains (Berenson 138).

[36] Brian Murray wants to paint him as "an artful imperial villain" (15), and maybe he was; but I refuse to view him so simplistically.

[37] The description on the website: <https://omanisilver.com/contents/en-us/d240_Omani_Slavery.html> offers additional information about the tusks, known as the "Kilimanjaro Tusks," which weighed 237 and 225 pounds; the tusks reportedly belonged to a bull elephant captured by an Omani hunter on the slopes of Kilimanjaro. There is some conflict on different websites about ownership and location of these magnificent tusks.

[38] As examples, Russell West published "Space and Language in the Private Diary: Conrad's Congo Diaries" in 1999, but his focus was largely on rhetorical structures and linguistic analysis. Jakob Lothe's essay "Conrad and Travel Literature" sees Conrad's literary potential in the discourse of his diary, arguing for its status as "fragmented autobiography" (47). Of course Najder's invaluable discussion and publication of both journals are important as are Richard Curle's introductory remarks to his pamphlet edition of the manuscript.

[39] Stanley is reprinting his comments published in the *Daily Telegraph*, November 12, 1877.

Notes 299

[40] After arguing animatedly with Sir Sidney Colvin about Gambetta in 1917, Conrad admits later in a letter to him that "He *was* a great man, especially in regard of the other makers of the 3rd Republic" (*CL* 6: 73, and referred to in Najder, *Joseph Conrad: A Life* 493).

[41] In fact, Stanley's gravestone in Pirbright Churchyard bears the inscription: "Henry Morton Stanley / Bula Matari / 1841-1904 / Africa."

[42] The Force Publique was a brutal military force formed by the Congo Free State comprised of white officers and an African soldiery from Congolese tribes and mercenaries from Zanzibar and West Africa.

[43] When referring to the published versions of these journals, I will italicize the title, but I'll use quotation marks when referring to the manuscripts. I'll entitle the first journal "The Congo Diary," but I should note that both journals at the Harvard Houghton Library bear the title "Up-river Book" because Conrad did not entitle the first journal notebook. Richard Curle published the first notebook journal after Conrad's death: first in *The Blue Peter* in October 1925, then in a privately printed edition by Strangeways and in *The Yale Review*, both of which appeared in January 1926. "The Congo Diary," along with "The Up-river Book" were subsequently published in Najder, *Joseph Conrad: Congo Diary and Other Uncollected Pieces* (1978) and in Stevens and Stape, *Last Essays* (2010).

[44] My quotations from Conrad's journals are found in the manuscripts which are not paginated and not always dated, but digitized versions of the manuscripts are available at the Harvard website: <https://digitalcollections.library.harvard.edu/catalog/990097771520203941_FHCL.HOUGH:3202521>; <https://digitalcollections.library.harvard.edu/catalog/990097771520203941_FHCL.HOUGH:3202522>.

[45] This illustration appears in Curle, *Joseph Conrad's Diary (hitherto unpublished) of his Journey up the Valley of the Congo in 1890*, in *The Blue Peter* 320.

[46] The illustration appears in Curle, *Conrad's Diary, The Yale Review* 255.

[47] This photograph is part of an Album kept in the Henry M. Stanley Archives (King Baudouin Foundation Collection held in trust at the RMCA). Inventory number: SA.5154.-36. <https://www.africamuseum.be/en/discover/focus_collections/display_object?objectid=32529>.

[48] The image is part of the International Mission Photography Archive, ca. 1860-ca.1960 at <Divinity.Library@yale.edu> and displayed as part of the University of Southern California Digital Library. Its description includes "[o]ver twenty porters who take a rest break in a clearing. Several people sit on their bundles. One man, perhaps the overseer, wears a hat and long cloak and stands holding a walking stick. The following information is printed on the back of the postcard: '*Belgische mission van Scheut. Kongo. Missions belges de Scheut.*'"

[49] Linking commodities and trade routes, Conrad identifies the local intoxicant, *malafu*, palm wine tapped from the Raphia palm, also referring two sentences prior to the "Palma Christi," conflating it with the oil palm;

but Conrad may be confusing Palma Christi, which produces castor oil, with the African oil palm which produces palm oil, next to ivory and, later, rubber, perhaps the most desirable African export due to the wide variety of its uses.

[50] Alphonse-Jules Wauters was editor in chief of the Belgian journal *Le Mouvement Géographique*, which was eventually taken over by the Belgian *Companie du Congo pour le Commerce et l'Industrie* with Wauters as secretary-general. Wauters, who never set foot in the Congo, was considered to possess the greatest knowledge of its geography. Additionally, he was, until 1890, a defender of the Belgian Congo, and a friend of Albert Thys, who hired Conrad as steamboat captain in the Congo. The map appears here: <https://lib.ugent.be/viewer/archive.ugent.be%3AA91C7B64-79A9-11E5-9523-EF6DD43445F2#?c=&m=&s=&cv=&xywh=3157%2C3203%2C1271%2C1035>.

[51] Hans van Marle remarks that another traveler in 1887 saw the same albino woman (59).

[52] Najder also adds information from a diary kept by Captain Duhst, who traveled part of the way downriver with Conrad and recorded that he was "continually sick with dysentery and fever" (*Joseph Conrad: A Life* 162).

[53] Stevens and Stape (CD, Stevens and Stape 134) transcribe this as "market color-tins" but I read it differently.

[54] Hans van Marle identifies the language as "Kikongo, the language of the Bakongo in the lower parts of the Zaire" (69).

[55] Grenfell and Comber go on to describe at some length executions and human sacrifices which are rather too gruesome to repeat here (361).

[56] Simmons and Stape (Introduction xxx) dispute the time of composition of the tale, arguing instead that it was written in about three weeks as I note in the next section.

[57] Robert Hobson's dissertation, "A Critical edition of 'An Outpost of Progress'" includes a very detailed discussion of the variants between the autograph manuscript, the Macmillan copyright copy, and *Cosmopolis* as well as other editions of the tale. Hobson's emphasis is largely on syntactical changes, correction of punctuation, and changes to eliminate redundance or contradiction. Where there is a substantive change identified by Hobson in the Macmillan pamphlet which subsequently appears in the *Cosmopolis* issue, I note that.

[58] The Macmillan pamphlet is extremely rare; I was lucky to discover, with the help of Bruce Cammack, Associate Librarian for Rare Books at Texas Tech University, that, while the collection at Texas Tech does not own a copy of the pamphlet, Indiana University does and digitized what is possibly the only extant copy: <https://urldefense.com/v3/__http://webapp1.dlib.indiana.edu/metsnav3/general/index.html*mets=http*3A*2F*2Fpurl.dlib.indiana.edu*2Fiudl*2Fgeneral*2Fmets*2FVAB6972&page=1__;IyUlJSUlJSU!!LNEL6vXnN3x8o9c!0EaGcfP1mN71Z51JY2X86ceFKM8MrCyQxULIotnu5_uMfzygvkEITOfSaxqOqXGXyKM$>.

[59] I've transcribed this passage without indicating the strikeouts which appear in the manuscript.

Notes

[60] See also Hobson's dissertation for a discussion of the elimination of this passage. Hobson's observations coincide with my own that there appears to be contradiction along with repetition which may have decided Conrad on cancellation.

[61] Jim Holstun suggests that the choice of epigraph may have been a "sneer at those eager for imperial romances [like Kipling's] and a radical reflection on the utility of empire in maintaining domestic rule" (209).

[62] See Brantlinger 261, among others, for the claim.

[63] Frederick Karl claims that "Stanley was a man after Conrad's own heart," arguing that Conrad may have seen something of himself and his own aspirations in Stanley's career (274-75). I sharply disagree; I think that Stanley was a man for Conrad to despise and thus Conrad placed the blame squarely on Stanley's shoulders for Congo atrocities as evidenced in his remark about the "newspaper stunt" and "the vilest scramble for loot" in "Geography and Some Explorers." Karl also speculates that Conrad may have read Stanley's books but stops short of pushing the point (275).

[64] The emphasis on this grave echoes two significant remarks in "The Congo Diary." On the 29th of July, Conrad describes a white man's grave, as I pointed out in the last chapter, which is marked by stones in the form of a cross, and in his sketch a few days earlier, July 26, he marks the spot where a white man died. Of course, Conrad doesn't only mention dead white men; we've seen that he witnesses the appalling sight of unburied, decomposing black men on his trek.

[65] Robert Hampson notes on this point that rather than describing African practices in relation to objects, the word *fetish* is used here to turn that around to question the European investment in ivory ("Objects" 11).

[66] See also Robert Hamner 178, on Conrad's ironic use of "maintained" as well as "pretend[ed] to keep a correct account."

[67] Sewlall 9; Hamner 179; Bhabha, *The Location of Culture* 86, among others.

[68] See John Stape, "Father Gobila, I presume?" for additional descriptions of the historical Gobila in Belgian accounts, especially Camille Coquilhat's *Sur le Haut Congo*. Norman Sherry in *Conrad's Western World* (126, 128, and 130-32) also identifies Gobila from Stanley's *The Congo and the Founding of Its Free State*, but Sherry is intent on matching Conrad's character with Stanley's historical figure, claiming that Conrad used the incidents from Stanley in his own tale. However, Sherry has no proof to offer that Conrad read Stanley and does admit that Conrad's references could have come from many other accounts by explorers and missionaries (132).

[69] Sherry mentions that matches were a mystery to African natives and that the missionary W. H. Bentley struck matches for the natives around Stanley Pool who "would have crowded for hours to see *mindele* [white man] strike a little stick on something, and a great flame ensue" (Bentley *Pioneering on the Congo* 1: 336, qtd. in Sherry 133).

[70] David Gill in "The Fascination of the Abomination: Conrad and Cannibalism" discusses the connection and sorts through contemporary evidence to establish if and how much cannibalism was practiced in central Africa.

[71] I'd like to point out again that Sherry contends that Conrad knew Stanley's work, but offers no proof while trying to tie "An Outpost of Progress" directly to Stanley – "I feel certain," Sherry writes, "that Conrad put together his story from these incidents related by Stanley" (129). I think it's all very well to want to believe that, but without irrefutable evidence that Conrad read Stanley, we cannot claim that he did. Throughout this book I've emphasized the unmistakable influence of Stanley *on the Congo*, he preceded Conrad in the Congo and blazed the trail Conrad would follow; but while I think it inevitable that Conrad could have gathered much information about Stanley not only while he was in the Congo from word of mouth but also later in the abundance of news accounts, I think he would have resisted reading any of Stanley's voluminous pages. But I also think it inevitable that as an agent of the Belgian Congo, Conrad may have seen maps derived from Stanley's publications, as it goes without question that Stanley forcibly filled in the map of central Africa.

[72] Several scholars remark on the connection, for example, Holstun 200, and Wiegandt 15.

[73] See Rutledge and Tally 7, 9, for a brief discussion of the outpost in "An Outpost of Progress" as a "crisis" heterotopia, where the individuals placed there are in a state of crisis.

[74] Stanley makes the connection between fever and exposure to the sun in *Congo* 2: 323; however this would likely have been common knowledge and common sense for most explorers and missionaries in the Congo.

[75] Peter Firchow suggests in a note that the Managing Director may be a "satirical sketch of Henry Morton Stanley," though, he acknowledges, Stanley himself railed against the agents sent to him from Belgium (221n20). It's inviting to think of Conrad (in the guise of Kayerts) sticking his tongue out at Stanley!

[76] An earlier version of this chapter, entitled "Kicking the Biscuit Tin: Conrad, Mass Culture, and Commodity Spectacle," appeared in *Various Dimensions of the Other in Joseph Conrad's Fiction* edited by Wiesław Krajka.

[77] I mean this term as it is used in Jacques Lacan's schematic of the three domains of human experience: the real, the imaginary, and the symbolic. Fred Botting attempts one explanation of this inexplicable term: "the real remains what *is,* an impossible, inexpressible, ineffable and undifferentiated space outside language. The real, then lies beyond systems of signification; it ex-ists outside Lacan's symbolic order. It is defined as that which cannot be defined, that which is alien to or resists signification, that which exceeds symbolization" (24). I would note additionally that Botting's definition is hardly the most conclusive or exhaustive as the explanations for the Lacanian *Real* shift from theorist to theorist. Based upon the work of Lacan, Fredric

Jameson, and Slavoj Žižek, my incorporation of the Real in discussing the novella is meant to negotiate a delicate balance between the historicity and the symbolism of Conrad's text.

[78] For a fine collection of essays including Lacoue-Labarthe's philosophical approach to Conrad's *"Heart of Darkness"* in his essay "The Horror of the West," see Nidesh Lawtoo's *Conrad's "Heart of Darkness" and Contemporary Thought*.

[79] See Tony C. Brown for a different interpretation of the presence of the Lacanian *Real* in "Heart of Darkness."

[80] Jakob Lothe elaborates on the relationship between the frame narrator and Marlow in his *Conrad's Narrative Method* 21-44.

[81] So much has been written by Conrad scholars in response to Chinua Achebe's attack on Conrad in "An Image of Africa" that I feel it unnecessary to add to that conversation, and, in fact, a discussion of it here would deflect from rather than enhance my reading of the novella.

[82] See Allen MacDuffie for a different interpretation of the link between the dice and ivory as well as the connection between commodities and waste.

[83] The phrase "pioneers of progress" echoes Conrad's earlier description of Kayerts and Carlier as "pioneers of trade and progress" in "An Outpost of Progress" (OP 82).

[84] Christopher GoGwilt writes compellingly about the mapping of Europe and Africa in this scene, arguing that there is a dis-ease with insisting upon England's "real work" on the African continent, "This ambivalent relation to the official images of the Empire complicates the reading of the map of Africa as a color-coding of Europe" (122).

[85] See Schopenhauer's "On Women" for an appalling discussion of women as "children their whole life long" (107). Owen Knowles, in "Who's Afraid of Arthur Schopenhauer?" reflects on the influence of Schopenhauerian pessimism more broadly in the nineteenth century and specifically on Conrad.

[86] The phrase is suggested by the title of Sven Beckert's important study of cotton textiles, *Empire of Cotton*.

[87] I should note here that Steiner's quotation of Obenga above is used in a more narrow context, where Obenga's original context expands the argument to "The *work of the historian of Africa* is becoming a continuous interdisciplinary dialogue" (Obenga 85, emphasis added).

[88] The information for the cloth worn by the woman from Acra was provided to me in e-mails from Helen Elands, independent researcher in African textiles, who confirmed the transculturation of the clothing depicted in the postcard in consultation with another researcher in textiles, Philip Sykas, at the Manchester Fashion Institute.

[89] See also Knowles' "Explanatory Notes" 446, for a brief description of the correspondence between Conrad's overland trek and Marlow's.

[90] Aldwin Roes writes that the "prevalence of Zanzibaris and Afro-Arabs" in the second half of the nineteenth century contributed to the violence in the Congo (28).

[91] Knowles' "Explanatory Notes" confirm the observation that Marlow's white companion is a reference to Conrad's companion on the overland journey, Prosper Harou (447).

[92] Conrad refers to Nselemba in his *Congo Diary*, the location is also known as Lemba, near the southeast border of Stanley Pool.

[93] The Levin catalog of Moses Levin's bead samples is an important resource for identifying the variety of beads in circulation in African trade in the mid to late nineteenth century. Together with *The Venetian Bead Book*, it is housed in the Museum of Mankind in the British Museum, London. For a descriptive essay on the catalog, see Karklins, "The Levin Catalogue."

[94] These statistics reinforce the link between Africans in the Congo and their descendants in the US.

[95] In the mid nineteenth century, women warriors formed the king's palace guard in Dahomey (Bay 201).

[96] In 1890, the length of brass wire was approximately fifteen inches, but could vary from district to district and could be shortened as it changed hands – note Marlow's measurement of nine inches (Weeks, *Congo Life* 40).

[97] See Mulhern for a well developed Marxist reading of commodity fetishism.

[98] Niland (82) reports that Cedric Watts even suggests a conspiracy against Kurtz in the sabotage of Marlow's steamer in *The Deceptive Text*.

[99] Hampson discusses the biscuit tin among other objects in Conrad's fiction ("Conrad's Objects" 6), and Valentine Cunningham acknowledges the Reverend Darby photograph illustrated later in this chapter in a wide-ranging discussion of the biscuit tin's appearance in "Heart of Darkness" and other works and argues further that its appearance in Conrad's "intensely anti-colonial" text, is one that British readers would recognize, implicating "British trade [...] in the Belgian horrors" (253).

[100] Knowles references this photograph in offering information about the Huntley and Palmers biscuit tin ("Explanatory Notes" 448).

[101] Knowles's "Explanatory Notes" offer a brief history of the biscuit making firm and cite Valentine Cunningham's reference to the photograph illustrated above (448).

[102] Niland suggests that Towson's manual, as a "thorough, systematic" text, stands in contrast to Marlow's "meandering tale," raising the question of the reliability of Marlow's narrative (83).

[103] Knowles offers more detail about the history of the harlequin ("Explanatory Notes" 452n98.20).

[104] Stanley details his discovery of Lake Leopold II in *The Congo* vol: 1, chap. 21.

[105] Firchow also notes the presence of Amazon fighting women in Dahomey, especially when they were in the news of a British attack on Benin in 1897, and he references Richard Burton's mention of a female fighting force in 1864 (25, 196n7).

Notes 305

[106] Kimberly Devlin provides a more detailed discussion of the gaze in the novella.

[107] Mariana Torgovnick writes that the "African woman is, for [her], the crux of *Heart of Darkness*" (154), and I agree, but I don't follow her assumption that the African woman dies because she is "unwilling to flinch" from the pilgrims' bullets (155). Torgovnick asserts that the woman's death "fulfills her role as an emblem of the African landscape […] and makes explicit the hidden reference of 'the feminine' and 'the primitive' to death" (155). I prefer to see the African woman as a premier sign of resistance, stalking off into the wilderness unbowed.

[108] Johanna Smith argues compellingly that Marlow's refusal to tell the Intended Kurtz's true last words conflate her name with "the horror" (181).

List of Illustrations and Permissions

Absolon, John. *The Greek Slave.* 1851. View in the East Nave of the Great Exhibition in the Crystal Palace. London. Hand-colored lithograph. *Recollections of the Great Exhibition of All Nations.* Lloyd. Public domain.

Beads Employed in the African Trade for Ivory. C 1863. Donated by Moses Lewin Levin. Museum number Af1863,0717.1. © The Trustees of the British Museum.

Belgian Trading Steamer. Upper Congo River. Huntley and Palmers foremost again. Around 1890. Rev R. D. Darby's Potos [sic] No. 17. Entitled *Biscuits in the Congo.* © Reading Museum (Reading Borough Council). All rights reserved. With kind permission.

Boma: Post Office, with Rail Tracks: On the Lower Left Two Tracks Leading onto the Jetty Can Be Distinguished. Boma Had the First Railway in the Belgian Congo …. It Was Opened on 4 March 1890. Circa 1912. Belgian Postcard. Public Domain.

Box of Bead Samplings. The Henry Morton Stanley collection of memorabilia. HO. 1954.72.53. Africa Museum. Stanley Archives, Coll. King Baudouin Foundation, entrusted to the AfricaMuseum, Brussels, Belgium. <https://www.africamuseum.be/de/discover/focus_collections/display_object?objectid=32415>.

Bridge over Lufu River. Cataract Region. [Stanley's handwriting]. Stanley Archives, Coll. King Baudouin Foundation, entrusted to the AfricaMuseum, Brussels, Belgium.

Chained Prisoners in Zanzibar. 1888-1890. Photo taken by J. Sturtz. Omani and Zanzibar Virtual Museum. Public domain. <https://omanisilver.com/contents/en-us/d240_Omani_Slavery.html>.

Clearing the Forest to Erect a Trading Factory on the Kasai. 1911-1912. Photograph taken by Alice Seeley Harris. Antislavery International. Bodleian Library. University of Oxford MSS. Brit.Emp. S. 17/B11(Box 11). Courtesy of Anti-Slavery International and the Family of Alice Seeley Harris. <http://antislavery.nottingham.ac.uk/items/show/052>.

The Colonizability of Africa. 1899. Harry H. Johnston. *A History of Colonization of Africa by Alien Races.* Map to face p. 275. Schomburg Center for Research in Black Culture. Jean Blackwell Hutson Research and Reference Division. The New York Public Library Digital Collections. Public domain. <https://digitalcollections.nypl.org/items/510d47df-fd22-a3d9-e040-e00a18064a39>.

Congo. Femme Acra. 28 July 1911. Postcard of African woman dressed in European cloths. Postcard image provided by Duncan Clarke, with kind permission. <http://adireafricantextiles.com>.

The Congo River from Stanley Pool to Bangala. 1884. Surveyed by George Grenfell and T. J. Comber. Public domain. <https://www.jstor.org/stable/1800407>.

Conrad's Drawing of Saddle Island. "Geography." "Geography," Original Manuscript 37. Public domain in US.

Cover Page. 30 April 1890. *"The Graphic" Stanley Number.* Public domain.

Cruikshank, George. *All the World Going to See the Great Exhibition of 1851.* 1851. Etching. Henry Mayhew, and George Cruikshank. *1851 or the Adventures of Mr. and Mrs. Sandboys and Family. Who Came Up to London to "Enjoy Themselves" and to See the Great Exhibition.* Public domain.

Daylight at Last! Illustration from *"The Graphic" Stanley Number* 21. Public domain.

Detail from *A Map of the Route of the Emin Pasha Relief Expedition through Africa. In Darkest Africa.* Vol. 2. In back pocket. Public domain.

Detail from *Preliminary Map and Plans of the Congo and its Tributaries.* George Grenfell. "Exploration of the Tributaries of the Congo, between Leopoldville and Stanley Falls." Public domain.

Detail from Stanley's *A Map of the Congo Basin. The Congo and the Founding of Its Free State.* Vol. 1. In back pocket. Public domain.

Drawing on verso of page marked at the top VI N. Conrad. "Up-river Book." Manuscript 1890. MS 46 (2). Houghton Library. Harvard University. Public domain in USA.

Elephant Tusk with Scenes of African Life. The Walters Art Museum. Baltimore. No permission required.

The *En Avant, A.I.A.*, and *Roi des Belges*. 1889. Leopoldville. Public domain. <https://en.wikipedia.org/wiki/En_Avant_(steam_launch)#/media/File:The_En_Avant_(L),_A.I.A._(C)_and_Roi_des_Belges_(R)_—_Leopoldville,_1889.jpg>.

Excerpt from Narrative. 27 July 1890. Conrad. "The Congo Diary." First journal in "Up-river Book." Manuscript 1890. MS Eng 46 (2). Houghton Library. Harvard University. Public domain in USA.

Fetish Idols. Stanley. *The Congo and the Founding of Its Free State* 1: 200. Public domain.

Gobela's, detail from *A Map of the Route of the Emin Pasha Relief Expedition Through Africa.* Henry Morton Stanley. *In Darkest Africa.* Vol. 2. Public domain.

Henry M. Stanley describing his travels to the Portuguese Expedition (Ivens, Capello, Serpa Pinto) at Loanda. [August or September 1877]. Oval-framed photograph, mounted on cardboard, with pencil inscription. Stanley Archives, Coll. King Baudouin Foundation, entrusted to the AfricaMuseum, Brussels, Belgium.

List of Illustrations and Permissions   309

An Idol or Fetish from Boma. Displayed on the table in front of Panel 11 "The Congo State Collection." *The Stanley and African Exhibition.* Figure 24. Illustration copied by Peter Crush from Steains' sketchbook, with kind permission of Peter Crush.
Illustration from Hermann von Wissmann. *My Second Journey through Equatorial Africa* 37. Public domain.
Illustration from John Brown Myers. *The Congo for Christ: The Story of the Congo Mission* 11. Public domain.
Illustration of the Conference of Berlin. 1 January 1884. *Illustrierte Zeitung.* Public domain. <https://commons.wikimedia.org/wiki/File:Kongokonferenz.jpg>.
Johann Hase. *1737 Map. Evolution of the Map of Africa.* Public domain. <https://library.princeton.edu/visual_materials/maps/websites/africa/maps-continent/1737%20hase.jpg>.
Keltie, J, Scott. *Central Africa after Stanley.* Illustration of the Central African map. "What Stanley Has Done for the Map of Africa" 53. Public domain.
Keltie, J. Scott. *Central Africa before Stanley.* Illustration of the Central African map. "What Stanley Has Done for the Map of Africa" 52. Public domain.
List of Congolese Days of the Week. 25 July 1890. Conrad. "The Congo Diary." First journal in "Up-river Book." Manuscript 1890. MS Eng 46 (2). Houghton Library. Harvard University. Public domain in USA.
Map of African Literature. 1873. William Winwood Reade. *The African Sketch-Book.* Vol.1. No copyright in USA. <https://library.si.edu/image-gallery/106330>.
Map of Congo Basin: Showing Path Traveled by Joseph Conrad Korzeniowski. Joseph Conrad Collection. General Collection. Beinecke Rare Book and Manuscript Library. Yale University. Public domain in the USA. <https://collections.library.yale.edu/catalog/15533524>.
A Map of the Route of the Emin Pasha Relief Expedition Through Africa. Henry Morton Stanley. *In Darkest Africa.* Vol. 2. In back pocket. Public domain. <https://texashistory.unt.edu/ark:/67531/metapth298428/m1/1/zoom/?resolution=12&lat=2525.3088315513496&lon=2966.3505115553794>.
Map of the Russias. Joseph Conrad Collection. General Collection. Beinecke Rare Book and Manuscript Library. Yale University. Public domain in the USA.
Map Showing the Western Half of Equatorial Africa. Henry Morton Stanley. *Through the Dark Continent.* Vol. 2. Public domain. <https://maps.princeton.edu/catalog/princeton-44558g13k>.
The Market in Matadi. 1899. Public domain. <https://en.wikipedia.org/wiki/Matadi#/media/File:108_Matadi._-_Le_marche.jpg>.
Mission Church, Congo. Ca. 1920-1940. Yale University. Divinity School. Day Missions Library. <https://digitallibrary.usc.edu/CS.aspx?VP3=DamView&VBID=2A3BXZSZU6X3B&SMLS=1&RW=1741&RH=962>.

Moll, Herman. *1710 Map. Evolution of the Map of Africa.* Public domain. <https://library.princeton.edu/visual_materials/maps/websites/africa/maps-continent/continent.html>.

Mpozo in section of Stanley's *Map of the Congo Basin. The Congo and the Founding of Its Free State.* Vol. 1. In back pocket. Public domain.

Mr. H. M. Stanley's Anglo-American Expedition for the Exploration of Central Africa – Bumbireh Hospitality. Illustration from *"The Graphic" Stanley Number* 12. Public domain.

Mr. H. M. Stanley's Return to England. The Illustrated News of the World. Saturday, 17 May 1980. Printed from the Original Blocks of *The Illustrated London News.* New York. Public domain.

Mtesa's Amazons. From a photograph by the Author. [*Through the Dark Continent* 1, to face page 314]. Public domain.

Mukimbungu in section of Stanley's *Map of the Congo Basin.* Annexed to *The Congo and the Founding of Its Free State.* Vol. 1. In back pocket. Public domain.

Page One. "An Outpost of Progress." GEN MSS 1207, Box 16. Joseph Conrad Collection. General Collection. Beinecke Rare Book and Manuscript Library. Yale University. Public domain in USA.

Papa Gobila of Mswata. Henry Morton Stanley. *The Congo and the Founding of Its Free State* 1: 508. Public domain.

Porters Stop to Rest. Ca. 1920-1940. Kangu, Congo. University of Southern California Digital Library. © Yale University Divinity School Library. <https://calisphere.org/item/bc4160ef70ff15ca1cd44e5c879415e9/>.

Rough Map of the Route Followed by Joseph Conrad on His Overland Journey in the Belgian Congo from Matadi to Nselemba. 1890. Richard Curle. *The Blue Peter* and the Strangeways privately printed pamphlet. Public domain in USA.

Section from F. Delhaye. *Croquis Hypsometrique du Congo Occidental.* Royal Museum for Central Africa. Public domain. <https://geocatalogue.africamuseum.be/geonetwork/srv/eng/catalog.search#/metadata/BE-RMCA-EARTHS-021312>.

Section of Stanley's *Map Showing the Western Half of Equatorial Africa.* 1874-1877. Public domain. <https://library.princeton.edu/visual_materials/maps/websites/africa/stanley/stanley-map3.jpg>.

Section of To Day's Road. 3 July 1890. Conrad. "The Congo Diary." First journal in "Up-river Book." Manuscript 1890. MS Eng 46 (2). Houghton Library. Harvard University. Public domain in USA.

Section of To Day's Road. 5 July 1890. Conrad. "The Congo Diary." First journal in "Up-river Book. Manuscript 1890. MS Eng 46 (2). Houghton Library. Harvard University. Public domain in USA.

Section of To Day's Road. 31 July 1890. Conrad. "The Congo Diary." First journal in "Up-river Book. Manuscript 1890. MS Eng 46 (2). Houghton Library. Harvard University. Public domain in USA.

The Shattered Remains of Russian Heroes Who Were Killed Near 203 Metre Hill, Port Arthur. 1905. Photograph retrieved from the Library of

List of Illustrations and Permissions 311

Congress. Underwood. No restrictions on publication. <https://www.loc.gov/item/2002712252/>.
Sketch of Conrad's Route along the Congo. January 1926. Richard Curle. *Conrad's Diary. The Yale Review* 255. Public domain.
Sketch on July 26, 1890. Conrad. "The Congo Diary." First journal in "Up-river Book." Manuscript 1890. MS Eng 46 (2). Houghton Library. Harvard University. Public domain in USA.
Sketch on July 28, 1890. Conrad. "The Congo Diary." First journal in "Up-river Book." Manuscript 1890. MS Eng 46 (2). Houghton Library. Harvard University. Public domain in USA.
Sketch on July 30, 1890. Conrad. "The Congo Diary." First journal in "Up-river Book." Manuscript 1890. MS Eng 46 (2). Houghton Library. Harvard University. Public domain in USA.
The Slave Coast. C. 1914. A John Bartholomew map. Public domain. <https://en.wikipedia.org/wiki/File:The_Slave_Coast_on_a_John_Bartholomew_%26_Co._map_published_c._1914_(part).jpg>.
The Stanley and African Exhibition. Cover Illustration. *The Stanley and African Exhibition: Catalogue of the Exhibits.* London. Victoria Gallery. Courtesy of the Smithsonian Libraries and Archives. Washington D. C. <https://library.si.edu/image-gallery/100201>.
Stanley Recruits His Strength with Bovril. Advertisement in *"The Graphic" Stanley Number* 29. Public domain.
Stanley's Expedition to Relieve Emin Pasha. 1890s. Henry Stanley Picture Card. © Reading Museum (Reading Borough Council). All rights reserved. With kind permission.
To Day's March, July 4, 1890. "The Congo Diary." First journal in "Up-river Book." Manuscript 1890. MS Eng 46 (2). Houghton Library. Harvard University. Public domain in USA.
To Day's March, July 8, 1890. "The Congo Diary." First journal in "Up-river Book." Manuscript 1890. MS Eng 46 (2). Houghton Library. Harvard University. Public domain in USA.
Togoland Beauties. Photograph reproduced in Alan Bourchier Lethbridge. *West Africa the Elusive* facing p. 72. Public domain.
The Two Large Ivory Tusks Showing in the Background Zanzibar Door. 1898. Colored postcard based on photograph by Gomes & Sons, photographers. Public domain. <https://omanisilver.com/contents/en-us/d240_Omani_Slavery.html>.
Theed, William the Younger. *Africa.* 1864-1869. The Albert Memorial. Public domain. <https://victorianweb.org/sculpture/theed/index.html>.
Ulu (Saddle Island), an Ephemerally-used Continental Island, Naghi cluster. 8 June 2014. Photo Ian J. McNiven. McNiven 45. With kind permission of the author.
Universal Exhibition of Vienna. 1873. Illustration on Huntley and Palmers website. With kind permission of the Reading Museum (Reading Borough Council). <http://www.huntleyandpalmers.org.uk/

ixbin/hixclient.exe?a=query&p=huntley&f=generic_theme.htm&_IXFIRST_=1&_IXMAXHITS_=1&%3dtheme_record_id=rm-rm-global_content2&s=NEgqBZGxkr6)>.

View of Mpozo Station and River from Vivi. Henry Morton Stanley. *The Congo and the Founding of Its Free State* 2: 218. Public domain.

Watching the Battle of the Yalu. Photo JLP 532 LA 1 #11732. Jack London Collection. Jack London Photographs and Negatives. The Huntington Library. San Marino, CA. No copyright restriction.

Wyld, James. *Map of Central Africa.* Detail. Public domain. <https://www.christies.com/en/lot/lot-3975937>.

Works Cited

Achebe, Chinua. "An Image of Africa." *Research in African Literatures* 9.1 (spring 1978): 1-15.
Adorno, Theodor. *Aesthetic Theory.* Trans. Robert Hullot-Kentor. U of Minnesota P, 1997.
---. "A Portrait of Walter Benjamin." *Prisms.* Trans. Samuel Weber and Sherry Weber. MIT P, 1983. 227-42.
Aitchison, Leslie. *A History of Metals.* 2 vols. Interscience, 1960.
Aitken, W. C. *The Early History of Brass and the Brass Manufactures of Birmingham.* Billing, 1866.
Altic, Mirela. "Henry Morton Stanley – Exploration and Mapping of the Congo River (1874-1877) – solving the last great mystery of the African continent." *International Cartographic Association/Association Geographique Internationale,* 2005. N.pag. <https://icaci.org/files/documents/ICC_proceedings/ICC2005/htm/pdf/oral/TEMA25/Session%202/MIRELA%20ALTIC.pdf>.
---. "Pondering a Sketch by Conrad." Message to the author. 23 Sept. 2021. E-mail.
Anstey, R. T. "British Trade and Policy in West Central Africa Between 1816 and the Early 1880's." *Transactions of the Historical Society of Ghana* 3.1 (1957): 47-71.
Armstrong, Isobel. "Languages of Glass: The Dreaming Collection." Buzard, Childers, and Gillooly 55-83.
Auerbach, Jeffrey. "The Great Exhibition and Historical Memory." *Journal of Victorian Culture* 6.1 (January 2001): 89-112.
---. *The Great Exhibition of 1851: A Nation on Display.* Yale UP, 1999.
Ball, Jeremy. "The History of Angola." *Oxford Research Encyclopedia of Africa.* Nov. 2017. <https://www.academia.edu/en/69619393/The_History_of_Angola>.
Banning, Emile, *Africa and the Brussels Geographical Conference.* Trans. Richard Major. Low, 1877.
Barnard, A. "Wool Buying in the Nineteenth Century: A Case History." *Bulletin of Economic Research* 8.1 (1956): 1-12.
Bassett, Thomas J. "Indigenous Mapmaking in Intertropical Africa." *The History of Cartography. Volume Two, Book Three: Cartography in the Traditional African, American, Arctic, Australian, and Pacific Societies.* Ed. David Woodward and G. Malcolm Lewis. U of Chicago P, 1998. 24-48.
Bay, Edna G. *Wives of the Leopard: Gender, Politics, and Culture in the Kingdom of Dahomey.* U of Virginia P, 1998.
Beachey, R. W. "The East Arican Ivory Trade in the Nineteenth Century." *The Journal of African History* 8.2 (1967): 269-90.

Beckert, Sven. *Empire of Cotton: A Global History.* Knopf, 2015.
Bell, Morag, Robin Butlin, and Michael Heffernan. "Introduction: Geography and Imperialism, 1820-1940." *Geography and Imperialism, 1820-1940.* Ed. Morag Bell, Robin Bultin, and Michael Heffernan. Manchester UP, 1995. 1-12.
Belloc, Hilaire, and Basil Temple Blackwood. *The Modern Traveller, by H.B. and B.T.B.* Arnold, 1898.
Benjamin, Walter. *The Arcades Project.* Trans. Howard Eiland and Kevin McLaughlin. Harvard UP, 1999.
---. *Charles Baudelaire: A Lyric Poet in the Era of High Capitalism.* Trans. Harry Zohn. Verso, 1999.
---. "The Work of Art in an Age of Mechanical Reproduction." *Illuminations: Essays and Reflections.* Ed. Hannah Arendt. Trans. Harry Zohn. Schocken Books, 1968. 217-52.
Bennett, Tony. "The Exhibitionary Complex." *New Formations* 4 (spring 1988): 73-102.
Bentley, William Holman. *Pioneering on the Congo.* 2 vols. The Religious Tract Society, 1900.
Berenson, Edward. *Heroes of Empire: Five Charismatic Men and the Conquest of Africa.* U of California P, 2011.
Bergmann, Bettina. "Introduction to the Art of Ancient Spectacle." *The Art of Ancient Spectacle.* Ed. Bettina Bergmann and Christine Kondoleon. National Gallery of Art, 2000. 8-35.
Bhabha, Homi. *The Location of Culture.* Routledge, 1994.
---. "Signs Taken for Wonders: Questions of Ambivalence and Authority under a Tree outside Delhi, May 1817." *Critical Inquiry* 12.1 (1985): 144-65.
Biebuyck, Daniel. *The Arts of Zaire.* 2 vols. U of California P, 1985.
Bierman, John. *Dark Safari: The Life and the Legend of Henry Morton Stanley.* Knopf, 1990.
Bingham, Colin, ed. *Wit and Wisdom: A Public Affairs Miscellany.* Melbourne UP, 1982.
Böhme, Hartmut. *Fetishism and Culture: A Different Theory of Modernity.* De Gruyter, 2014.
Botting, Fred. "Relations of the Real in Lacan, Bataille and Blanchot." *SubStance* 23.1 (1994): 24-40.
Bow Bells: A Weekly Magazine of General Literature and Art, for Family Reading 17.424 (September 11, 1872): 169-92.
Brantlinger, Patrick. *Rule of Darkness: British Literature and Imperialism.* Cornell UP, 1988.
Brown, Tony C. "Cultural Psychosis on the Frontier: The Work of Darkness in Joseph Conrad's *Heart of Darkness.*" *Studies in the Novel* 32.1 (spring 2000): 14-28.
Burton, Sir Richard. *The Lake Regions of Central Africa: From Zanzibar to Lake Tanganyika.* 2 vols. The Narrative P, 2001.

Works Cited

Buszczynski, Stefan. *La Décadence de l'Europe*. Librairie du Luxembourg, 1867.
Buzard, James, Joseph W. Childers, and Eileen Gillooly, eds. *Victorian Prism: Refractions of the Crystal Palace*. U of Virginia P, 2007.
Candido, Mariana P. "The Expansion of Slavery in Benguela during the Nineteenth Century." *International Review of Social History* 65 (2020): 67-92.
Carabine, Keith. "Conrad the European: 'Autocracy and War' and 'The Heroic Age.'" *Yearbook of Conrad Studies (Poland)* 1 (2005): 77-91.
---. *The Life and Art: A Study of Conrad's "Under Western Eyes."* Rodopi, 1996.
Carter, Paul. *The Road to Botany Bay: An Exploration of Landscape and History*. Knopf, 1988.
Casey, Brendan. "Cook, Conrad and the Poetics of Error." *JASAL: Journal of the Association for the Study of Australian Literature* 20.2 (2020): 1-12.
Chambers, Helen. *Conrad's Reading: Space, Time, Networks*. Palgrave Macmillan, 2018.
---. "'A Sort of Still Uproar': Conrad's Reading of Periodicals." *Conrad First: The Joseph Conrad Periodical Archive*. <http://www.conradfirst.net/conrad/scholarship/authors/chambers.html>.
Chekhov, Anton. *The Island: A Journey to Sakhalin*. Trans. Luba Terpak and Michael Terpak. Washington Square P, 1967.
Clarence-Smith, W. G. "Slavery in Coastal Southern Angola, 1875-1913." *Journal of African Studies* 2. 2 (April 1976): 214-23.
Cohen, Margaret. *Profane Illumination: Walter Benjamin and the Paris of Surrealist Revolution*. U of California P, 1993.
Conrad, Joseph. Author's Note. Knowles, *Youth, Heart of Darkness, The End of the Tether* 5-10.
---. Author's Note. Simmons and Stape, *Tales of Unrest* 5-10.
---. "Autocracy and War." *The Fortnightly Review* 461 (1 July 1905): 1-21.
---. "Autocracy and War." *North American Review* 181.584 (July 1905): 33-55.
---. "Autocracy and War." Stape, *Notes on Life and Letters* 71-93.
---. "Autocracy and War." *Notes on Life and Letters. The Uniform Edition of the Works of Joseph Conrad*. Dent, 1924. 88-114.
---. "The Congo Diary." Untitled Manuscript. 1890. MS Eng 46 (2). Houghton Library. Harvard University. [Listed as "Up-river book."]
---. "The Congo Diary." Stevens and Stape, *Last Essays* 123-37.
---. "Geography (The Romance of Travel)." Original Manuscript. GEN MSS 1207 Box 7. General Collection, Beinecke Rare Book and Manuscript Library. Yale University.
---. "'Geography'": *Ur*-Version of "'Geography and Some Explorers.'" Stevens and Stape, *Last Essays* 381-390.
---. "Geography and Some Explorers." *National Geographic Magazine* 45.3 (March 1924). 241-74.
---. "Geography and Some Explorers." Stevens and Stape, *Last Essays* 3-17.
---. "Heart of Darkness." GEN MSS 1207. Box 25. General Collection. Beinecke Rare Book and Manuscript Library. Yale University.

---. "Heart of Darkness." Knowles, *Youth, Heart of Darkness, The End of the Tether* 43-128.
---. "The Heart of Darkness." Incomplete typescript. 36 p. *Joseph Conrad Collection of Papers*. The Henry W. and Albert A. Berg Collection of English and American Literature. The New York Public Library.
---. "The Heart of Darkness." [Part One]. *Blackwood's Edinburgh Magazine* 165.1000 (Feb. 1899): 193-220.
---. *The Mirror of the Sea*. Harper, 1906.
---. "An Outpost of Progress." GEN MSS 1207. Box 16. Joseph Conrad Collection. Beinecke Rare Book and Manuscript Library. Yale University.
---. "An Outpost of Progress." Macmillan, 1896.
---. "An Outpost of Progress." (Part I) *Cosmopolis* 18 (June 1897): 609-20.
---. "An Outpost of Progress." (Part II) *Cosmopolis* 19 (July 1897): 1-15.
---. "An Outpost of Progress." Simmons and Stape, *Tales of Unrest* 77-99.
---. *A Personal Record*. Ed. Zdzisław Najder and J. H. Stape. Cambridge UP, 2008.
---. "Tales of the Sea." Stape, *Notes on Life and Letters* 46-49.
---. "The Romance of Travel." *Countries of the World*. Ed. J. A. Hammerton. 1 (February, 1924). xvii-xxvii.
---. "Up-river book." Manuscript, 1890. MS Eng 46 (2). Houghton Library. Harvard University. [This item consists of two manuscript journals: the first unnamed, later entitled *The Congo Diary* by Richard Curle, and the second bears the title "Up-river book" in Conrad's handwriting].
---. "Up-river Book, 1890." Najder, *Congo Diary* 17-44.
---. "Up-river Book." Stevens and Stape, *Last Essays* 138-68.
Coombes, Annie. *Reinventing Africa: Museums, Material Culture and Popular Imagination*. Yale UP, 1994.
Cooper, James Fenimore. *The Last of the Mohicans; a Narrative of 1757*. Vol 2. Miller, 1826.
Corley, T. A. B. *Quaker Enterprise in Biscuits: Huntley and Palmers of Reading, 1822-1972*. Hutchinson, 1972.
Cosgrove, Denis. "Introduction: Mapping Meaning." *Mappings*. Ed. Denis Cosgrove, Reaktion Books, 1999. 1-23.
Cotter, Charles H. "John Thomas Towson (1804-81): His Contributions to Navigation." *Journal of Navigation* 30.2 (1977): 220-31.
Cowper, William. *The Works of William Cowper: His Life, Letters, and Poems*. Tegg, 1851.
Crush, Peter. *Exhibiting Cultures (Minkisi, a Case Study in Signification)*. 2002. Diss. Wimbledon School of Art. <https//studylib.net/doc/7897954/exhibiting-cultures--minkisi--a-case-study-in-signification>.
Cunliffe, Marcus. "America at the Great Exhibition of 1851." *American Quarterly* 3.2 (summer 1951): 115-26.
Cunningham, Valentine. *In the Reading Gaol: Post-modernity, Texts, and History*. Blackwell, 1994.

Works Cited

Curle, Richard, ed. *Conrad's Diary. The Yale Review* 15 (January 1926): 254-66.
---. Introduction. Curle, Richard. *Joseph Conrad's Diary of His Journey up the Valley of the Congo in 1890.* Strangeways 5-13.
---.Introduction. Curle, Richard. *Conrad's Diary. The Yale Review* 254-59.
---.Introduction. Curle, Richard. *Joseph Conrad's Diary of His Journey up the Valley of the Congo in 1890. The Blue Peter* 319-21.
---, ed. *Joseph Conrad's Diary of His Journey up the Valley of the Congo in 1890. The Blue Peter: The Magazine of Sea Travel* 5.43 (October 1925): 319-25.
---, ed. *Joseph Conrad's Diary of His Journey up the Valley of the Congo in 1890.* Privately Printed by Strangeways. January 1926.
Daerden, Peter. "Cartographic Entries in Stanley's Sketch Books." *Brussels International Map Collectors' Circle Newsletter* 21 (January 2005): 11-14.
Davies, Laurence. "'Don't You think I am a lost soul?' Conrad's Early Stories and the Magazines." *Conradiana* 41 (spring 2009): 7-28.
---. "More on railways and Saddle Island." Message to the author. 30 May 2021. E-mail.
Davis, Richard Harding. "The Japanese-Russian War – Battles I Did Not See." *Notes of a War Correspondent.* Scribner's, 1911. 213-36.
Debord, Guy. *The Society of the Spectacle.* Trans. Donald Nicholson-Smith. Zone, 1995.
Devlin, Kimberly. "The Scopic Drive and Visual Projection in *Heart of Darkness.*" *Modern Fiction Studies* 52.1 (Spring 2006): 19-41.
Dickens, Charles. "The Noble Savage." *Household Words. A Weekly Journal* 154 (June 11, 1853): 337-39.
Donovan, Stephen. "Conrad's Unholy Recollection." *Notes and Queries* 49.1 (March 2002): 82-84.
---. "'That Newspaper Fellow – What's His Name?' Joseph Conrad on W. T. Stead." *NewsStead: A Journal of History and Literature* 17 (fall 2000): 3-10.
Driver, Felix. *Geography Militant: Cultures of Exploration and Empire.* Blackwell, 2001.
Dubin, Lois Sherr. *The History of Beads: From 100,000 B. C. to the Present.* Rev. ed. Abrams, 2009.
Dumas, Alexandre. *The Three Musketeers.* Routledge, 1878.
Elands, Helen. Messages to the author. 24 March and 7 April, 2019. E-mails.
Eltis, David, and Lawrence C. Jennings. "Trade between Western Africa and the Atlantic World in the Pre-Colonial Era." *The American Historical Review* 93.4 (1988): 936-59.
Fernandez-Armesto, Felipe. *Near a Thousand Tables: A History of Food.* Free P, 2002.
Fincham, Gail, Jeremy Hawthorn, and Jakob Lothe, eds. *Outposts of Progress: Joseph Conrad, Modernism and Post-Colonialism.* U of Capetown P, 2015.
Firchow, Peter. *Envisioning Africa: Racism and Imperialism in Conrad's "Heart of Darkness."* UP of Kentucky, 2000.

Flaubert, Gustave. *Bouvard et Pécuchet*. Trans. and Introduction A. J. Krailsheimer. Penguin, 1976.

Forfeitt, Reverend J. Lawson. "A Gift from African Native Christians." *The Missionary Herald of the Baptist Missionary Society* (1 Jan. 1891): 7.

Francis, Andrew. *Culture and Commerce in Conrad's Asian Fiction*. Cambridge UP, 2015.

Francis, Peter, Jr. *The Glass Trade Beads of Europe: Their Manufacture, Their History, and Their Identification*. Lapis Route, 1988.

Freud, Sigmund. *The Interpretation of Dreams: The Complete and Definitive Text*. Trans. James Strachey. Basic, 1955.

Friedman, Kajsa. *Catastrophe and Creation: The Transformation of an African Culture*. Routledge, 2016.

---. "From Religion to Magic." *Modernities, Class, and the Contradictions of Globalization: The Anthropology of Global Systems*. Ed. Kajsa Ekholm Friedman and Jonathan Friedman. Rowman, 2008. 29-88.

"From the New Gibbon." *Blackwood's Edinburgh Magazine*. 165.M (February 1899): 241-49.

Fyfe, Christopher. "Freed Slave Colonies in West Africa." *The Cambridge History of Africa*. Vol. 5. Ed. John E. Flint. Cambridge UP, 1977. 170-99.

Gentes, Andrew A. "The Institution of Russia's Sakhalin Policy, From 1868 to 1875." *Journal of Asian History* 36.1 (2002): 1-31.

Gerzina, Gretchen. "Virginia Woolf, Performing Race." *The Edinburgh Companion to Virginia Woolf and the Arts*. Ed. Maggie Humm. Edinburgh UP, 2010. 74-87.

Gibbon, Edward. *The History of the Decline and Fall of the Roman Empire*. 4 vols. Harper, 1836.

Gill, David. "The Fascination of the Abomination: Conrad and Cannibalism." *The Conradian* 24.2 (autumn 1999): 1-30.

Glave, E. J. "The Congo River of To-day." *The Century Magazine* 34.4 (February 1890): 618-20.

---. "Cruelty in the Congo Free State." *The Century Magazine* 54.5 (September 1897): 699-714.

GoGwilt, Christopher. *The Invention of the West: Joseph Conrad and the Double-Mapping of Europe and Empire*. Stanford UP, 1995.

Gold, John R., and Margaret M. Gold. *Cities of Culture: Staging International Festivals and The Urban Agenda, 1851-2000*. Routledge, 2005.

"The Graphic." *Stanley Number* 30 April 1890.

Greenblatt, Stephen. *Renaissance Self-Fashioning: From More to Shakespeare*. U of Chicago P, 1980.

Greenhalgh, Paul. *Ephemeral Vistas: The Expositions Universelles, Great Exhibitions and World's Fairs, 1851-1939*. Manchester UP, 1988.

Grenfell, George. "Exploration of the Tributaries of the Congo, between Leopoldville and Stanley Falls." *Proceedings of the Royal Geographical Society and Monthly Record of Geography* 8.10 (October 1886): 627-34.

---, and T. J. Comber. "Explorations by the Revs. George Grenfell and T. J.

Comber, on the Congo, from Stanley Pool to Bangala, and up the Bochini to the Junction of the Kwango." *Proceedings of the Royal Geographical Society and Monthly Record of Geography* 7.6 (June 1885): 353-73.
Griffith, John W. *Joseph Conrad and the Anthropological Dilemma: "Bewildered Traveller."* Oxford UP, 1995.
Griffiths, Andrew. *The New Journalism, the New Imperialism and the Fiction of Empire, 1870-1900*. Palgrave Macmillan, 2015.
---. "Seeking the Sources of *Heart of Darkness:* The African Narratives of late-Victorian Explorers and Journalists." *Continents Manuscrits* 11 (2018). 1-17. <http://journals.openedition.org/coma/2694>.
Haddon, A. C., W. J. Sollas and G. A. J. Cole. "On the Geology of Torres Straits." *The Transactions of the Royal Irish Academy* 30 (1892-1896): 419-76.
Hamner, Robert. "The Enigma of Arrival in 'An Outpost of Progress.'" *Conradiana* 33 (fall 2001): 171-87.
Hampson, Robert. "Conrad, the 'Polish Problem' and Transnational Activism." *Conradiana* 46 (2014): 21-38.
---. "Joseph Conrad's Objects." *Fathom: A French e-journal of Thomas Hardy Studies* 6 (2019): 1-16. <https://journals.openedition.org/fathom/970>.
---. "'An Outpost of Progress': The Case of Henry Price." *Conrad in Africa: New Essays on "Heart of Darkness."* Ed. Attie de Lange and Gail Fincham with Wiesław Krajka. Social Science Monographs – Maria Curie-Skłodowska U. Distributed by Columbia UP, 2002. 211-30. Vol. 11 of *Conrad: Eastern and Western Perspectives*. Ed. Wiesław Krajka. 30 vols. to date. 1992- .
---. "'A Passion for Maps': Conrad, Africa, Australia, and South-East Asia." *The Conradian* 28.1 (spring 2003): 34-56.
Harley, J. B. "Deconstructing the Map." Cartographica[to slowo kursywa] 26.2 (spring 1989): 1-20.
Harrison, Austin. "The German Press." *National Review* 44.262 (December 1904): 632-41.
Hawker, George. *The Life of George Grenfell, Congo Missionary and Explorer.* Revell, 1909.
Hay, Eloise Knapp. *The Political Novels of Joseph Conrad: A Study*. U of Chicago P, 1963.
Herbert, Eugenia W. *Red Gold of Africa: Copper in Precolonial History and Culture*. U of Wisconsin P, 1984.
Hibbard, Andrea. "Distracting Impressions and Rational Recreation at the Great Exhibition." Buzard, Childers, and Gillooly 151-70.
Hobsbawm, Eric. *The Age of Capital: 1848-1875*. Vintage, 1996.
Hobson, Robert. "A Critical Edition of Joseph Conrad's 'An Outpost of Progress.'" 1977. Diss. Texas Tech U.
---. "A Textual History of Conrad's 'An Outpost of Progress.'" *Conradiana* 11 (1979): 143-63.
Hochschild, Adam. *King Leopold's Ghost*. Houghton, 1998.

Holstun, Jim. "'Mr. Kayerts. He is Dead': Literary Realism and Conrad's 'Outpost of Progress.'" *English Literary History* 85.1 (spring 2018): 191-220.

Hunt, Herbert J. *Balzac's Comédie Humaine*. Athlone P, 1959.

Huxley, Thomas H. "On the Natural History of the Man-Like Apes." *Man's Place in Nature and Other Anthropological Essays*. Hill, 1904.

Hyman, Linda. "The Greek Slave by Hiram Powers: High Art as Popular Culture." *Art Journal* 35.3 (spring 1976): 216-23.

Inikori, Joseph E. *Africans and the Industrial Revolution in England: A Study in International Trade and Economic Development*. Cambridge UP, 2002.

Jameson, Fredric. *The Political Unconscious: Narrative as a Socially Symbolic Act*. Cornell UP, 1981.

Jeal, Tim. *Stanley: The Impossible Life of Africa's Greatest Explorer*. Yale UP, 2007.

Jean-Aubry, Gérard. *The Sea Dreamer: A Definitive Biography of Joseph Conrad*. Archon, 1967.

Johnson, Peter. "The Geographies of Heterotopia." *Geography Compass* 7.11 (2013): 790-803.

Johnston, Sir Harry Hamilton. *British Central Africa*. Methuen, 1897.

---. *George Grenfell and the Congo*. 2 vols. Hutchinson, 1908.

---. *A History of the Colonization of Africa by Alien Races*. Cambridge UP, 1905.

---. "A Visit to Mr. Stanley's Stations on the River Congo." *Proceedings of the Royal Geographical Society and Monthly Record of Geography* 5.10 (October 1883): 569-81.

Kainz, Wolfgang. "Cartography and the Others – Aspects of a Complicated Relationship." *Geospatial Information Science* 23.1: 52-60. <https://doi.org/10.1080/10095020.2020.1718000>.

Kanes, Martin. *Père Goriot: Anatomy of a Troubled World*. Twayne, 1993.

Karklins, Karlis. "The Levin Catalogue of Mid-19th-Century Beads." *Beads: Journal of the Society of Bead Researchers* 16 (2004): 39-50.

Karl, Frederick R. *Joseph Conrad, The Three Lives: A Biography*. Farrar, 1979.

Keltie, J. Scott. "What Stanley has Done for the Map of Africa." *Science* 15.364 (January 1890): 50-55.

Kember, Joe, John Plunkett, and Jill A. Sullivan, eds. *Popular Exhibitions, Science and Showmanship,1840-1910*. Routledge, 2012.

Kennedy, Dane, ed. *Reinterpreting Exploration: The West in the World*. Oxford UP, 2014.

Kerridge, Eric. "Wool Growing and Wool Textiles in Medieval and Early Modern Times." *The Wool Textile Industry in Great Britain* Ed. J. Geraint Jenkins. Routledge, 1972. 19-33.

Klehm, Carla. "Trade Tales and Tiny Trails: Glass Beads in the Kalahari Desert." *The Appendix* 2.1 (January 2014). N.p. <http://theappendix.net/issues/2014/1/trade-tales-and-tiny-trails-glass-beads-in-the-kalahari-desert>.

Works Cited

Knadler, Stephen. "At Home in the Crystal Palace: African American Transnationalism and The Aesthetics of Representative Democracy." *ESQ: A Journal of the American Renaissance* 56.4 (2011): 328-62.
Knowles, Owen, "Copy-texts." Knowles, *Youth, Heart of Darkness, The End of the Tether* 303-07.
---. "Explanatory Notes." Knowles, *Youth, Heart of Darkness, Th End of the Tether* 431-65.
---. Introduction. Knowles, *Youth, Heart of Darkness, The End of the Tether* xxvii-lxviii.
---. "'Who's Afraid of Arthur Schopenhauer?': A New Context for Conrad's Heart of Darkness." *Nineteenth Century Literature* 49.1 (1994): 75-106.
---, ed. *Youth, Heart of Darkness, The End of the Tether.* Cambridge UP, 2010.
Korzeniowski, Apollo. "Poland and Muscovy." *Conrad under Familial Eyes* Ed. Zdzisław Najder. Trans. Halina Carroll-Najder. Cambridge UP, 1983. 75-87.
Krzyżanowski, Ludwik. "Joseph Conrad's 'Prince Roman': Fact and Fiction." *The Polish Review* 1.4 (autumn 1956): 22-62.
Lacan, Jacques. *The Seminar of Jacques Lacan, Book XI: The Four Fundamental Concepts of Psychoanalysis* Ed. Jacques-Alain Miller. Trans. Alan Sheridan. Norton, 1998.
Lack, Clem. "The Achievements of James Cook, Navigator, Humanist, Anthropologist." *Journal of the Royal Historical Society of Queensland* 9.1: 7-77.
Lawtoo, Nidesh, ed. *Conrad's "Heart of Darkness" and Contemporary Thought: Revisiting The Horror with Lacoue-Labarthe.* Bloomsbury, 2012.
Le Bon, Gustave. *The Crowd: A Study of the Popular Mind.* Macmillan, 1896.
Leslie, Esther. *Walter Benjamin: Overpowering Conformism.* Pluto, 2000.
Lethbridge, Alan. *West Africa the Elusive.* Bale, 1921.
Lindfors, Bernth, ed. *Africans on Stage: Studies in Ethnological Show Business.* Indiana UP, 1999.
---. "Charles Dickens and the Zulus." Lindfors 62-80.
Livingstone, David. *The Last Journals of David Livingstone in Central Africa. From Eighteen Hundred and Sixty-Five to His Death* Ed. Horace Waller. Harper, 1875.
---. "A Map of the Forest Plateau of Africa Shewing the Great Rivers and Lakes." *Livingstone's 1871 Field Diary: A Multispectral Critical Edition.* <http://livingstone.library.ucla.edu/1871diary/site_guide.htm>.
---. *Missionary Travels and Researches in South Africa.* Murray, 1857.
---, and Charles Livingstone. *Narrative of an Expedition to the Zambezi and Its Tributaries.* Murray, 1865.
Lothe, Jakob. "Conrad and Travel Literature: From Conrad's 'Up-river Book' and 'Congo Diary' (1890) via *Heart of Darkness* (1899) to Redmond O'Hanlon's *Congo Journey* (1996)." *Journeys, Myths and the Age of Travel: Joseph Conrad's Era.* Ed. Karin Hansson. U of Karlskrona/ Ronneby, 1998. 36-54.

---. *Conrad's Narrative Method.* Oxford UP, 1989.
MacDuffie, Allen. "Joseph Conrad's Geographies of Energy." *English Literary History* 76.1 (2009): 75-98.
Mahood, Molly. *The Colonial Encounter: A Reading of Six Novels.* Rowman, 1977.
Marle, Hans van. "Letters, 1959-2000." *A Joseph Conrad Archive: The Papers of Hans van Marle." The Conradian* 30.2 (autumn 2005): 19-143.
Martens, Daisy S. *A History of European Penetration and African Reaction in the Kasai Region of Zaire, 1880-1908.* 1980. Diss. Simon Fraser U.
Martin, Phyllis M. "Contesting Clothes in Colonial Brazzaville." *Journal of African History* 35 (1994): 401-26.
---. "Power, Cloth and Currency on the Loango Coast." *African Economic History* 15 (1986): 1-12.
Marx, Karl. *Capital: A Critique of Political Economy.* Vol. 1. Ed. Frederick Engels. Trans. Samuel Moore and Edward Aveling. Marx/Engels Internet Archive. Marxists.org. <www.marxists.org/archive/marx/works/download/pdf/Capital-Volume-I.pdf>.
Mayhew, Henry and George Cruikshank. *1851: The Adventures of Mr. and Mrs. Sandboys, Their Son and Daughter, Who Came up to London to Enjoy Themselves and See the Great Exhibition.* Stringer, 1851.
McKay, Ian. "The Congo, I presume. (Bids and Pieces)." *Mercator's World* 8.1 (January-February 2003): 58+. <https://go.gale.com/ps/i.do?p=AONE&u=googlescholar&id=GALE%7CA96993496&v=2.1&it=r&sid=googleScholar&asid=df283518>.
McNiven, Ian J. "Precarious Islands: Kulkalgal Reef Island Settlement and High Mobility Across 700 km of Seascape, Central Torres Strait and Northern Great Barrier Reef." *Quarternary International* 385 (2015): 39-55.
Meredith, Martin. *Elephant Destiny: Biography of an Endangered Species in Africa.* PublicAffairs, 2001.
Miller, John. "Representation, Race and the Zoological Real in the Great Gorilla Controversy of 1861." Kember, Plunkett, and Sullivan 153-66.
Mirzoeff, Nicholas. *An Introduction to Visual Culture.* Routledge, 1999.
Montesquieu, Albert de, ed. *Voyages de Montesquieu.* Vol. 1. Gounouilhou, 1894.
Mulhern, Francis. "Critical Considerations on the Fetishism of Commodities." *English Literary History* 74.2 (2007): 479-92.
Murray, Brian. "Building Congo, Writing Empire: The Literary Labours of Henry Morton Stanley." *English Studies in Africa* 59.1 (2016): 6-17.
Myers, John Brown. *The Congo for Christ: The Story of the Congo Mission.* 3rd ed. Partridge, 1905.
Najder, Zdzisław. "Conrad's European Vision." *The Conradian* 37.1 (spring 2012): 46-57.
---, ed. *Joseph Conrad: Congo Diary and Other Uncollected Pieces.* By Conrad. Doubleday, 1978.
---. *Joseph Conrad: A Life.* Trans. Halina Najder. Camden, 2007.

Works Cited

Nielsen, Ruth. "The History and Development of Wax-Printed Textiles Intended for West Africa and Zaire." *The Fabrics of Culture: The Anthropology of Clothing and Adornment*. Ed. Justine M. Cordwell and Ronald A. Schwarz. Mouton, 1979. 467-98.

Niland, Richard. *Conrad and History*. Oxford UP, 2009.

Obenga, T. "Sources and Specific Techniques Used in African History: General Outline." *General History of Africa I: Methodology and African Prehistory*. Ed. J. Ki-Zerbo. California: UNESCO, 1981. 72-86.

Official Descriptive and Illustrated Catalogue of the Great Exhibition of the Works of Industry of All Nations. 3 vols. Spicer, 1851.

"On the Congo." *New York Herald. Henry M. Stanley Archives*. 30 Oct. Royal Museum for Central Africa. Newspaper Cutting. Item 5360.

Pakenham, Thomas. *The Scramble for Africa: White Man's Conquest of the Dark Continent from 1876 to 1912*. Harper, 1991.

Pallaver, Karin. "'A recognized currency in beads'. Glass Beads as Money in Nineteenth Century East Africa: The Central Caravan Road." *Money in Africa*. Ed. Catherine Eagleton et al. The British Museum, 2009. 20-29.

Pawlowski, Merry M. "Kicking the Biscuit Tin: Conrad, Mass Culture, and Commodity Spectacle." *Various Dimensions of the Other in Joseph Conrad's Fiction*. Ed. Wiesław Krajka. Maria Curie-Skłodowska UP and Columbia UP, 2020. 13-49. Vol. 29 of *Conrad: Eastern and Western Perspectives*. Ed. Wiesław Krajka. 30 vols. to date. 1992- .

Pettitt, Claire. *Dr. Livingstone, I Presume? Missionaries, Journalists, Explorers, and Empire*. Harvard UP, 2007.

---. "Exploration in Print: From the Miscellany to the Newspaper." Kennedy 80-108.

Pietz, William. "Fetishism and Materialism: The Limits of Theory in Marx." *Fetishism as Cultural Discourse*. Ed. Emily Apter and William Pietz. Cornell UP, 1993. 119-51.

---. "The Problem of the Fetish, I." *Review of English Studies: Anthropology and Aesthetics* 9 (spring 1985): 5-17.

---. "The Problem of the Fetish, II." *Review of English Studies: Anthropology and Aesthetics* 13 (spring 1987): 23-45.

Polish Pomerania (Pomorze). Polish Library of Facts. 4. Polish Information Service, 1933.

Pye, Gillian. "Introduction: Trash as Cultural Category." *Trash Culture: Objects and Obsolescence in Cultural Perspective*. Ed. Gillian Pye. Lang, 2010. 1-14.

Pynchon, Thomas. *Mason & Dixon*. Holt, 1997.

Qureshi, Sadiah. "Meeting the Zulus: Displayed Peoples and the Shows of London, 1853-57." Kember, Plunkett, and Sullivan 183-98.

Reade, Winwood. *The African Sketch-book*. Vol 2. Elder, 1873.

Recollections of the Great Exhibition, 1851. Lloyd, 1851.

Reid, J. S. "Tacitus as Historian." *The Journal of Roman Studies* 11 (1921): 191-99.

Richards, Thomas. *The Commodity Culture of Victorian England: Advertising and Spectacle, 1851-1914*. Stanford UP, 1990.

Riffenburgh, Beau. *The Myth of the Explorer*. Oxford UP, 1994.

Robinson, Arthur H. "Rectangular World Maps – No!" *Professional Geographer* 42.1 (1990): 101-04.

Rockel, Stephen J. *Carriers of Culture: Labor on the Road in Nineteenth-Century East Africa*. Heinemann, 2006.

---. "Decentering Exploration in East Africa." Kennedy 172-94.

---. "Enterprising Partners: Caravan Women in Nineteenth Century Tanzania." *Canadian Journal of African Studies/Revue Canadienne des Études Africaines* 34.3 (2000): 748-78.

Roes, Aldwin. "Towards a History of Mass Violence in the État Indépendent du Congo, 1885-1908." *South African Historical Journal* 62.1 (2010): 634-70. Reprint: White Rose Research Online 1-49. <http://eprints.whiterose.ac.uk/74340/>.

Rubery, Matthew. *The Novelty of the Newspapers: Victorian Fiction after the Invention of The News*. Oxford UP, 2009.

---. "On Henry Morton Stanley's Search for Dr. Livingstone, 1871-72." *Britain, Representation and Nineteenth-Century History*. Ed. Dino Franco Felluga. <https://branchcollective.org/?ps_articles=matthew-rubery-on-henry-morton-stanleys-search-for-dr-livingstone-1871-72>.

Ruppel, Richard. *A Political Genealogy of Joseph Conrad*. Lexington, 2015.

Ruskin, John. "The Opening of the Crystal Palace Considered in Some of Its Relations to the Prospects of Art." *Lectures on Architecture and Painting with Other Papers, 1844-1854*. Allen, 1904. 417-32.

Rutledge, Thais, and Robert Tally, Jr. "Formed by Place: Spatiality, Irony, and Empire in Conrad's 'An Outpost of Progress.'" *Transnational Literature* 9.1 (November 2016): 1-16.

Said, Edward. "Narrative, Geography, Interpretation." *New Left Review* 1.180 (March/April 1990): 81-97.

Samarin, William J. "The State's Bakongo Burden Bearers." *The Workers of African Trade*. Ed. Catherine Coquery-Vidrovitch and Paul E. Lovejoy. Sage, 1985. 269-92.

Schopenhauer, Arthur. "On Women." *Studies in Pessimism: A Series of Essays*. Trans. T. Bailey Saunders. Allen, 1913. 103-24.

Sciama, Lidia D. "Gender in the Making, Trading and Uses of Beads: An Introductory Essay." Sciama and Eicher 1-46.

---, and Joanne B. Eicher, eds. *Beads and Bead-Makers: Gender, Material Culture and Meaning*. Berg, 1998.

Sciarini, Natalia. "Form Submission from: Archives at Yale: Ask a Question." Message to the author 28 July, 2021. E-mail.

Sewlall, Harry. "'Masquerading philanthropy': Conrad's Image of Africa in 'An Outpost of Progress.'" *The English Academy Review* 23.1 (2007): 1-14. <https://doi.org/10.1080/10131750608540421>.

Works Cited

Shakespeare, William. *Henry the Fourth*. Part 2. *The Oxford Shakespeare*. Ed. Stanley Wells and Gary Taylor. Oxford UP, 2005. 537-68.
Sherry, Norman. *Conrad's Western World*. Cambridge UP, 1971.
Simmons, Allan H., and J. H. Stape. Introduction. Simmons and Stape xxv-lxii.
---, eds. *Tales of Unrest*. By Conrad. Cambridge UP, 2012.
---. "The Texts." Simmons and Stape 175-244.
Smith, Johanna M. "'Too Beautiful Altogether': Ideologies of Gender and Empire in *Heart of Darkness*." *Heart of Darkness, Complete, Authoritative Text with Biographical and Historical Contexts, Critical History, and Essays from Five Contemporary Critical Perspectives*. Ed. Ross C. Murfin. 2nd ed. Bedford, 1996. 169-84.
Stanard, Matthew. *Selling the Congo: A History of European Pro-Empire Propaganda and the Making of Belgian Imperialism*. U of Nebraska P, 2011.
Stanley, Sir Henry Morton. *The Autobiography of Sir Henry Morton Stanley*. Ed. Dorothy Stanley. Houghton, 1909.
---. *The Congo and the Founding of Its Free State: A Story of Work and Exploration*. 2 vols. Harper, 1885.
---. *The Exploration Diaries of H. M. Stanley*. Ed. Richard Stanley and Alan Neame. Vanguard P, 1961.
---. "Geographical Results of the Emin Pasha Relief Expedition." *Proceedings of the Royal Geographical Society and Monthly Record of Geography* 12.6 (June 1890): 313-31.
---. *How I Found Livingstone: Travels, Adventures, and Discoveries in Central Africa*. Low, 1872.
---. *In Darkest Africa or the Quest, Rescue, and Retreat of Emin Governor of Equatoria*. 2 vols. Scribner's, 1891.
---. "On the Congo." Newspaper cutting from *The New York Herald*. 30 Oct. 1882. *Africa Museum*. Item 5360. Scrapbook (Newspaper Cuttings) with press cuttings from 1873-1874. 1878. 317. <https://archive.org/details/inventory-of-the-henry-m.-stanley-archives/page/317/mode/2up>.
---. *Stanley's Despatches to the New York Herald, 1871-72, 1874-77*. Ed. Norman Bennett. Boston UP, 1970.
---. *Stanley's First Opinions: Portugal and the Slave Trade*. Rodrigues, 1883.
---. *Through the Dark Continent*. 2 vols. Low 1878.
The Stanley and African Exhibition: Catalogue of the Exhibits. The Victoria Gallery, 1890.
Stape, J. H. "Apparatus." Stape, *Notes on Life and Letters* 309-82.
---. "Conrad's Voyage to Africa: Footnotes to a Journey." *The Conradian* 38.2 (autumn 2013): 108-12.
---. "Father Gobila, I presume? Sources for 'An Outpost of Progress.'" *The Conradian* 35.1 (spring 2010): 132-37.
---. Introduction. Stape, J. H. *Notes on Life and Letters* xxxv-liii.
---. Notes. Stape, J. H. *Notes on Life and Letters* 391-447.

---, ed. *Notes on Life and Letters*. By Conrad. Cambridge UP, 2004.
---. "The Texts: An Essay." Stape, J. H. *Notes on Life and Letters* 209-308.
Stead, W. T. "Bismarck and His Boswell." *The Review of Reviews* 18 (July-December 1898): 404-10.
---. "Russia: 'Ghost, Ghoul, Djinn, etc.': The Fantastic Rhetoric of Mr. Conrad." *The Review of Reviews* 32 (July-December 1905): 51-52.
Steains, W. J. "Notebooks Containing Drawings of the Objects in the *Stanley and African Exhibition*, 1890." British Museum. Museum of Mankind. Africa A-N. Vols. 1 and 11.
Steiner, Christopher B. "Another Image of Africa: Toward an Ethnohistory of European Cloth Marketed in West Africa, 1873-1960." *Ethnohistory* 32.2 (spring 1985): 91-110.
Stevens, Harold Ray, and J. H. Stape, eds. "The Congo Diary." Stevens and Stape 123-37.
---."Emendation and Variation." Stevens and Stape 273-348.
---. "The Essays." Stevens and Stape 202-63.
---. "Explanatory Notes." Stevens and Stape 400-73.
---, eds. *Last Essays*. By Conrad. Cambridge UP, 2010.
---. "Up-river Book." Stevens and Stape 138-68.
Stine, Linda France, Melanie A. Cabak, and Mark D. Goover. "Blue Beads as African-American Cultural Symbols." *Historical Archaeology* 30.3 (1996): 49-75.
Stott, Rebecca. "The Dark Continent: Africa as Female Body in Haggard's Adventure Fiction." *Feminist Review* 32.1 (1989): 69-89.
Stowe, Harriet Beecher. *Uncle Tom's Cabin, or Life among the Lowly*. Jewett, 1853.
Strother, Z. S. "Dancing on the Knife of Power: Comedy, Narcissism, and Subversion in the Portrayals of Europeans and Americans by Central Africans." *Through African Eyes: The European in African Art, 1500 to Present*. Ed. Nil O. Quarcoopome. Institute of Arts, 2009.
Swafford, Kevin R. "'In the Thick of It': the (Meta)Discourse of Jack London's Russo-Japanese War Correspondence." *Pacific Coast Philology* 50.1 (2015): 82-102.
Tacitus. *The Annals of Tacitus*. Books 1-6. Trans. Aubrey V. Symonds. Macmillan, 1906.
Tallis, John. *The Illustrated Atlas, and Modern History of the World, Geographical, Political Commercial & Statistical*. 3 vols. Ed. R. Montgomery Martin. Tallis, 1851.
---. "1851 Map." *Evolution of the Map of Africa*. <https://library.princeton.edu/visual_materials/maps/websites/africa/maps-continent/continent.html>.
---. *Tallis's History and Description of the Crystal Palace and the Exhibition of the World's Industry in 1851*. 3 vols. Tallis, 1852.
Tanner, Henry Schenck. *Map of Africa*. <https://exhibits.stanford.edu/maps-of-africa/catalog/ms639jm9954>.

Works Cited

Taunt, Lieutenant E. H. "Report: US Navy Congo River Expedition of 1885." *Naval History and Heritage Command.* <https://www.history.navy.mil/research/library/online-reading-room/title-list-alphabetically/u/us-navy-congo-river-expedition-1885.html#rep>.

Theed, William the Younger. *Africa* (1864-1869). The Albert Memorial. <https://victorianweb.org/sculpture/theed/index.html>.

Torgovnick, Mariana. *Gone Primitive: Savage Intellects, Modern Lives.* U of Chicago P, 1990.

Trivellato, Francesca. "Murano Glass, Continuity and Transformation (1400-1800)." *At the Centre of the Old World: Trade and Manufacturing in Venice and Venetian Mainland, 1400-1800.* Ed. Paola Lanaro. Centre for Reformation and Renaissance Studies, 2006, 143-84.

---. "Out of Women's Hands: Notes on Venetian Glass Beads, Female Labour and International Trades." Sciama and Eicher 47-82.

Tythacott, Louise. "From the 'fetish' to the 'specimen': the Ridyard African Collection at the Liverpool Museum 1895-1916." *Collectors: Expressions of Self and Other.* Ed. Anthony Shelton. Horniman Museum, 2001. 157-79.

Vansina, Jan. *Being Colonized: The Kuba Experience in Rural Congo, 1880-1960.* U of Wisconsin P, 2010.

Verhaeghe, Charlotte, et al. "Shell and Glass Beads from the Tombs of Kindoki, Mbanza Nsundi, Lower Congo." *Beads: Journal of the Society of Bead Researchers* 26.23-24 (2014): 23-34.

Vincent, Frank. *Actual Africa, or, The Coming Continent.* Appleton, 1895.

Vivan, Itala. "Geography, Literature and the African Territory: Some Observations on the Western Map and the Representation of Territory in the South African Literary Imagination." *Research in African Literatures.* 31.2 (summer 2000): 49-70.

Volavkova, Zdenka. "Nkisi Figures of the Lower Congo." *African Arts.* 5.2 (winter 1972): 52-59+84.

Wack, Henry Wellington. *The Story of the Congo Free State.* Putnam's, 1905.

Wall, Brian. *Theodor Adorno and Film Theory: The Fingerprint of Spirit.* Palgrave Macmillan, 2013.

Waller, Horace. *"Ivory, Apes, and Peacocks;" An African Contemplation.* Stanford, 1891.

Ward, Herbert. *Five Years with the Congo Cannibals.* Chatto, 1890.

Warodell, Johan. "Conrad's Unpublished Map of His Congo Journey: A Note." *The Conradian* 42.2 (autumn 2017): 64-68.

---. "Query: Joseph Conrad's Unpublished 'Map of the Russias.'" *Notes and Queries* 64.4 (December 2017): 681-82.

---. "The Writer at Work Hand-Drawn Maps in Conrad's Manuscripts." *Conradiana* 48 (spring 2016): 25-46.

Weeks, John H. *Among Congo Cannibals.* Lippincott, 1913.

---. *Congo Life and Folklore.* The Religious Tract Society, 1911.

Weigandt, Kai. "Humans and Animals in Conrad's 'An Outpost of Progress.'" Fincham, Hawthorne, and Lothe 3-17.
Wells, Colin. *The Roman Empire*. 2nd ed. Harvard UP, 1984.
West, Russell. "Space and Language in the Private Diary: Conrad's Congo Diaries." *Marginal Voices, Marginal Forms: Diaries in European Literature and History*. Ed. Rachael Langford and Russell West. Rodopi, 1999. 107-25.
White, Andrea. *Joseph Conrad and the Adventure Tradition: Constructing and Deconstructing the Imperial Subject*. Cambridge UP, 1993.
White, James P. "The Sanford Exploring Expedition." *The Journal of African History* 8.2 (1967): 291-302.
Wisnicki, Adrian. "Charting the Frontier: Indigenous Geography, Arab-Nyamwezi Caravans, and the East African Expedition of 1856-59." *Victorian Studies* 51.1 (autumn 2008): 103-37.
Wissmann, Hermann von. *My Second Journey Through Equatorial Africa from the Congo to The Zambesi in the Years 1886 and 1887*. Trans. Minna Bergmann. Chatto, 1891.
Withers, Charles. *Zero Degrees: Geographies of the Prime Meridian*. Harvard UP, 2017.
Wyld, James. "Map of Central Africa." (1874). Personal copy of Henry Morton Stanley, privately owned. <https://www.christies.com/en/lot/lot-3975937>.
---. "Wyld's New Map of Central Africa Shewing All the Most Recent Discoveries & Explorations." 1890. *Maps of Africa: An Online Exhibit, a Digital Collection of African Maps at the Stanford University Libraries*. <https://exhibits.stanford.edu/maps-of-africa/catalog/yz026hv8042>.
Youngs, Tim. *Travellers in Africa: British Travelogues, 1850-1900*. Manchester UP, 1994.
Zdrada, Jerzy. "Apollo Korzeniowski's *Poland and Muscovy*." *Yearbook of Conrad Studies* 4 (2008-2009): 21-96.
Žižek, Slavoj. *Looking Awry: An Introduction to Jacques Lacan through Popular Culture*. MIT P, 1991.

Index of Nonfictional Names

Achebe, Chinua 303, 313
Adorno, Theodor 287, 290, 313, 327
Aitchison, Leslie 265, 313
Aitken, W. C. 266, 267, 313
Altic, Mirela xii, 85, 90, 159, 160, 313
Anstey, R. T. 145, 313
Armstrong, Isobel 30, 296, 313
Arnold, Matthew 118
Auerbach, Jeffrey 28, 29, 32, 35, 36, 296, 313

Ball, Jeremy 197, 313
Banning, Emile 230, 313
Barnard, A. 251, 313
Bartholomew, J. G. 96, 311
Bassett, Thomas J. 81, 313
Baudelaire, Charles 29, 30, 290, 314
Bay, Edna G. 284, 304, 313
Beachey, R. W. 244, 251, 268, 269, 313
Beckert, Sven 252, 303, 314
Bell, Morag 80, 81, 314
Belloc, Hilaire 110, 314
Benjamin, Walter 26-30, 287, 290, 294, 313-15, 321
Bennett, James Gordon, Jr. 105, 115-118
Bennett, Norman 298, 325
Bennett, Tony 30, 314
Bentley, William H. (Rev.) 11, 140, 141, 167, 169, 172, 179, 183, 301, 314
Berenson, Edward 44, 102, 110, 112, 113, 115-19, 127, 298, 314
Bergmann, Bettina 42, 314
Bhabha, Homi 217, 278, 279, 301, 314
Biebuyck, Daniel 296, 314
Bierman, John 101-03, 105, 109, 110, 125-27, 314

Bingham, Colin 65, 314
Bismarck, Otto von 55, 56, 61, 62, 65, 109, 296, 326
Blackwood, Basil T. 110, 314
Blackwood, William 235, 242
Bobrowski, Tadeusz 74, 330
Böhme, Hartmut 211, 212, 314
Botting, Fred 302, 314
Brantlinger, Patrick 297, 301, 314
Brown, Tony C. 303, 314
Burton, Sir Richard 41, 46, 88, 96, 98, 100, 105, 260-63, 265, 266, 304, 314
Busch, Moritz 61
Buszczynski, Stefan 24, 315

Candido, Mariana 199, 315
Capello, Brito 197, 198, 308
Carabine, Keith xiii, 17, 21, 22, 296, 315, 329, 330
Carter, Paul 240, 241, 271, 315
Casement, Roger 144-46,168
Casey, Brendan 97, 315
Chambers, Helen 44, 114, 120, 315
Chekhov, Anton 53, 315
Clarence-Smith, W. G. 199, 315
Cohen, Margaret 30, 315
Coleridge, Samuel Taylor 212
Comber, Thomas J. (Rev.) 11, 169, 179-84, 218, 300, 308, 318, 319
Conrad, Jessie 10, 56, 97, 142, 188, 235
Cook, James (Captain) 68, 79, 96-98, 114, 129, 293, 315, 321
Coombes, Annie 44, 46-48, 50, 316
Cooper, James Fenimore 228, 229, 316
Cosgrove, Denis 72, 84, 297, 316
Cowper, William 37, 38, 316
Cruikshank, George 27, 308, 322

329

Index of Nonfictional Names

Crush, Peter 51, 52, 296, 308, 316
Cunliffe, Marcus 32, 316
Cunningham, Valentine 304, 316
Curle, Richard x, xi, 10, 11, 75, 76, 142, 143, 147-53, 156, 158, 163, 164, 167, 172, 173, 295, 298, 299, 310, 316, 317

Daerden, Peter 106, 317
Darby, E. D. (Rev.) 273, 304, 307
Darwin, Charles 41
Davies, Laurence xi, xiii, 69, 191, 232, 292, 297, 317
Davis, Richard Harding 59, 317
Davray, Henri-Durand 19
Debord, Guy 29, 30, 317
Delcommune, Alexandre 201
Delcommune, Camille 201
Delhaye, F. 76, 77, 310
Dickens, Charles 40, 317, 321
Dilke, Charles 191
Donovan, Stephen 60, 100, 105, 114, 317
Driver, Felix 45, 107, 128, 296, 317
Du Chaillu, Paul 41, 46, 50, 88
Dubin, Lois Sherr 15, 259, 263, 317
Dumas, Alexandre 228, 317

Elands, Helen 303, 317
Eltis, David 14, 253, 317
Emin Pasha (Eduard Schnitzer) 10, 44, 76, 92, 111, 112, 275, 276

Ferdinand, Franz (Archduke of Austria) 65, 296
Fernandez-Armesto, Felipe 39, 317
Firchow, Peter 185, 302, 304, 317
Flaubert, Gustave 224, 318
Forfeitt, J. Lawson 199, 200, 318
Foucault, Michel 224
Francis, Andrew 18, 25, 318
Francis, Peter, Jr. 262, 318
Franklin, John 68, 96, 98, 241

Freud, Sigmund 13, 241, 318
Friedman, Kajsa 210, 212, 214, 318
Fyfe, Christopher 199-201, 318

Galsworthy, Ada 23, 61
Galsworthy, John 19, 175, 242
Gambetta, Leon 135, 299
Garnett, Edward 187, 188, 201, 235
Gentes, Andrew A. 53, 318
Gerzina, Gretchen 45, 318
Gibbon, Edward 20, 21
Gill, David 302, 318
Glave, E. J. 128, 129, 196, 318
GoGwilt, Christopher 24, 25, 279, 297, 303, 318
Gold, John 42, 318
Gold, Margaret 42, 318
Gordon, Charles 110, 191
Gosse, Joseph 144, 145
Grant, James Augustus (Col.) 41, 46, 47
Greenhalgh, Paul 31, 35, 37, 42, 43, 318
Grenfell, George 11, 12, 178-84, 204, 205, 218, 300, 308, 318, 320
Griffith, John W. 21, 319
Griffiths, Andrew 297, 319

Haddon, A. C. 70, 319
Hamner, Robert 11, 187, 188, 301, 319
Hampson, Robert xiii, 19, 22-24, 71, 197, 199, 218, 301, 304, 319
Harley, J. B. 82, 319
Harou, Prosper 146, 169, 171, 258, 304
Harris, Alice Seeley 207, 208, 307
Harrison, Austin 82, 319
Hase, Johann 86, 87, 309
Hawker, George 274, 319
Herbert, Eugenia 265, 266, 319
Hinde, Sidney 196
Hobsbawm, Eric 31, 34, 319
Hobson, Robert x, 189, 190, 193-95, 300, 301, 319

Index of Nonfictional Names

Hochschild, Adam   108, 319
Holstun, Jim   301, 302, 320
Hunt, Herbert J.   230, 320
Huxley, Thomas H.   41, 320
Hyman, Linda   32, 34, 35, 320

Inikori, Joseph   252, 265, 320
Ivens, Roberto   197, 198, 308

Jacques, W. H.   21, 175
Jameson, Fredric   13, 239, 303, 320
Jeal, Tim   108, 120, 196, 198, 320
Jean-Aubry, Gérard   12, 142, 176, 188, 320
Jennings, Lawrence   14, 253, 317
Johnson, Peter   224, 225, 320
Johnston, Harry Hamilton   95, 96, 108, 179, 183, 266, 307, 320

Kainz, Wolfgang   83, 320
Kamienski, Henryk   21
Kanes, Martin   230, 320
Karklins, Karlis   304, 320
Karl, Frederick R.   201, 301, 320
Keltie, James Scott   84-86, 309, 320
Kember, Joe   320, 322, 323
Kennedy, Dane   320, 323, 324
Kerridge, Eric   250, 320
Kirk, John   101, 105, 110, 111, 117
Klehm, Carla   259, 263, 320
Knadler, Stephen   33, 321
Knowles, Owen   13, 236, 242, 303, 304, 315, 316, 321, 329
Koch, Ludwig (Captain)   11, 15, 176, 177, 264
Korzeniowski, Apollo   23, 74, 321, 328
Krzyżanowski, Ludwik   73, 74, 321

Lacan, Jacques   13, 241, 285, 302, 314, 321, 328
Lack, Clem   97, 321
Lacoue-Labarthe, Philippe   303, 321
Lawtoo, Nidesh   303, 321
Le Bon, Gustave   226, 227, 321

Leopold II of Belgium   8, 45, 47, 66, 68, 76, 77, 90, 91, 96, 106-11, 125, 191, 196, 207, 223, 230, 250, 272, 319
Lerman, Dragutin   185
Leslie, Esther   7, 26, 27, 321
Lessing, Julius   28
Lethbridge, Alan   255, 311, 321
Lindfors, Bernth   40, 321
Livingstone, David (Rev.)   15, 40, 44, 47, 68, 84, 85, 88, 91, 94-96, 99-103, 106, 114-17, 119, 120, 125, 128, 129, 251, 260, 265-67, 284, 293, 298, 321, 323-25
London, Jack   59, 312, 326
Lothe, Jakob   298, 303, 317, 321, 328, 329

MacDuffie, Allen   303, 322
Mackinnon, William   110, 111
Mahood, Molly   223, 322
Marle, Hans van   142, 173, 176, 300, 322
Martens, Daisy S.   206, 322
Martin, Phyllis M.   252, 256, 322
Marx, Karl   26, 322, 323
Mayhew, Henry   296, 308, 322
McClintock, Leopold   68, 79, 96, 98
McKay, Ian   298, 322
McNiven, Ian J.   70, 311, 322
Meldrum, David   235, 236
Meredith, Martin   125, 129, 269, 322
Miller, John   41, 42, 322
Mirzoeff, Nicholas   5, 295, 322
Moll, Herman   86, 87, 297, 309
Montesquieu, Albert de   322
Montesquieu, Charles Louis de   259, 322
Mulhern, Francis   304, 322
Murray, Brian   118, 119, 122, 124, 298, 322
Myers, John   150, 169, 170, 309, 322

Index of Nonfictional Names

Najder, Zdzisław x, 11, 19, 21, 114, 142, 143, 156, 158, 164, 167, 173, 176, 179-81, 185, 298-300, 316, 321, 322
Nielsen, Ruth 253, 323
Niland, Richard 21, 24, 304, 323

Obenga, T. 255, 303, 323

Pakenham, Thomas 66, 107, 108, 125, 323
Pallaver, Karin 260, 263, 323
Park, Mungo 47, 96, 98, 114, 293
Parke, Thomas (Dr.) 46, 298
Pettitt, Claire 117, 323
Pietz, William 211, 212, 214, 323
Pinto, Serpa 197, 198, 308
Powers, Hiram 33, 34, 38, 320
Pye, Gillian 27, 323
Pynchon, Thomas 84, 297, 323

Quinn John 296
Qureshi, Sadiah 40, 323

Rashid ben Mohammed (Reshid) 125
Reade, Winwood 88, 89, 309, 323
Reid, J. S. 20, 323
Richards, Thomas 6, 26, 29, 30, 324
Riffenburgh, Beau 102, 105, 115, 118, 324
Robinson, Arthur H. 83, 324
Rockel, Stephen J. 100, 101, 171, 324
Roes, Aldwin 303, 324
Rubery, Matthew 61, 99, 297, 324
Ruppel, Richard 18, 324
Ruskin, John 28, 324
Rutledge, Thais 302, 324

Said, Edward 80, 81, 324
Samarin, William J. 155, 324
Sanguszko, Roman (Prince) 73
Schopenhauer, Arthur 303, 321, 324
Sciama, Lidia D. 259, 263, 324, 327
Sciarini, Natalia 297, 324
Sewlall, Harry 217, 301, 324
Sherry, Norman 185, 301, 302, 325
Simmons, Allan H. 188, 190, 191, 224, 300, 315, 316, 325
Smith, Johanna M. 305, 325
Speke, John Hanning 41, 46, 47, 88, 92, 98, 100
Stanard, Matthew 196, 325
Stanley, Henry Morton (Bula Matari) 8-12, 41, 43-45, 47, 51, 66-68, 76, 77, 83-86, 88-95, 96, 99-108, 110-23, 125-29, 133-47, 149-56, 160, 164, 165, 168, 172, 175, 182, 196-200, 202, 213, 218, 219, 222, 223, 230, 231, 239, 245-47, 252, 258, 260, 261, 263, 265-67, 271, 272, 274, 275, 277, 281, 282, 284, 286, 289-93, 297-99, 301, 302, 304, 307, 309, 312-14, 317, 320, 322-325, 328
Stape, J. H. x, 8, 17, 56, 67-69, 130, 142, 144, 146, 158, 164, 167, 173, 174, 188, 190, 191, 224, 229, 295-97, 299-01, 315, 316, 325, 326
Stead, W. T. 60-62, 117, 118, 317, 326
Steains, William J. 50, 308, 326
Steiner, Christopher B. 254, 255, 304, 326
Stevens, Harold Ray x, 8, 67-69, 130, 142, 143, 146, 158, 164, 167, 173, 174, 297, 299, 300, 315, 316, 326
Stine, Linda France 263, 326
Stott, Rebecca 16, 283, 284, 326
Stowe, Harriet Beecher 34, 326
Strother, Z. S. 2-4, 295, 326
Swafford, Kevin R. 59, 326

Tacitus 6, 20-22, 323, 326
Tallis, John 87, 296, 297, 326

Index of Nonfictional Names

Tally, Robert, Jr.   302, 324
Tanner, Henry Schenck   85, 86, 297, 326
Tasman, Abel   79, 88, 97
Taunt, Emory H. (Lt.)   11, 183-86, 327
Theed, William   48-50, 311, 327
Thys, Albert   10, 46, 300
Tib, Tippu (aka Tippu Tip)   111, 125, 127, 128, 183,
Torgovnik, Mariana   305, 327
Towson, John   278-81, 304, 316
Trivellato, Francesca   259, 327
Tythacott, Louise   296, 327

Underwood, Arthur   144, 145
Unwin, Fisher   12, 187, 201

Vansinsa, Jan   206, 207, 327
Verhaeghe, Charlotte   259, 327
Vincent, Frank   208, 209, 327
Vivan, Itala   81, 327
Volavkova, Zdenka   211, 327

Wack, Henry   203, 204, 327
Wall, Brian   287, 327
Waller, Horace   46, 129, 321, 327
Warodell, Johan   xiii, 71, 72, 74, 76, 78, 81, 327
Ward, Herbert   165, 327
Wauters, Alphonse-Jules   160, 300
Weeks, John   157, 158, 210, 267, 304, 327
Wells, Colin   20, 328
West, Russell   298, 328
White, Andrea   xiii, 21, 189, 328
Wiegandt, Kai   302, 328
Wisnicki, Adrian   98, 328
Wissmann, Hermann von   202, 204-07, 209, 309, 328
Withers, Charles   82, 328
Wyld, James   92, 93, 312, 328

Youngs, Tim   111, 120, 328

Zdrada, Jerzy   328
Žižek, Slavoj   277, 303, 328

Published volumes of the series
Conrad: Eastern and Western Perspectives
Editor: Wiesław Krajka

I 1992 Carabine, Keith, Owen Knowles, and Wiesław Krajka, eds. *Conrad's Literary Career*

II 1993 Carabine, Keith, Owen Knowles, and Wiesław Krajka, eds. *Contexts for Conrad*

III 1994 Morzinski, Mary. *Linguistic Influence of Polish on Joseph Conrad's Style*

IV 1995 Lothe, Jakob, ed. *Conrad in Scandinavia*

V 1996 Kurczaba, Alex S., ed. *Conrad and Poland*

VI 1998 Carabine, Keith, Owen Knowles, with Paul Armstrong, eds. *Conrad, James and Other Relations*

VII 1998 Davis, Laura L., ed. *Conrad's Century:The Past and Future Splendour*

VIII 1999 Krajka, Wiesław, ed. *Joseph Conrad: East European, Polish and Worldwide*

IX 2000 Lucas, Michael, A. *Aspects of Conrad's Literary Language*

X 2001 Fincham, Gail, Attie de Lange, with Wiesław Krajka, eds. *Conrad at the Millennium: Modernism, Postmodernism, Postcolonialism*

XI 2002 Lange, Attie de, Gail Fincham, with Wiesław Krajka, eds. *Conrad in Africa: New Essays on „Heart of Darkness"*

XII 2003 Carabine, Keith, and Max Saunders, eds. *Interrelations: Conrad, James, Ford and Others*

XIII 2004 Krajka, Wiesław, ed. *A Return to the Roots: Conrad, Poland and East-Central Europe*

XIV 2005 Krajka, Wiesław, ed. *Beyond the Roots: The Evolution of Conrad's Ideology and Art*

XV 2006 Paccaud-Huguet, Josiane, ed. *Conrad in France*

XVI 2007 Gőbel, Walter, Hans Ulrich Seeber, and Martin Windisch, eds. *Conrad in Germany*

XVII 2008 Bobrowski, Tadeusz. *A Memoir of My Life*. Trans. and ed. Addison Bross

XVIII 2009 Krajka, Wiesław, ed. *Joseph Conrad: Between Literary Techniques and Their Messages*

XIX 2010 Krajka, Wiesław, ed. *In the Realms of Biography, Literature, Politics and Reception: Polish and East-Central European Joseph Conrad*

XX 2011 Sokołowska, Katarzyna. *Conrad and Turgenev: Towards the Real*

XXI 2012 Acheraïou, Amar, and Nursel Içőz, eds. *Joseph Conrad and the Orient*

XXII 2013 Krajka, Wiesław, ed. *From Szlachta Culture to the 21st Century, Between East and West. New Essays on Joseph Conrad's Polishness*

XXIII 2014 Krajka, Wiesław, ed. *„Wine in Old and New Bottles": Critical Paradigms for Joseph Conrad*

XXIV 2015 Curreli, Mario, ed. *Conrad in Italy*

XXV	2016	Brodsky, G. W. Stephen. *Joseph Conrad's Polish Soul. Realms of Memory and Self.* Ed. George Z. Gasyna
XXVI	2017	Maisonnat, Claude. *Joseph Conrad and the Voicing of Textuality*
XXVII	2018	Krajka, Wiesław, ed. *Joseph Conrad's Authorial Self: Polish and Other*
XXVIII	2019	Krajka, Wiesław, ed. *Some Intertextual Chords of Joseph Conrad's Literary Art*
XXIX	2020	Krajka, Wiesław, ed. *Various Dimensions of the Other in Joseph Conrad's Fiction*
XXX	2021	Acheraïou, Amar, and Laëtitia Crémona, eds. *Joseph Conrad and Ethics*
XXXI	2022	Pawlowski, Merry M. *Joseph Conrad and Material Culture: From the Rise of the Commodity Transcendent to the Scramble for Africa*